The Joyless Economy

THE PSYCHOLOGY
OF HUMAN SATISFACTION

Revised Edition

TIBOR SCITOVSKY

New York   Oxford
OXFORD UNIVERSITY PRESS
1992

TO ELISABETH
who provided the stimulus, the comfort, and
many of the ideas for writing this book

Oxford University Press

Oxford   New York   Toronto
Delhi   Bombay   Calcutta   Madras   Karachi
Petaling Jaya   Singapore   Hong Kong   Tokyo
Nairobi   Dar es Salaam   Cape Town
Melbourne   Auckland

and associated companies in
Berlin   Ibadan

Published by Oxford University Press, Inc.,
200 Madison Avenue, New York, New York 10016

Library of Congress Cataloging-in-Publication Data
Scitovsky, Tibor.
The joyless economy : the psychology of human satisfaction
/ Tibor Scitovsky. —Rev. ed.
p. cm.
Includes bibliographical references and index.
ISBN 0–19–507346–0
ISBN 0–19–507347–9 (pbk.)
1. Consumer satisfaction.   2. Motivation research (Marketing)   I. Title.
HF5415.3.S355 1992
658.8'34—dc20   91–18743

1 3 5 7 9 8 6 4 2

Printed in the United States of America
on acid-free paper

FOREWORD

Most people in advanced industrial economies confront a problem much like the one confronting a man I saw depicted in a cartoon many years ago. Having died and gone to heaven, he was sitting on a cloud playing his harp in the company of two other angels. His desperation was apparent as he asked them, "You mean this goes on *forever?*" The difficulty in both cases is that persistently high material comfort levels tend to undermine traditional sources of pleasure. Indeed, there can be little real joy in the lives of people whose every appetite is gratified almost instantaneously.

When the first edition of Tibor Scitovsky's *The Joyless Economy* articulated this message in 1976, most economists simply were not ready for it. The profession was on a roll, triumphantly extending the neoclassical model into one new area after another. Most of us were in no mood to be distracted by Professor Scitovsky's penetrating criticisms. Even so, *The Joyless Economy* managed to attract a loyal band of enthusiastic supporters, and it continues to be cited by scholars from many disciplines. Yet it never quite made it into the economics mainstream.

In the intervening years, however, evidence against certain predictions of the neoclassical model has continued to mount.

More important, much of this evidence has become widely dissem-
inated in the profession. Our new *Journal of Economic Perspectives*,
for example, devotes its regular "Anomalies" column to an assess-
ment of it. Almost everyone who has confronted this evidence is
troubled by it, and younger economists appear particularly inclined to rethink our conventional approach. It has become increasingly clear that theories and evidence from psychololgy have
something useful to contribute to this reassessment. So Oxford's
release of *The Joyless Economy*'s revised edition comes at an especially opportune moment. This time, I think, the profession is
primed for Professor Scitovsky's message.

His first four chapters present what remains one of the most
artful and accessible summaries of what psychologists know about
human motivation. Economists will learn that the concept of utility
in economic models corresponds to the psychologist's notion of
comfort; and they will see substantial evidence against the idea
that people are comfort maximizers. As Professor Scitovsky explains, our utility-maximization model leaves out the psychological concept of pleasure, which is the fleeting state that occurs in the
transition from discomfort to comfort. As he convincingly demon-
strates, there are many human behaviors that are difficult to
explain without invoking the concept of pleasure.

The comfort-pleasure distinction is important for both normative and positive analysis. One normative message of traditional
neoclassical economics, for example, is that happiness will rise if
the level of consumption either rises or becomes more uniform
over time. But the comfort-pleasure distinction informs us that
neither change is a sufficient condition for increased satisfaction.
On the contrary, Professor Scitovsky shows why we often do
better when consumption is both lower and more variable over
time.

Although I am sure Professor Scitovsky did not intend *The Joyless
Economy* as a self-help manual for those trying to kick a drug habit
and members of the leisure class, his book is filled with acute
observations about how consumption activities might be restruc-
tured to the benefit of both these groups. Its subject matter and

engaging style will continue to appeal to intelligent lay readers and scholars from a variety of disciplines. Its most enduring value, however, will be as a source of guidance and inspiration for economists whose goal is to predict human behavior and to analyze the welfare consequences of different institutional arrangements.

There are stimulating ideas aplenty in this volume. The challenge for the next generation of economists is to discover how to formalize these ideas and integrate them into the existing body of neoclassical thought. We can be confident that careful research along these lines will yield high returns indeed.

Robert H. Frank
Professor of Economics
Cornell University

PREFACE

This book was written more than 15 years ago in an America very different from the one we are living in today. Ours was then the world's richest nation. Thirty years of unbroken prosperity had almost doubled the average person's income in real terms and yet people seemed to be missing something. The book analyzed the psychology of human motivation and satisfaction in order to explain why such unprecedented and fast-growing prosperity had left its beneficiaries unsatisfied. To devote a whole book to explaining that paradox may seem frivolous today, when a decade of misrule, corruption, and neglect of public health, education, the poor, and our country's infrastructure have created many much more pressing economic and social problems. On the other hand, to know what motivates us, what our needs are, and which unsatisfied need explains the disappointment even of the affluent among us is necessary for fully understanding why our youth and the unemployed poor turn so easily to drugs, why violence is on the rise, and even helps to explain the deterioration of the environment.

The disappointment I am referring to is boredom: people's need to keep busy and their failure to find the right stimulus to keep them busy. As Blaise Pascal, the French catholic philosopher and scientist put it in his *Pensées* 350 years ago: "I have discovered that all human evil stems from one fact alone: Man's inability to sit still."

Boredom creates no problem for hard-working men and women whose labor leaves them no time to sit still long enough to relax, get rested, and start fidgeting. The problem only plagues people with leisure—more leisure than they know what to do with. Up until Pascal's time, men of leisure whiled away much of their leisure time with riding, bloodsports, dueling, jousting, and with intrigue, murder, war, and aggression against their fellow men. Violence seems to be men's instinctive outlet for their pent-up energies; and combining it with danger, especially danger they feel confident of overcoming, makes it all the more exciting and satisfying. Less cruel leisure activities were available in their time, but gambling and card games, their ladies' pastimes, were insufficient to satisfy the need for stimulating activity of strong, energetic men with nothing to do. They lacked the education and discipline necessary to enjoy more constructive excitements and leisure activities. Today, we are much more civilized, but not civilized enough to enable everybody to escape both boredom and the more objectionable means of relieving it.

Civilization consists in originating stimulating activities other than violence and back-breaking labor, developing the skills needed to exercise and enjoy those activities, and making available the education needed to learn the requisite skills and discipline. By now, the number and variety of enjoyable benign interests has become enormous: they comprise scientific research, exploration, literature, art, sports, games of skill and chance, and the offerings of the entertainment industry, among many other things. We need them all, considering that scientific research in turn is forever increasing our leisure and with it our need for nondestructive leisure activities to keep us busy. They differ greatly in the degree of exertion they involve, the intensity of the stimulus they provide, and the amount of skill, education, discipline, and perseverance their enjoyment requires. Such differences cater to different people's differing temperaments, tastes, and abilities; unfortunately, however, the most stimulating benign activities are usually also the ones whose enjoyment requires the most skill and perseverance, whereas the people most avid for strong stimulus are seldom the most able and willing to acquire the skills and discipline necessary for their enjoyment.

Advancing civilization would advance our happiness if our education for enjoying leisure by putting it to good use increased in step with the increase in our leisure. Problems arise when it does not, and they are the problems this book sets out to explore.

The first part of the book presents a simple account of the psychological theory of motivation. It relates our feelings of pain and pleasure to the physiology of the brain, explains the complex relationship between those two feelings, and shows that boredom is as powerful a drive as hunger, making our psychological need to relieve it with stimulating physical or mental activities as urgent as are our physiological needs for food, drink, or sex. That, to my mind, is the most valuable part of the book because, quite apart from its use for the purpose at hand, motivation theory is interesting and fascinating in its own right, since all its findings seem to be confirmed by introspection and add to one's self-knowledge and understanding of others.

The second part of the book puts the theories of the first part into practice. It compares our chosen life-style to that which Europeans choose, documents our excessive demand for comfort, and shows how our Puritan tradition, work ethic, and educational system all contribute to depriving us of many of the skills and tastes necessary for the enjoyment of the more stimulating and creative leisure activities. That is why we try to satisfy our need for stimulation with activities that require no or negligible skill but soon turn out to be insufficiently stimulating and so leave us bored and dissatisfied.

Most of the conclusions reached, especially those concerning our overuse of comfort, are equally valid today. I argue in the book that people's too great love of comfort deprives them of some of life's pleasures; I would add now that it also harms their environment. Comfort seems to be the most costly source of human satisfaction in terms of the depletable resources and ecological degradation of our planet. If international comparisons of standards of living are to be trusted, the Swedes, Norwegians, Swiss, and ex-West Germans are as well off today as Americans, yet they consume less than half the energy and generate less than half the household waste per head of population than we do—presumably, because their life-style goes easy on comfort, but makes up for it on other sources of satisfaction. It would greatly benefit the environment if they, not we, were the world's leaders of fashion as far as life-style is concerned.

Some other aspects of our life-style, however, seem to have changed noticeably since the time to which my statistics refer. I mention in the book the emergence in this country of a counterculture, in revolt against its parents' Puritan ethic, searching for a more meaningful life-style but too young for their tastes to show up yet in the statistics (p. 151). By today, they have become part of the dominant generation, and their newfound interest in the quality of life has become apparent. Indeed, I originally wanted to revise that part of the book and bring its factual data up-to-date, only to find that most of them are unavailable for the 1980s, partly because statistics are part of this country's infrastructure on whose upkeep our previous and present administrations are trying to economize, and partly also because several international comparisons I had found useful and made much use of in the original edition have not been repeated.

With not enough documentary evidence to support my impressions of recent developments in our way of life, I decided to change nothing in the first twelve chapters of the book, let Chapters 8 through 12 stand as a record of the use we then made of our postwar prosperity, and encourage readers to note and judge for themselves the changes in our attitudes that have occurred over the past 15–20 years. The only and very minor change was to add more up-to-date figures in Tables 7 and 8, where they show a notable difference between then and now; and readers must excuse the retention of the present tense of the 1976 edition even where it refers to conditions that have greatly changed in the interim. To deal with those changes, I have improved and slightly expanded the last chapter, dividing it into two separate (thirteenth and fourteenth) chapters, and added the text of an address given a couple of years ago as an appendix. Moreover, I would also like to say a few words here about recent developments.

The two salient novelties in our American way of life are the increased interest in culture and the quality of life of an affluent, college-educated upper class, and, at the opposite end of the income and education scale, the increased violence and drug abuse of our newly emerging underclass. Both had been cursed with more leisure than they knew what to do with, they both revolted— the former against their parents' ways, the latter against society— and they both escaped their predicament, though in very different ways.

The first group's growing concern with the quality of life is reflected by the great increase in the availability of the many supplies that constitute the ingredients of the good life. I have in mind the increase in cultural activities, the improved quality of our domestic wines, the increased sophistication of restaurants, bakeries, delicatessens, and the gradual emergence of the new kind of bookshops that aim at providing the public with the broadest possible choice rather than just maximizing the sale of bestsellers and standard works, to mention just a few. I discussed and tried to document the increased interest in the performing arts and other cultural activities in my address reprinted in the Appendix. The data it contains pertain only to the San Francisco Bay area; and while similar changes are said to have occurred also elsewhere, I do not really know how representative my small sample is. In any case, I suspect that this kind of change is still restricted to the fortunate few with enough money, education, and energy to learn how to use their leisure in an enjoyable and constructive way.

The other group whose lifestyle has changed under the same pressure of excessive leisure but in the opposite direction is our new underclass of the unskilled poor, among them especially the black male youths of the inner cities, products of our worst schools and school dropouts, holding down unsatisfactory, unstimulating jobs and many of them chronically jobless. Their difficulty to find a job and the long stretches of unemployment between their short, dull, temporary jobs have been increasing throughout the postwar period; and by now, about half of the 16–19 age group of black males is out of work, as is a not much smaller proportion of the 20–24 age group. That is a tragic situation, rendered hopeless by employers' regrettable though understandable reluctance to hire people with long histories of past unemployment or intermittent employment.

In addition to poverty and miserable living conditions, these youngsters also suffer from the ordeal of unrelieved boredom, every day for weeks and months, from morning to night, with nothing to do or look forward to. They are unskilled and unprepared for making enjoyable and socially acceptable use of their unwanted full-time leisure, with most of them not even literate enough to pass the time with reading. Our society tries at least to give them food and shelter; less or nothing is done to relieve their no less urgent need for something to do. Yet, many of them, just like many of all the other, less disadvantaged youngsters, need stronger medicine against boredom than what TV, movies, and hanging out in the street can provide. At present, the only sources of excitement accessible to them seem to be violence, crime, illegal activities, and addictive drugs; and our singular lack of success in fighting such behavior with punitive measures indicates the great urgency of young people's need for adequate stimulation to escape boredom and release their unused energies. The only effective way therefore of coping with crime, drug trafficking, and drug addiction is to offer work, make-work, or any meaningful activity for those who need it, to educate our new underclass along with the rest of the population in the skills of some benign forms of leisure along with those of work, and provide them with opportunities to exercise both those skills, because that alone will wean them from activities destructive to others or themselves.

This book was not written to address that problem; but by learning about the more general issues it does deal with, the reader should also gain new insight into the nature, origin, and possible solution *also* of that problem. Let me just add that despite the word "joyless" in the title, this was by far the most enjoyable of my books to write, and I very much hope that some of the joy its writing gave me will also be found in its reading.

Menlo Park, Calif.   T. S.
June 1991

PREFACE TO FIRST EDITION

This book was written by an economist, but it is concerned with matters not hitherto considered part of economics. People's tastes, the way they spend their money and arrange their lives, are matters economists have always regarded as something they should observe, but must not poke their noses into. They seem to feel that analyzing people's tastes and their motivation would be an invasion of privacy and an abrogation of consumer sovereignty, and that it might expose them to the charge of pretending to know better than the consumer himself what is good for him. Instead, economists assume that the consumer is rational; in other words, they assume that whatever he does must be the best thing for him to do, given his tastes, market opportunities, and circumstances, since otherwise he would not have done it. The great advantage of such an approach is that it enables economists to look upon the consumer's actual behavior as a faithful reflection of his preferences and, conversely, to regard his preferences as revealed by his behavior. That assumption, together with its implications, is known as the theory of revealed preference; on it are based many of the economists' arguments, conclusions, recommendations.

I consider that approach unscientific, and I am trying in this book to lay the groundwork for something both humbler and better. The scientific approach, to my mind, is to observe behavior—different people's behavior in similar situations and the same person's behavior in different situations—in order to find, contained in those observations, the regularities, the common elements, the seeming contradictions and the resolution of those contradictions which then become the foundations of a theory to explain behavior. That has been the approach of behavioral psychologists. Accordingly, I shall use their work, their experimental findings and the theories they evolved to fit those findings, as the basis for my attempt to explain the consumer's behavior and his motivation. Therefore, after my introductory chapter, where I state the economist's position and stress the need for him to look deep into the consumer's soul, I give, in the next three chapters (Two, Three, and Four), a detailed but simple account of how psychologists view and explain behavior. Let me warn the reader that whenever I discuss psychology, I will be talking about *physiological* psychology—more particularly, motivational psychology, that part of the body of physiological psychology which is most relevant to establishing, extending, and correcting, where necessary, the economists' theory of consumer behavior.

The psychologists' theory is remarkable in that each statement they make is supported by experimental evidence. I quote examples as we go along, just to give the flavor. Those examples show how much more realistic and convincing psychological theory is than the economists' sweeping assumption of rational behavior. Not that our behavior is irrational; it simply turns out to be much more complex and subtle than those who merely assume rationality are wont to believe. When we behave rationally, we seek the best available choice or the best compromise between mutually incompatible considerations; one can go very wrong, however, in identifying the available choices and the relevant considerations.

To link the psychologists' and economists' approaches, I have (in Chapter Five) placed economic activity and economic welfare into the psychologists' much larger framework. The result is a clear separation of economic and non-economic satisfactions; a discussion of that curious borderline case, the satisfaction of work; and a better understanding of what determines whether a particular source of satisfaction will or will not be within the realm of economics. The economic satisfactions, which receive most of the public's attention, turn out to be a small part of the total, although they are, of course, the part over whose volume and distribution we have the most control. I then try (in Chapter Six) to reconcile some of the economists' and psychologists' classifications of sources of satisfaction and also to round out my earlier chapters' individualistic approach by including social motivation. Psychologists have a much broader view of man's behavior and motivation than economists do; I am extending that view even further by including the satisfactions of status, philanthropy, altruism, and the like. Another topic I introduce here is our tendency to take for granted the good things of life and become addicted to them.

T. S.

CONTENTS

THE JOYLESS ECONOMY

CHAPTER ONE

Introduction: Plutocracy and Mob Rule

The middle of the twentieth century may well turn out to have been the high point of our national existence. We saw ourselves in the forefront not only as a nation, but also as individuals. The American consumer was on top of the world, freely spending the world's highest income on the world's most copied and coveted life-style.

The glory, alas, was short-lived. We started losing our self-confidence while still on the ascendant. With hardly a change in objective circumstances, the American consumer's picture of himself changed drastically in the short span of hardly more than a decade. Our proud self-image of the sovereign consumer shrank to that of the pitiful character of a Caspar Milquetoast, the helpless consumer who gets oppressed and harassed, cheated and shortchanged, even poisoned, from every side. Why such a great and sudden change in the way in which we see ourselves?

Part of the reason, no doubt, is our growing realization that technical and economic progress also has a dark side to it. We are gaining increasing scientific evidence of the cumulative harm to health, environment, and future generations created by our reckless brandishing of weapons, extermination of pests, squandering of resources, popping of pills, ingesting of food additives, and use or overuse of every mechanical aid to our comfort and safety.

When drawbacks accompany advantages, it is natural to blame those who tout the advantages. But we would like to retain the advantages and therefore seek the remedy in tighter control over producers and their relation with consumers. We demand that the same scientific resources be brought to looking into the possible harm a product might do as are customarily applied to exploring its benefits; and we want government agencies to protect us against irresponsible producers and our irresponsible selves. Thanks to Ralph Nader and the public's recognition of the soundness of his cause, much badly needed progress has already been made in that direction, though much remains yet to be done.

But is there not another reason for our increasing frustration with our freely chosen lives? Could it not be that we seek our satisfaction in the wrong things, or in the wrong way, and are then dissatisfied with the outcome? That is the question this book is asking and trying to answer. It is a difficult question to deal with because we are accustomed to blaming the system or the economy and have gotten out of the habit of seeking the cause of our troubles in ourselves. That was an approach popular in past, more religious, ages, which focused their attention on man's transgression of the Laws of God. We gradually dismantled the Laws of God and came to believe in man as the final arbiter of what is best for him.

That was a bold idea and a proud assumption, but it set back by generations all scientific inquiry into consumer behavior, for it seemed to rule out—as a logical impossibility—any conflict between what man chooses to get and what will best satisfy him.

Economists today consider the two synonymous. They accept unquestioningly the consumer's judgment of what is best for him, his tastes as the outcome of that judgment, and his market behavior as the reflection of his tastes. Economists will not analyze the motivation of consumer behavior, claiming that that would be beyond their competence and that it would inevitably involve an improper judgment: that of judging one man's way of making the best of his life by another man's standards. As a result, the economist's approach to his subject tacitly assumes that consumers know what they are doing and are doing the best they can, so that the economist's only task is to see to it that the economy delivers what consumers want.

That approach overlooks the fact that tastes are highly variable, easily influenced by example, custom, and suggestion, constantly changed by the accumulation of experience, and modified by changing prices and the availability of some satisfactions and the unavailability of others. It also overlooks the possibility that the same influences that modify our tastes might also modify our ability to derive satisfaction from the things that cater to our tastes. In short, the economist's standard procedure of postulating that each consumer knows best what is good for him and trusting the consumer's behavior to reflect that knowledge seems to me unscientific. What I propose to do instead is to look into the consumer's behavior, analyze its motivation, and then draw whatever conclusions follow from such an investigation.

The market transmits information among competitors and between buyer and seller, thereby harmonizing their actions. Economists regard all such harmony as evidence that the bill of goods the economy produces conforms to consumer tastes. But in truth, the market is quite impartial. It puts pressure to conform on buyers and sellers alike, and most of the conforming is done by those whose behavior is the most flexible. Although both consumers and producers benefit from the other party's conforming to their wishes, producers have the greater power and influence. U.S. producers and merchants spend 2 1/2 per cent of the GNP on advertising—ample indication of their willingness to use that power. Harmony therefore, between consumer preferences and the pattern of production may simply indicate the adaptation of man's tastes to the rigid requirements of the productive system, and that would hardly be a cause for self-congratulation. We do not know which is more flexible, consumer behavior or producer behavior. Nor do we know who does most of the conforming. And we must not prejudge the issue. Economists know a lot about what makes producers tick, while they know almost nothing about the motivation of consumers. Surely, knowledge of what makes consumers tick is just as important as knowledge of the way producers make decisions.

Probing into consumer behavior and its motivation should give economists a better understanding of what harmony between consumption and production patterns really signifies, a better judgment of how well the economy performs, and a better basis for developing and recommending policies to improve its performance.

Ideally, an understanding of consumer behavior could accomplish even more than that. By long-established tradition, economists have been advisers to governments. The economist assumes that people are maximizers: consumers by seeking the greatest satisfaction and businessmen by trying to obtain the highest profit. And with this assumption, the economist focuses on the nature and desirability of the outcome of such maximizing behavior under various institutions, conditions, and public policies. He does not consider it his business to question the consumers' conpetence at maximizing whatever they maximize, nor does he advise them how best to do it.

Not so long ago, the economist took the same stand-offish, hands-offish attitude toward businessmen's competence at maximizing profits. But then, when he started to study and understand the difficulties businessmen face in trying to maximize profits, he gradually became more adept at handling some of those difficulties than the businessmen themselves were, and he soon found himself a much sought-after expert who could advise corporations on how to predict trends, economize costs, increase efficiency, and raise profits.

Can economists also appreciate the problems a consumer

faces as he budgets his income and arranges his life, and can they do something similar about that? It is too early to tell. I cannot quite visualize myself or my colleagues in the role of family economist, holding office hours or paying house calls on consumers, advising them about what to consume. On the other hand, if we succeed in dissecting consumer satisfaction into its components and laying bare the forces that make the consumer push away one thing and reach out for another, perhaps we will be able to help him understand his own behavior better and make it more rational. Who knows? Perhaps this book may help its readers to become better consumers.

Although economists have never analyzed the nature and origin of consumer preferences, others have, so we need not start from scratch. Psychologists have done a lot of work on the motivation of man's behavior, of which consumer behavior is a part. Moreover, the scientific method of at least some psychologists—mostly those who are known as physiological psychologists—is very similar to the economist's; they too observe behavior and from that infer its motivation. The main difference is that while economists observe man's market behavior in real-life situations, physiological psychologists observe many more kinds of behavior, mostly under carefully controlled experimental conditions, and they do not confine themselves to man. In any case, the two disciplines mesh well, and I will try to integrate parts of them into a larger and more general theory of man's striving for satisfaction.

Among the reasons for the economist's refusal to probe into consumers' motivation was his belief that every consumer is his own master, free to follow his personal tastes and inclinations independently of other consumers' tastes and inclinations, and that the economy can, at least in the realm of private goods, accommodate different consumers' different tastes all at the same time. That belief, known as the doctrine of consumer sovereignty, is a gross oversimplification, especially in our age of mass production, when almost nothing gets produced that cannot be produced in the thousands.

People exercise freedom of choice whenever they use money to pay for goods and services and are free to decide what to buy and in what quantities. That freedom must not be confused with consumer sovereignty. The consumer is sovereign insofar as his choice influences the nature and quantity of the goods and services produced.

In centrally planned economies, for example, central planners make the production decisions, but they allow their decisions to be more or less influenced by the buying public's preferences as revealed by sales. The extent of that influence is the measure of consumer sovereignty in the planned economy. Our claim for the free enterprise economy is that all its production decisions are determined solely by the free choice of buyers, so that consumer sovereignty is fully realized. Even if we accept this proud claim, it leaves some of the most important questions unanswered. There are millions of consumers. Are all of them sovereign? Are they equally sovereign? And, if not, what determines their relative influence on the nature and quantity of goods and services produced?

The standard answer to those questions is to say that the market is like a voting machine in which dollars spent by consumers are counted as votes. The more a consumer spends, the greater his voting power. Therefore, consumer sovereignty in a free enterprise economy is a plutocracy, the rule of the rich, where each consumer's influence on what gets produced depends on how much he spends. Plutocracy is a serious weakness in an economy, but we try to eliminate its excesses and make it more palatable by progressive taxation, public relief, and the free or subsidized provision of some of our basic necessities.

In addition, our economy provides a much more powerful antidote to the rule of the rich: the economies of scale. Thanks to the technology of mass production, things bought by many people can be produced more cheaply than those bought by only a few. The poor always have the advantage of numbers; those of the poor who all want the same thing can usually have it at a lower price, and that lower price, with respect to that particular thing, offsets their poverty. In the modern economy, therefore, wherever economies of scale lead to important reductions in cost, plutocracy is combined with mob rule: the crowd's ability to get those things on whose desirability its members agree. One of the main goals of advertising is to promote such agreement.

Rule of the rich and rule of the crowd sound like a curious combination, but that combination is, in fact, the rule imposed by modern capitalism. Also, their combination is better than either of them by itself, because each mitigates the shortcomings of the other. The inequalities of plutocracy would be much harder to bear if modern technology and mass production did not make many of the essentials of life accessible to almost everybody. Our sense of fairness does not demand that some statistical index of income inequality stay below some crucial numerical value, but it does demand that, whatever the inequalities of income, everybody should be given equal access to the basic necessities of life. One of the blessings of mass production is that it caters to this demand.

It is more difficult to appreciate the shortcomings of mob rule and the tempering of them by plutocracy. To render production cheap, the seller must extend his market; he can best do this by catering to desires everybody shares. These desires—beyond that for the essentials of life—consist in the primitive, unsophisticated desires, or variants of desires, which the most simple-minded segment of the consuming public shares with the rest. By catering to these desires the seller fulfills the important economic function of creating the conditions necessary for reaping the economies of scale, cheapening his product, and making that product accessible to all; but at the same time, he also discourages and discriminates against more sophisticated tastes and so pulls down the level of the public's average taste. These two effects, the good and the bad, seem to be, regrettably but inevitably, linked in our economy; hence my choice of the derogatory term, "mob rule," for the blessings of mass production under capitalism. We blame the film industry for encouraging a juvenile mentality with its "family" and "adult" movies; but we cannot in reason chide businessmen for doing whatever it takes to maximize profits while at the same time we rely on profit maximization as the economy's guiding principle.

A person finds his tastes well catered to if he is conformist enough to share them with millions of others, because the things he then wants are profitable to mass produce and to sell at prices lowered by mass production. By contrast, a person with eccentric tastes who wishes to pursue a divergent life-style will be discouraged by the high prices or unavailability of the things he wants. If he is a millionaire as well as an eccentric, he can afford both to pay the high prices and to have the unavailable things made available, which, after all, is usually just a matter of paying even higher prices. The more advanced the economy, the greater the economies of scale, and the greater the difference in price between what is mass-produced and what is not, between conformity to the established life-style and preference for a divergent one.

Readers who lack compassion for the rich may be all for having eccentric millionaires pay through the nose, probably on the ground that any price discrimination which helps to mitigate inequalities is for the good. But such an attitude is based on a misunderstanding. It is not millionaires whom the mob rule of our economy discriminates against and exacts a high price from, but eccentrics. A square millionaire—and probably most *are* square—pays much the same price as a square hard-hat does for the goods he buys. His higher purchasing power and greater consumer sovereignty are therefore fully proportionate to his higher income and wealth. It is the eccentrics, the people who want something different, who find life expensive in our economy, irrespective of whether they are rich or poor. The eccentric millionaire has become a byword, because he alone among eccentrics can afford to put his eccentricity into practice. Most of the others are forced by the high cost of eccentricity to give it up and conform instead.

"Eccentric" and "square" may be frivolous words, but the public's need for varied experiences, different life-styles, and the chance to try out new things and new sources of satisfaction is a serious matter—indeed, it is essential if society is to make good use of its economic opportunities and growing affluence in its search for the good life. Modern technology creates great possibilities, but it also pushes us toward standardization and uniformity, both of which inhibit our ability to exploit the possibilities it creates. This is one of the problems of our times, and it is part of the subject matter of this book.

It should now be apparent that the economists' representation of the consumer as someone whose tastes are set, who knows what he wants and fails to achieve it only for lack of means, is quite inadequate. The inadequacy of their picture of man has kept the profession from even considering the influences that mould the dominant life-style and push us all toward accepting and adopting it. It has also kept economists from recognizing and exploring that most important motive force of behavior, including consumption behavior—man's yearning for novelty, his desire to know the unknown. The yearning for new things and ideas is the source of all progress, all civilization; to ignore it as a source of satisfaction is surely wrong.

PART I

The Psychology and Economics of Motivation

CHAPTER TWO

Between Strain and Boredom

Modern economics and psychology originated with the rationalist philosophers of the eighteenth century. Both disciplines claim Jeremy Bentham as an ancestor, although soon after his day they went their very separate ways. One of Bentham's shrewd psychological observations was that the second cup of coffee or the second helping of a dish is less enjoyable than the first, and the economists enshrined it into their celebrated Law of Diminishing Marginal Utility. But in the twentieth century they expurgated even that tiny bit of psychology, and today the economist's theory of consumer behavior is limited to exploring the logical implications of the assumption of man's rationality.

The same eighteenth-century philosophers who explained man's behavior by the proud assumption of rationality attributed the not very different behavior of dumb animals to instinct; the psychologists, luckily for them, chose instinct as their starting point for studying the motivation of behavior. That set a course they still follow, although the shortcomings of the concept of instinct gradually became apparent and led to its replacement by a related but more satisfactory concept, "drive."

Hunger, thirst, pain, feelings of heat and cold, sexual desire—
all are manifestations of biological disturbances which were
originally believed directly to motivate action designed to eliminate the disturbance and restore the equilibrium of the organism. The mechanism whereby a disturbance creates a drive,
and the resulting activity restores equilibrium and so eliminates
the drive, is known by such names as "drive theory," "stimulus-response (or S-R) theory," and "homeostasis." Originally,
homeostasis, the organism's tendency to act like a thermostat,
had a narrower meaning; it only meant what today is known as
physiological homeostasis, the autonomic, involuntary action of
organs and muscles whereby, say, the temperature of the body
and the chemical composition of the blood are maintained at a
steady level, or a foreign body is washed out of the eye by involuntary weeping. Later the concept was broadened to include
"psychological homeostasis"—voluntary actions prompted by
various drives. After all, these voluntary actions complement
and are very similar to the involuntary actions: all of them aim
at maintaining the organism's environment in the steady state
most conducive to survival and comfort.[1]

Since biological drives cannot explain all action, the theory
was soon extended; secondary or learned drives were added to
the primary or biological drives. It is now believed, however,
that even the primary and secondary drives together cannot
explain all behavior, and that a more general framework is
needed to supplement or supplant the drive theory.

AROUSAL [2]

Just as instinct lost its usefulness as an explanatory principle
when the number of instincts distinguished grew into the thousands, so the drive theory is waning because of the proliferation
of drives. But there are even better reasons for seeking to explain behavior in terms other than drive theory.

The first is that the drive theory of behavior implies that the
organism is inert unless some disturbance or deprivation gener-

ates a drive and so leads to activity to eliminate the disturbance. This is now believed to be wrong.

> Observation of animals and people . . . indicates that much time and energy is taken up by brief, self-contained, often repetitive acts which are their own reason, . . . autonomously motivated, and not . . . small contributions to some remote, critically important aim. The organism scratches itself, stretches, shakes its head, grunts or chirps, looks around, examines an irrelevant item of the environment, picks its nose or its teeth, rocks back and forth, shifts its position, twists a paperclip out of shape, cracks its knuckles, doodles, looks at a picture on the wall, and so on *ad infinitum.*" [3]

Human beings and the higher animals, in addition to performing such brief acts, also engage in a variety of more sustained and complex activities that are equally hard to explain in terms of drive theory and need satisfaction.

The other reason for the psychologists' new explanation of behavior is the neurophysiologist's growing knowledge and changed view of the functioning of the brain. Just as the organism was believed to be quiescent except when bent on or engaged in satisfying some need, so too nerve cells and the central nervous system as a whole were also believed to be inert except when stimulated by some impulse. That idea, too, has been proved wrong. We now know that nerve cells can and do fire spontaneously; and that the central nervous system is continually active, whether the organism is awake or asleep, stimulated or not. The brain's activity, known as arousal, or activation, is manifest in electrical impulses which can be monitored by means of an electroencephalograph, and they appear on the electroencephalogram as waves, called EEG waves. The faster the electric discharges of neurons, the higher the level of arousal and the greater the frequency of EEG waves (measured in cycles per second). Moreover, EEG waves register the firing of not one neuron, but many, and the amplitude of a wave measures the sum of all the electrical discharges of all the neurons firing at a given moment in a given part of the brain. When the firing is slow, it is also quite synchronous: all the nerve cells fire at the same time, which makes the slow EEG waves fairly regular and large in amplitude. Faster firing, on the other hand, goes with lack of synchrony, with different nerve cells firing at different moments, which is why the fast EEG waves are rather irregular and small in amplitude.

Different brain waves correspond to different levels of agitation, though we do not yet know how, nor whether one causes the other. Neurophysiologists have named these waves—alpha, beta, gamma, and so on. The best known and most easily identifiable are the slow (8 to 13 cycles/second), synchronous, and therefore high amplitude and fairly regular alpha waves, which appear when the subject is at rest but awake and completely relaxed.

The level of arousal, measured by the frequency, amplitude, and synchrony of EEG waves, depends on the stimulation the central nervous system receives from outside, through the senses (exteroceptive stimulation), from the muscles and internal organs of the organism (enteroceptive stimulation), and from within the brain itself (cerebral stimulation); but it never sinks to zero as long as the organism is alive. Indeed, death is now in the process of being redefined as the stopped activity of the brain, not the heart. Moreover, the level of arousal when the organism is in a state of rest varies over a twenty-four-hour period. It is lowest during sleep; "after waking, higher organisms typically show an increasing degree of alertness, then a relatively long period with a gradual rise and, later, a gradual decline, and, finally, a sharper decline toward drowsiness and a return to the sleeping state." [4]

The level of arousal, of course, can be not only measured, it can be felt. We feel ill or well, we experience pain or pleasure, and when we do, we are sensing our level of arousal. Moreover, because we seek pleasure and try to avoid pain, the concept of arousal is central to the explanation of behavior. Without continuous activity of the brain, without incessant firing of its nerve cells, there cannot be any response to stimuli. A high arousal is associated with vigilance and quick response; it makes the senses more sensitive to stimuli, increases the brain's capacity to process information, readies the muscles for action, and so shortens the total reaction time that elapses between an incoming sensation and the response through action. It makes you feel excited, emotional, anxious, and tense. On the other hand, when you feel slow, less than vigilant, lax, and drowsy, you are in a state of low arousal. The parts of the brain which are involved in such continuous activity, and which provide and regulate the organism's alertness, are known as the "arousal system."

All stimulation is now believed to have two parallel effects on the central nervous system: it activates direct neural pathways to the associative areas of the brain, those parts which do the thinking and decision-making, thus transmitting specific information about each specific stimulus for possible action. At the same time it causes a diffuse, non-specific, general raising of the activation level of the arousal system, which increases alertness and so provides a more appropriate background for the efficient and prompt functioning of the brain's direct stimulus-response mechanism.[5]

The effects of various stimuli on the level of arousal seem to be additive, however different their nature and sources might be, so that total arousal is the sum of the arousing effect of each stimulus taken separately. This means that total arousal depends on total stimulation from all the senses, muscles, endocrine secretions, and the brain itself.[6] It also seems likely that arousal always rises with total stimulation, although here there are some qualifications. For the level of arousal is measured not only by the frequency and lack of synchrony of the electrical impulses recorded on the electroencephalograph, but also by such indices of the activity of the sympathetic nervous system as the galvanic (electric) conductance of the skin, muscle tension, blood pressure, heartbeat, dilation of the pupil of the eye, and so on.[7] There is a high, but not a perfect, correlation between these and the frequency, amplitude, and synchrony of brain waves. The correlation seems especially to break down at the extremes. It seems, for example, that prolonged very low levels of total stimulation can lead to restlessness and cause some indicators of arousal (though not, apparently, the electrical activity of the brain) to rise, whereas too much stimulation occasionally lowers some manifestations of arousal, causing the person to be dazed and bemused, as if some protective device kept extremely strong stimuli from overtaxing the excitatory capacity of his nervous system.[8]

We are beginning to realize that what we now call arousal, or activation, may well have several components—for example, cortical arousal, as measured by brain waves, and the arousal of the autonomic (involuntary) nervous system, as measured by the other indices just mentioned. Little is known at this stage about the distinction between the two, about their interaction and respective functions, but, since they seem to be highly correlated, we may safely ignore the distinction here.

The level of arousal or activation is interesting in two contexts. First of all, the efficient performance of every task requires an appropriate degree of alertness and attention to assure a prompt and proper response to sensory stimuli, their collation with information stored up in the organism's memory, and the making and executing of the requisite decisions. Laboratory experiments have established a functional relationship between behavioral efficiency and arousal level. A particularly simple and striking example is that people are better able to memorize poetry and to solve arithmetic problems when they raise their arousal level, even if they do so by the simple means of tensing their hand muscles by grasping and compressing a dynamometer.[9]

Efficiency increases with the level of arousal at first, but it declines beyond a certain point. The level of arousal at which efficiency reaches its maximum is generally different for different types of activities, higher for simple, lower for difficult tasks, and also higher for physical, lower for mental activities.[10] Many activities, especially physical ones, provide, through enteroceptive stimulation, the right amount of stimulus for the level of arousal most appropriate for that activity, but this is not always the case, especially not at the beginning of an activity or at a time of sudden change to a new activity. The arousal level often fails to provide the right background for efficient action. Consider the "paralysis of terror," a state in which a person, suddenly finding himself in extreme danger but with enough time to escape, is unable to do so because his arousal level is too low and rises too slowly to reach the level he needs in time for him to make the quick decision and quick move required by the situation.[11] On the other hand, an American World War II study of soldiers in battle shows that the emotional stress of battle tends to raise arousal to too high a level, so that no more than 20 to 25 per cent of men under attack manage to fire their rifles, let alone use them efficiently.[12]

Man, being aware of the need to attain and maintain the proper activation level for efficient action, will often try deliberately to raise or lower it. The warming-up exercises of athletes, the use of pep pills and coffee to keep alert for intellectual activity, singing to keep awake while driving—all are ways in which we deliberately raise our arousal level for efficiency's sake; counting sheep to promote sleep, waiting a while to calm down before reacting to another person's objectionable behavior, and resting in a quiet room, as is the practice of some surgeons before they go into surgery, all are attempts to lower arousal to its appropriate level.

The second and, from my point of view, even more important fact about arousal is that its level has much to do with our general feeling of well- or ill-being, and thus with motivating behavior. The arousal of the autonomic nervous system may be more relevant here than is the arousal of the cortex, but we need not concern ourselves with such detail.

We all know that excessive stimulation and consequent extreme levels of arousal are unpleasant. Tension, anxiety, jumpiness, restlessness, irritability, frantic behavior, and panic are some of the symptoms of extreme arousal; so are the pain and discomfort which accompany biological deprivations or "tissue needs." All of these (including lack of sleep) are known to raise arousal.

I said earlier that different stimuli, whatever their source, are additive in their effect of raising arousal. That is why we can help a person in pain by making him lie down, loosening his clothing, and otherwise making him comfortable, all of which eliminate other stimuli and so help to lower arousal. Similarly, and for the same reason, we can, within limits, substitute food for sleep and sleep for food. Since both hunger and lack of sleep increase arousal, we can stay awake longer by eating more often, and bear hunger better with more sleep.

Just as too much stimulation and the resulting too high arousal are unpleasant and prompt a desire to end them, so too little (or no) stimulation is also unpleasant and leads to a desire for more. This is not widely realized, but it is amply documented. Its first scientific recognition probably came during the Korean war, when American prisoners of war were successfully brainwashed under no more pressure than prolonged stimulus deprivation by solitary confinement. Since then, a number of controlled experiments have amply confirmed the fact that such deprivation can be very painful. In one experiment, the subjects, well paid, well fed, and well provided for during the experiment, were required merely to lie quietly in a sound-proof room, wearing frosted glass goggles and gloves with cuffs to exclude all possible stimulation. All of them went through a short, initial period of sleep or relaxation, but then they began to feel the effects of sensory deprivation, which they found very hard to bear. They developed a regular hunger for external stimulation, and they found relief and enjoyment even in things as dull as an old stock-market report and a talk addressed to six-year-olds on the dangers of alcohol. The pain of no stimulation was so great that most subjects, after the first four to eight hours, suffered headaches, nausea, confusion, fatigue, hallucinations, and a temporary impairment of various mental faculties.[13] Other experiments of stimulus deprivation have yielded similar results; they all confirm prisoners' accounts of the ordeal of solitary confinement and of having nothing to do, nothing to occupy or distract them. As one man, in a remarkable account of solitary confinement (in a Nazi prison), put it, "variety is not the spice of life, it is the very stuff of it." [14]

While these experiments deal with the effects of no or virtually no stimulation, those of little stimulation are not very different. Experiments with mechanical, repetitive, and undemanding tasks have shown gradual deterioration of the quality of the work, coupled with the subjects' increasing dissatisfaction, anger with the experimenter, attempts to introduce variety into the situation or into the way of doing the work, and longing for other things they would have liked to do. [15] Indeed, that reaction is sufficiently common and widely known as to require no controlled experiments to establish it. Almost everybody knows how painful and unpleasant work which is too simple and too repetitive can be if we have to keep at it for long without relief. As a rule, it is not the work as such, but its failure to provide variety and stimulus which is unpleasant. Work is unpleasant only because it compels us to stay with it beyond the point where it has become completely mechanical and uninteresting, and to do it without the relief of also doing or thinking about something else at the same time. Sitting in a waiting room alone, with nothing to read, and nothing to do, watch, or listen to, would be just as painful if we did not have the relief of being able to jump up and pace from time to time and so raise our activation level.

Such unpleasant states are the extreme consequences of extremely high and extremely low levels of total stimulation; there is a wide intermediate range between them. But if very high and very low levels of stimulation are painful to the point that they cause major disturbances and pathological symptoms, lesser deviations from the normal are also unpleasant. Indeed, psychologists postulate the existence of an optimum level of total stimulation and arousal, one which is optimal in the sense that it gives rise to a feeling of comfort and well-being. This, probably, is not stable over time, but varies with the wakefulness cycle. Deviations from the optimum level of total stimulation are believed to give rise to feelings of boredom when it is below the optimum and feelings of strain, fatigue, or anxiety when it is above, and these unpleasant feelings seem the greater the longer the duration of the divergence and the greater its extent. They are believed, therefore, to constitute the inducement to try to bring back arousal to its optimum level. In short, psychologists picture the organism as striving to maintain its arousal level at or near its optimum.[16]

The concept of an optimum level of arousal, tentatively advanced by a number of psychologists, is likely to require refinement or modification. For example, stimulus-deprivation experiments have shown that most people rather enjoy, in the beginning, the lack of stimulation and the complete relaxation (or sleep) it leads to; only after the first few hours does its prolongation become at first boring, then painful and hard to bear. The concept of the optimum, therefore, may be better interpreted somewhat loosely, as an average over a finite period rather than as an exact rate at a moment of time. After a lot of excitement we welcome a period of quiet, just as a little extra stimulation relieves too uneventful a period; and most of us might well prefer some alternation of high and low arousal to a completely even level of serenity, as long as that alternation averages out to an optimal dose.

While all agree that the optimum level of total stimulation is intermediate between too much and too little, opinions differ on whether the optimum level of arousal, which optimum total stimulation gives rise to, is also at an intermediate level, or whether it is at a minimum. Those who believe that arousal always rises with total stimulation obviously adhere to the first view. However, Professor Daniel Berlyne, one of the most important writers in the field, cites evidence that sensory deprivation raises arousal as measured by some indices, and he then argues that the level of arousal first falls, then rises, with total stimulation, with the lowest level of arousal defining the optimum.[17]

That controversy is still unresolved; it too may have to do with the distinction between the two kinds of arousal already mentioned. In any case, it leaves unaffected the (for us, relevant) conclusion that the most pleasant level of total stimulation is intermediate between too much and too little. For the sake of simpler exposition, I shall tentatively assume that arousal always increases with stimulation, so that the optimum is at an intermediate level both of stimulation and of arousal. That assumption will greatly simplify the presentation of much of what follows, although no part of my argument hinges on it.[18]

PERSONALITY [19]

The concept of arousal, if not the term, is familiar to most people. It is what we have in mind when we speak of someone's being tense or drowsy, anxious or easy-going, having much or little nervous energy, or when we use the well-worn clichés about phlegmatic Englishmen, high-strung Frenchmen, and excitable Italians. The concept of arousal, or something very close to it, is best known and most used in measurements of personality. The type-casting of personality, so popular in the past, has given way to personality measurement on a one- or two-dimensional continuum. One— perhaps the only—dimension, which is variously named anxiety, emotionality, or "strength of the nervous system," is what here would be called arousability or the average level of arousal. Most familiar, perhaps, is Jung's classification of people on an extroversion-introversion scale. A number of personality inventories have been assembled for this purpose; with their aid we can rank people on a continuous scale or classify them into at least two groups of introverts and extroverts. Measurements of the average arousal levels of people so classified show that there is a significant difference between introverts and extroverts, which suggests that personality has very much to do with average arousal.[20]

One purpose of personality measurement is to predict human behavior. People with a given personality have a number of characteristics and characteristic tastes in common; by identifying some of these, some others can be predicted. There is much evidence to show that people's performance of different tasks depends on their personality. For example, it is well established experimentally that introverts do many tasks best in the morning while extroverts do the same tasks best in the afternoon. The explanation is simple. We know that to each activity there corresponds a certain level of arousal at which it will be the most efficiently performed. We also know that people's normal, at-rest arousal level changes: it gradually rises in the course of the day, from a low point on waking to a high point late in the day when the decline toward drowsiness and sleep sets in. At some point of the wakefulness cycle, everybody's arousal reaches the level at which he can best perform a given task, but introverts reach it earlier in the day, because their average arousal, and with it their whole wakefulness cycle, is at a higher absolute level.[21]

That is just one of many ways in which personality affects performance. This book, however, is concerned with behavior, with the ways in which people seek satisfaction, and those ways too are much influenced by personality. Extroverts seek excitement, outside stimulation, contact with other people; they tend to be playful, adventurous, unruly, given to gambling and to taking risks. Introverts, on the other hand, are concerned, anxious to abide by rules, and persistent; they tend to be withdrawn, self-sufficient, shunning excitement.

Such characteristics and many others fall into place and are simply explained when we bear in mind the low average arousal of the one group and the high average arousal of the other. The low arousal of extroverts makes them often seek means of raising it toward the optimum, which explains their greater need of excitement and adventure; the high arousal of

introverts explains their lesser need of raising it and their consequent preference for a safer and quieter life. The same difference in their average levels of arousal also explains the extroverts' higher consumption of stimulants, such as coffee, tea,
tobacco, and the introverts' greater need and consumption of
depressants, such as alcohol—a difference in market demand
which is statistically well documented. Similarly explained and
equally well documented is the influence of personality on sexual behavior.

> Extraverts are more likely than introverts to have pre-marital in
> tercourse . . . extra-marital intercourse . . . intercourse very
> early in life . . . intercourse with several different people over a
> given period of time . . . affairs with more than one person at a
> time . . . intercourse in more than one position. Extraverts are
> more likely to indulge in "perverted" practices, like fellatio and
> cunnilingus . . . to get along well with persons of the opposite
> sex . . . [and they] are less likely than introverts to resort to
> homosexual practices . . . masturbation.[22]

These theoretical predictions have been tested and fully borne
out by a small British questionnaire survey specifically designed
to test them; they have also been borne out by a much larger
and less detailed West German survey.[23] There is quite a long
list also of many other differences in behavior, all of which can
be similarly explained.

We tend to think of people as having different tastes, but in
fact they have different types of personalities. If the typical behavior of high arousal people is to seek to lower their arousal
and of low arousal people to seek to raise theirs, then the optimum level of arousal the two groups seek must be very much
the same—certainly more nearly the same than their average
levels of arousal. In other words, their aims and tastes in what
they consider optimal arousal are similar, though their points of
departure are different; it is this latter which accounts for differences in their behavior.

Here is the first of many contrasts between the psychologist's and the economist's view of man. The economist registers differences in what people consume and regards them as evidence of differences in what he calls "revealed preferences." The psychologist is not content to accept these and stop there; he tries to penetrate beneath the surface to find the causes and explanation of the differences.

AROUSAL REDUCTION

The foregoing has, I hope, given an inkling of the meaning of arousal, of its quantitative nature, and of some of the uses to which the concept can be put. "Level of excitement" is perhaps the simplest and shortest definition of it, which also explains its role in motivating behavior. For it seems obvious that we should dislike and try to avoid both too much and too little excitement. That shows the importance of the concept of an optimum level of excitement, arousal, and total stimulation.

Let us now settle down to a more systematic discussion of the role of arousal in human motivation. The concept of an optimum level of arousal or total stimulation makes the discussion fall conveniently under two headings: the reduction of total stimulation when this is too high, and its raising when it is too low. Arousal reducing can easily and quickly be presented here, since it deals with essentially the same type of behavior already discussed in terms of the drive theory or drive reduction theory. Arousal raising, which has been the subject of some of the most interesting and imaginative work in modern psychology, we will discuss later.

Pain, hunger, thirst, extremes of temperature, and the other biological need deprivations are all known to raise arousal, and this seems generally true of all disturbances, physical and mental, real and imagined. Somewhat surprisingly, even fatigue and lack of sleep are arousing, a fact most parents observe in their children, whose mounting excitement, jumpiness, and hyperactivity often signify their need for bed. Heightened arousal provides the inducement for action aimed at eliminating the disturbance and so bringing down the arousal level; at the same time it readies the organism for such action. We seem here to have returned to the theory of homeostasis or drive theory. Now, however, we picture the disturbance as something that leads to heightened arousal, and the action as aimed at reducing arousal. The advantage of our new picture is that it yields greater generality than the drive-reduction model and can be used to explain more than just a narrow range of physiological disturbances.

For instance, in terms of the drive reduction theory, it is easy to see that the physiological changes manifested in hunger should lead to action that secures food, but it is not at all easy to explain in these terms why someone with a full stomach should engage in storing up food for future contingencies. As soon as we introduce heightened arousal into the picture the difficulty is removed. Thinking of a problem can make us tense and raise our arousal level in much the same way as does the actual experiencing of it. Organisms capable of forethought will be motivated in very similar ways, whether they deal with an actual, a prospective, or an imagined situation. Getting food when we are hungry, laying in supplies for the weekend, and saving part of our income to have something to live on during retirement turn out to be very similar actions, for all of them are motivated by our heightened arousal, whether it is due to hunger or the thought of hunger.

Obviously, the number and range of activities prompted by heightened arousal and aimed at lowering it are very great. They include activities aimed at satisfying just about every need, whether biological or social, basic or acquired, present or future, real or imagined. Psychologists believe that every unsatisfied need heightens the arousal level, thereby both motivating the organism and readying it for activities which can satisfy that need. The activity, while it lasts, usually maintains or raises yet further the heightened arousal level, thereby assuring maximum efficiency in the performance and completion of the activity.

As to the connection between the feeling of a need and the carrying out of an activity to satisfy that need, modern psychology tends to regard all such activity as learned. This again is in strong contrast to the economist's approach, in which action and the need it satisfies are indissolubly linked. Eating, for example, psychologists believe to be a learned, not an instinctive, response, based on memory of the experience that the organism can still hunger and relieve its discomfort. They used to attribute most animal behavior to instinct, because no prolonged learning process was evident. They now believe, however, that the learning process is faster in lower organisms and slower in higher ones, because the speed of learning depends on the size of the brain and the ratio of the associative areas to the sensory areas within it. A lower organism is capable only of relatively simple responses, but it learns these very much faster than a higher organism does. Thus, an animal's seemingly instinctive behavior is probably a response that was *learned* in minutes or seconds, although the same response might take hours or days for a higher animal or for man to learn.[24]

From the economist's point of view, arousal reduction or drive reduction is especially important, because almost all of man's economic activities, consumption as well as production, fall into this category. No wonder the economist's model of consumer behavior also comes closest to that half of the psychologist's theory. But very different and quite alien to economics and the economist's way of thinking is the other half of the psychologist's theory of the motivation of behavior, which deals with the raising of too low arousal.

CHAPTER THREE

The Pursuit of Novelty[1]

What does an organism do when all its needs are satisfied, all its discomforts eliminated? The original answer, nothing, is now generally recognized to have been wrong.

Perfect comfort and lack of stimulation are restful at first, but they soon become boring, then disturbing. At that stage the organism actively seeks stimulation. Fighting boredom is the opposite of relieving discomfort: the one raises too low, the other lowers too high, an arousal level. They are opposites also in that, while discomfort is usually specific and is fully relieved only by satisfying the particular need causing it, boredom is general and can be escaped through a great variety of activities. Boredom, therefore, is much harder to analyze, because we must deal with the whole gamut of activities capable of fighting boredom, but try at the same time to find what their common element is which explains their ability to stimulate.

PHYSICAL STIMULATION

The simplest remedy for too low arousal is bodily exercise. To realize this, we need only recall the warming-up exercises of athletes and the stretching exercises of sleepers when they awake. Animals and children usually fight boredom by moving around and fidgeting. There is some evidence that many laboratory animals manage to do about as much running or moving around as they would in the wild. Perhaps the incessant pacing of some zoo animals shows the same thing.

Not only is bodily exercise a good weapon against boredom; it is also pleasant. It seems the most pleasant when it fully engages our skill and prowess. In sports we usually try to do our best, not because of outside pressure, but for our own satisfaction. Playing tennis with an equally good partner is the most fun; playing with a much weaker opponent is dull, because it is too easy, while playing with a much stronger one is discouraging, because it overtaxes one's capacity. Competitive sports and games are popular because the pleasantness of exercise is maximized by the full exertion of our strength and skills called forth by competition. The higher animals also engage in playful combat and other forms of competitive behavior.

MENTAL STIMULATION

The other source of stimulation is mental exercise. By that we mean recreation, entertainment, spectator sports, games, art, philosophy, the satisfaction of scientific and idle curiosity, and any other mental activity taken up not to fill a need, but to avoid boredom. Such activities, satisfying no biological need but undertaken for their own sake and valued for the stimulation they provide, are not peculiar to man; they are common also in animals. There is hardly a species of animal that has not been observed to engage in play and exploration for the sheer fun of it.[2] Much of what is known on the subject comes from animal experiments; the psychologist's use of the technical term, "exploratory behavior," shows that his study of the subject began with and still largely centers on the observation of animals.

Exploration of the environment can often be looked upon as

the gathering of information for future use. When so regarded, it is called *extrinsic exploration*, to distinguish it from *intrinsic exploration*, which cannot be so regarded. (A spayed dog, for example, pampered and overfed, will nevertheless sniff at street-corners and explore the shrubbery, presumably out of idle curiosity and just for fun. Intrinsic exploration, then, is an activity engaged in for its own sake, solely for pleasure.) [3]

But even intrinsic exploration has something to do with survival, as suggested by the use of the word "exercise." Every organ, every sense, every skill needs exercise to remain usable; all our faculties are known to deteriorate very rapidly without exercise. To mention just one statistic: when you are forced to take complete bed rest, you lose approximately 3 per cent of general muscular strength per day.

Exercise therefore, even if lacking in motivation, is hardly useless. To find enough stimulation to avoid boredom is literally a matter of life and death for retired people—it may become that for our entire civilization if, God forbid, further technical progress manages to take all physical and mental effort out of economic activity.[4]

The usefulness of useless activity is a paradox, and one comes up against yet another paradox when trying to explain why mental exercise is stimulating. We are concerned here with stimulus sought and enjoyed for its own sake and not followed, nor meant to be followed by response such as action or change in behavior. Yet, when one asks why a sight, sound, thought, or piece of news should arouse the central nervous system, the only plausible answer is that it prepares the organism for action. When an organism has eaten, drunk, made love, and is fully satiated and comfortable in all other respects, only a threat to its existence would move it to action. Any new feature or unexpected change of the environment might, potentially, pose such a threat and so require attention and possible response. An efficient response, however—and one such is the decision whether or not to respond—requires heightened arousal. Evolutionary theory, therefore, leads us to expect everything new or unexpected to be arousing. This expectation is fully borne out by the evidence. Observation and experiments alike show that anything new, not new in the sense of being situated later in time, but new in being surprising, different from what went before and was expected, will catch the attention and be stimulating.

But this fails to explain why potential threats to survival should be not only stimulating, but pleasantly so. New and surprising sensations are sometimes frightening and shunned, at other times attractive and sought after. The apparent conflict is resolved when we distinguish differences in degree. The new and surprising is always stimulating, but it is attractive only up to a limited degree, beyond which it becomes disturbing and frightening. Attractiveness first increases, then diminishes with the degree of newness and surprisingness. That kind of relation is common in psychology, and will recur so often in later pages that it is worth illustrating here. It takes the shape of a graph looking like an inverted U (see Fig. 1).

The inverted U-shaped curve which relates the pleasantness of a sensation to its intensity is sometimes called a Wundt curve, in honor of the first psychologist to postulate such a relation (1874). It was experimentally confirmed in 1928 by Engel, who tested the reaction of animals to varying degrees of taste sensations (saltiness, sourness, sweetness); since then, it has been confirmed in many other, widely divergent areas of experience, which suggests that it may represent a universal law.[5]

Here in a nutshell is the theory I am setting out to document and develop. The fact is that the most pleasant is on the borderline with the unpleasant. I hardly need say that the borderline is occasionally blurred, that it is differently placed for different people, and that it can shift with changing circumstances even for the same person.

What is not new enough and surprising enough is boring; what is too new is bewildering. An intermediate degree of newness seems the most pleasing. That immediately raises the further question, what determines the optimal and most satisfy-

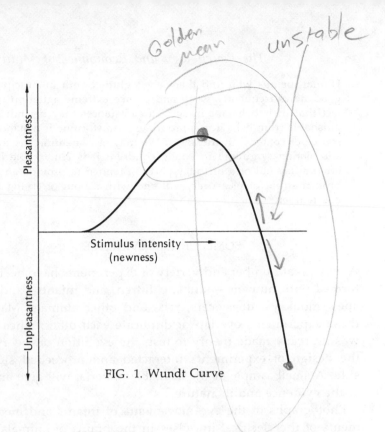

FIG. 1. Wundt Curve

ing degree of newness? The answer has been sought in the relation between the quantity of information and degree of surprisingness that a sensation contains and the brain's capacity to process information and relate it to the information already stored in its memory. It seems that a flow of information that is either too easy and too familiar or too fast and too unfamiliar should be less pleasant than something in between, and the most pleasant seems to be what fully engages the brain's information-processing capacity.

The idea that the most pleasant lies between the extremes of too little and too much was well known to the philosophers of ancient Greece. They talked a lot about the "Golden Mean" and preached moderation in everything. Our modern age seems to have all but forgotten that truth, although there are many, many reminders that too much of a "good thing" can be a bad thing.

Human beings who find themselves glutted with unanticipated good news frequently weep and evince extreme agitation. The fact that their behavior in such circumstances may be indistinguishable from behavior appropriate to misfortune is a standard source of comedy on the stage. We may also mention the overstimulation syndrome in young children. It is remarkable how often a day out or a birthday party, intended to provide an unbroken string of pleasures, will end with a bout of crying and bad temper.[6]

SOME OF THE EVIDENCE

A very great number and variety of experiments have been performed with humans—adults, children, and infants—and with apes, monkeys, dogs, cats, rats, and other animals. Many of these experiments overlap or duplicate each other; since there was no ready-made theory to test, the evolution of theory and the design of experiments interacted and proceeded side by side. A small sample of the available material will give an idea of the evidence and its nature.

Photographs of the eye movements of infants and measurements of the electrical impulses in the brains of animals have established that anything new or unexpected in the environment attracts attention and heightens arousal. Such photographs and measurements also show that as the repetition of an event renders it less new and less surprising, it gets less attention and becomes less arousing. A sufficient number of repetitions of an event can extinguish all reaction to it. Again, by monitoring the brain waves of a group of cats, psychologists have shown that a loud sound "at first evoked a burst of irregular high-frequency EEG waves of low magnitude like those commonly associated with anxiety or great effort. For each succeeding presentation, the EEG arousal reaction became shorter and the changes in frequency and amplitude less in degree. After some 30 trials, this arousal reaction had essentially disappeared." [7]

Tests of responses to repeated stimulation show the same result.

> Fear is more likely to be in evidence when the novel stimulation is first encountered: an animal is likely to retreat and keep away from novel features of the environment. . . . As the novel stimulation is repeated . . . these reactions gradually give way to approach and inspection. Finally, when the loss of novelty has gone further still, exploration declines and the stimulation that attracted it comes to be ignored.[8]

In man, adult subjects exposed to an unfamiliar rhythmic pattern several times in succession judged this unpleasant at first, then pleasant, and finally indifferent. Six-month-old children, exposed to an unfamiliar falsetto voice, at first exposure reacted with vocalization and movement indicative of displeasure, but these declined in intensity and duration until the fourth exposure caused "interested looking in the direction of the sound."[9]

Experiments designed to let subjects choose between different degrees of novelty which are simultaneously available show much the same result. The simplest and best known of these is the alternation experiment.[10] Animals placed in the starting alley of a Y- or T-shaped maze, with equal rewards offered in its two arms, tend, in successive runs, to alternate between the left and the right arm significantly more often than they would if their choice were random. Many organisms, ranging from the rat down to the cockroach and the earthworm, engage in such "spontaneous alternation."

In one variant of the experiment the animal was placed in opposite arms of a cross-shaped maze in alternate runs. This was done to test whether "fatigue of the turning-response used in the previous trial" might not be the true explanation. The results ruled this out.[11] This finding was confirmed by another variant in which one of the two arms of a maze remained the same and the other was changed between successive runs by varying its length, its shape, or the location or quantity of food in it. Most rats took the varying path more frequently than the other. In yet another variant, rats were shown, but prevented from entering the two arms of a maze. One arm was white and the other black. Before the rats were allowed to enter, one arm was changed so as to make it the same color as the other; the animals reliably chose the arm that had been altered.[12] All this seems to show conclusively that the animal seeks to expose himself to stimuli that are as different as possible from what he has been experiencing in the recent past.

Psychologists do not use mazes to test human subjects, naturally, but they do use corresponding experiments. In one of these the subjects expose themselves as often as they wish to sensations (usually patterns and pictures) of varying degrees of surprisingness, complexity, or incongruity, and then the psychologist counts the number of times the subjects choose to view each of them. The results show that people tend to look longer and more frequently at more complex or more surprising patterns, as if they are trying to master them fully and understand their complexity.

More interesting, perhaps, are the multiple-choice experiments, because they show up the inverted-U shape of the dependence of pleasingness on degree of novelty or complexity. A report on the observations of five-week-old infants states that "the subject looks neither at what is too familiar, because he is in a way surfeited with it, nor at what is too new, because this does not correspond to anything in his schemata."[13] In a more elaborate experiment, several infants were allowed to familiarize themselves with five toys, after which they could choose from six groups of toys, each containing five toys. The first group contained the five familiar toys, the second contained four of the familiar toys and one unfamiliar toy, and so forth, with the sixth group containing five unfamiliar toys. Most of the infants avoided the first and the last group; they preferred those groups which contained a mixture of familiar and unfamiliar toys. This behavior was significantly different from that of a control group which had not been previously exposed to any of the ten toys used in the experiment. Similar experiments with animals yielded much the same result.

The same type of experiment, slightly extended, has also been used to demonstrate psychological growth, the increasing sophistication of tastes which results from the accumulation of learning and experience. In one such experiment with rats, the animals were introduced into a complex maze whose different parts contained objects or were painted with patterns of different degrees of complexity. The preferences of the animals were then inferred from the length of time they spent in each part of the maze. After an initial quick survey of the whole maze, different animals settled down in different parts of it, revealing differences in tastes, perhaps explained by different previous experiences. However, daily repeated exposure of the same animals to the same experiment revealed a change of preferred location in many of them, and the overwhelming majority of the changes in location (twelve out of thirteen in one experiment) showed a shift in tastes toward greater complexity.[14]

That experiment has been repeatedly performed in slightly varying versions. Human subjects are usually asked to judge the pleasantness of random shapes of differing degrees of complexity (measured by the number of turns they contain); they, too, tend to regard those of intermediate degrees of complexity as the most pleasant, and they tend to shift their preferences toward the more complex with repeated exposure and increasing familiarity.

Another type of experiment shows how changed circumstances shift the dividing line between pleasing and disturbing degrees of newness. We know that different stimuli are additive in their effects of raising arousal; we would expect, therefore, a shift in preference toward lesser novelty at times when some other, altogether different stimulus already raises arousal. Rats which under normal conditions show a preference for the novel over the familiar arm of a maze manifest the opposite preference when aroused by hunger, by amphetamine injections, or even by a noisy environment.[15] Among humans, anxious people are known to find too exciting and therefore unpleasant many entertainments enjoyed by people who are not anxious.

These are only a few of the very large number of experiments which have served to establish and confirm two facts—that novelty has a stimulating effect and that people and animals generally prefer an intermediate degree of it. We have yet to survey the psychologists' findings on what exactly it is about novelty which makes it stimulating and attractive, and we must also look at their attempts to quantify and render measurable the substance that makes sensations stimulating and attractive.

Experiments measuring the arousing effect of such simple sensory inputs as light and sound have shown that the point of origin, that is, the level where there is no arousing effect, is not the absence of light or sound, but whatever level of it the organism is already experiencing and has adapted to. This point of origin has been called the adaptation level. It is divergences from the adaptation level that are arousing, and equal divergences in either direction are, within quite a wide range, equally arousing. For example, the sudden cessation of a clock's ticking is as striking as a new burst of sound after silence. Also, moderate divergences are pleasant, great divergences unpleasant. Sometimes this is graphically expressed by a so-called butterfly diagram, which is obtained by drawing two inverted U-shaped Wundt curves, one to the right and one to the left of the adaptation level as the point of origin.[16]

THREAT

People get a lot of satisfaction from participating in dangerous sports, watching horror movies, and reading crime stories. They also enjoy watching and find beautiful a thunderstorm from under shelter, the waves of the sea from the shore or from on board a good ship, and a fire in the fireplace or at a safe distance. Children are thrilled by being thrown into the air and caught again, by the make-believe cruelty of grown-ups (e.g.

pretend spanking), by the safe dangers of the amusement park, and by many other not-so-safe dangers as well. Animals show much the same willingness to expose themselves to danger.[17] And everybody—grown-ups, children, and animals alike—enjoys doing what is forbidden. At the same time, what is an enjoyable stimulus to one person can be a painful ordeal to another, more anxious person, or it can be insufficiently stimulating to a third, who is used to stronger fare. The excitements of children are usually dull for the grown-ups, since they have experienced them many times and are also more aware of the absence of danger.

In short, danger and the fear of danger are exciting; excitement within limits is pleasant; therefore, danger is pleasant as long as it is limited, controllable or under control, vicarious, or make-believe—and known to be such. However, the limitation or remoteness of the danger must not be too great, since that too takes away pleasantness. Tastes differ greatly as to the degree and nature of excitement considered enjoyable, and each person's taste depends largely upon his average arousal level.

Seeking limited danger, however, is only one of many ways of relieving boredom. For us it was a convenient starting point because the ability of danger to stimulate is so very obvious and because the pleasant thrill to be had from exposure to some types and degrees of danger is within most people's personal experience. But most forms of pleasant stimulation cannot be so simply explained, because their connection with potential threat to survival is often very remote, although the satisfaction they provide is not correspondingly smaller. How can we explain the enjoyment of art? After all, a violin concerto is no threat to survival, yet many people will pass up a rousing murder story, which has at least a vicarious threat, in order to enjoy a concerto. Where does that leave the theory that explains stimulation by a threat and its pleasantness by an intermediate degree of stimulation and hence, presumably, by an intermediate degree of threat?

It all depends on what we mean by a "threat to survival."

Anything new, in the sense of anything unexpected, is a threat to our survival, because we do not know how to deal with it. Each of us, through the accumulation of personal experience, develops a view of the world, starting from day one. And that view is the basis of the strategy we use for living—for surviving. Which would be fine if it were not for the fact that the world changes all the time and so threatens to render our strategy obsolete. For that reason we must continually update our world view by perceiving new information, processing it, and relating it to our previously accumulated fund of knowledge, which it will complete or modify. By doing this we update our strategy of survival. And this holds for violin concertos just as much as it does for murder stories.

Here the inflow of information poses a problem, while our successful processing of that information resolves the problem. Successful processing, however, hinges on the amount of information to be processed staying within the limits imposed by the brain's information-processing capacity. That relation between the amount to be processed and our capacity to process is the basis of the psychologists' quantitative approach to the subject.

In short, to explain the pleasantness of listening to music, we were led to broaden the idea of a "threat" to include that of a "problem," and to extend the notion of "dealing with a threat" to include that of "resolving a problem." That generalization enables us to explain many things hitherto unexplained and focuses our attention on the measurement of stimulation and its pleasantness.

MEASUREMENT

Shannon, working in communication theory, developed a measure of information. He defined the unit of information, the "bit" (short for binary digit), as the binary logarithm [18] of the number of equally likely alternatives, because this is the number of two-way choices needed to transmit a given message without ambiguity.[19] The bit is the natural unit to use when information is transmitted by two-way choices, such as the closing or breaking of electric circuits in a computer or communication system, or the firing or non-firing of nerve cells in man's nervous system, because it shows the number of impulses (or relays) needed to transmit a given volume of information. For example, to learn on which of the sixty-four squares of a chessboard a coin is located from yes-or-no answers we have to ask at least six questions ($64 = 2^6$). The quantity of information those questions elicit is six bits.

Tentative estimates put an average adult's information-processing capacity at sixteen bits per second.[20] This corresponds to the average frequency (16 cycles/second) of beta waves—that is the rate of firing of nerve cells when the organism is in an alert state. When information is not a flow over time but available simultaneously and distributed in space, as in a picture, we must relate the pieces of information contained in all parts of the picture and group them as a whole. Since the eyes scan the picture and perceive its different parts at different times, the observer must be able, while looking at one part, to keep in mind all other parts. The ability to do that depends on "short-term memory"—that is, the ability to hold many bits of information while considering them all together. The Germans have a good word for it: *Gegenwartsdauer*, duration of the present. Experiments have shown this to extend up to ten seconds in the adult. Man's capacity to process spatially distributed information therefore may be as high as 160 bits.[21]

The next step would be to compare these estimates of the brain's capacity to estimates of the amount of information contained in various sensory inputs. The information content of some abstract paintings, drawings, even of mime, has been estimated, and these estimates bear out the tentative guess that the most enjoyable and aesthetically most pleasing objects and sensations are those whose information content is close to the upper limit of man's information-processing capacity.[22] That, however, is precious little, and further work along these lines is slowed by the necessity to deal with two problems. One is created by the difficulty of ascertaining the quantity of information a person perceives, as distinguished from the information his environment contains. The other stems from the fact that the quantitative relation between the information to be processed and the brain's capacity to process it is not the only determinant of the pleasantness of novelty.

ATTENTION

Because our environment contains very much more information than our brains can process, we always single out for attention only a small part of it, suppressing or inhibiting our sensory perception of the rest. We are occasionally conscious of deliberately focusing our attention—in the midst of a lively party we try to catch one person's words and to blot out the noise of everybody else's. Mostly, however, we are not conscious and not deliberate about such sensory selection, because our attention is automatically caught by the most striking, potentially most threatening novel feature of our environment.

Psychologists have established that there is involuntary blocking of the sensory perception of relatively unimportant information. They have found, for example, that the "neural activity of the cochlea [inner ear], recorded through electrodes imbedded in the cochlear nuclei of unanesthetized cats and evoked by exposure to tones of substantial intensity, can be markedly reduced by exposing the cats to the sight of mice in a bell jar or to the odor of fish." [23]

Indeed, it is difficult for us to pay attention to a piece of music or a book at a time when some greater and more urgent threat demands our immediate attention. That is why in times of great personal or national stress or calamity, our desire for temporary relief and distraction cannot be satisfied by a gentle, slow-moving novel, but demands the greater potential threat of, say, a tense mystery. [24] When we are faced with a crisis, we may realize that dwelling on it will do no good, but we cannot suppress our involuntary tendency to focus our attention on it, because it is the greatest threat to our welfare. The danger or horror in the story helps our conscious selves fool our subconscious minds into accepting the threat of the story, however vicarious, as greater and therefore more worthy of attention than the genuine threat of our real life problem. Man's instinctive feeling that the necessities of life have higher priority than its enjoyments probably stems from the rigid priorities the central nervous system imposes by always focusing attention on whatever happens to be, at a given moment, the most urgent or the most threatening. However, once our attention is focused on something enjoyable, the mere fact that it is so focused proves that there is nothing more urgent, nothing more threatening at that time to interfere with our enjoyment. In other words, whatever our attention is focused on is shown, by that very fact, to be the most "threatening" of our concerns.

Threat or danger clearly plays an important role in both focusing our attention and determining the pleasantness of stimulation, but the kinds of threat relevant to each are very different, even if ordinary language tends to confuse them. Let us distinguish therefore the two kinds of danger. One is the danger or chance of a threat becoming reality; the other is the very different potential danger to my well-being should the threat become reality. Mountain climbing, for example, involves more danger of the second kind than solving crossword puzzles, because a false step can break my neck while an unsolved puzzle hurts only my ego. At the same time, I am in greater danger of failing to solve the puzzle than of failing to reach the mountain top if I happen to be bad at puzzles but good at climbing. The puzzle, therefore, poses a greater danger of the first kind. The two kinds of danger—chance of failure and consequences of failure—are totally different and independent; no wonder if their implications for man's behavior are also different.[25]

For my enjoyment of a stimulus, the likelihood of failure, the precise degree of danger of my failing at whatever problem or task I am tackling, is more important than the amount of danger

I would be exposed to in case of failure. There is more fun in a crossword puzzle whose difficulty matches my skill than in going on a climb which is too easy and unchallenging by my standards. How enjoyable a game of bridge is depends much more on how well the partners are matched than on how high the stakes are.

On the other hand, the *consequences* of failure are more important than its likelihood is in determining the priorities for my attention. I will keep my eyes and mind on the trail rather than on the crossword, despite the latter's greater challenge and difficulty. But once my attention is fixed on something, the stimulus enjoyment this provides depends mainly on my chance of success or danger of failure, which is determined in turn by my ability to handle the flow of information involved.[26]

REDUNDANCY

When I focus my attention, I reduce the information my brain must process, and I further reduce it when it is related to something already known to me. For to that extent it is not new information from my point of view; it is not in need of processing. That part of the information inflow is called redundant information, and its ratio to the total inflow of objective information is called relative redundancy. The other part of the objective information, the part new to me, is subjective information or subjective novelty; its ratio to the objective information is sometimes called relative information.

Think of the redundancy of language. A written text conveys 4.7 bits of information per letter, because there are twenty-six letters in the alphabet and $26 = 2^{4.7}$. That, however, is objective information, much of which is redundant. In English, different letters, sequences of letters, and sequences of words occur with different probabilities. Because I know English, I know those probabilities, however unconsciously, and the subjective information a letter conveys to me is inversely related to the probability with which I expect it to occur. After all, the function of information is to reduce uncertainty, and the more uncertainty a given piece of information reduces, the greater its quantity. Conversely, the more strongly I suspect something to be true, the less information is conveyed to me by verification of its truth.

The relative redundancy of the English language is estimated to be 50 per cent or higher.[27] In other words, the subjective information flow contained in an English text is around 2.3 bits per letter.[28] This means that when we write English, we are free to choose only half the letters; the other half are dictated by the laws of spelling, grammar, and syntax. That is why we can often understand and complete a partly heard sentence, make sense of misspelled words, use telegram style, abbreviations, and shorthand, and solve crossword puzzles. Redundancy in communication is far from useless; it keeps our messages intelligible in spite of errors or imperfect transmission. For example, when I write on an envelope not only the zip code, but also the name of the town, I provide redundant information in order to keep my letter from going astray in case I erred or my hand was illegible when writing down the zip code.

Redundancy is equally useful for information-processing. Information that is completely new, completely unrelated to anything we already know, can at best be committed to memory, which for most people is a difficult and unpleasant process. It is also quite slow: the rate at which adults can commit unfamiliar information to long-term memory is estimated at between 0.5 and 0.7 bits per second.[29] Most of the time we absorb information by relating it to what we already know, comparing it with and modifying the fund of information we have already stored in memory, but that is only possible when the incoming information is related to and linked with informational elements familiar to us. Every teacher knows how much easier it is for students to learn if they can relate the new with the familiar, be it by resemblance, parallelism, or contrast, and he will try to help his students by stressing or bringing in elements that establish such a relation. Redundant information, far from adding

to the burden on the brain's processing capacity, renders information-processing easier and more pleasant.

A completely unfamiliar sight, sound, taste or smell is bound
to be bewildering and therefore unpleasant. A fictional story, to
be enjoyable, must deal with characters and situations which
have some affinity to those we are familiar with. The same is
also true of news. A news item is interesting only if it deals
with subjects or people we already know, or know about; it is
usually the more interesting the more intimately we know
them.

In music, a melody never before heard and not fitting into
any musical tradition we are familiar with is likely to leave us
puzzled and uncomprehending. Some redundancy is already
provided when a piece of music is written in (and recognized as
written in) a given key, since the tones belonging to that key
can be expected to occur with greater frequency than others,
with the tonic and dominant of that key occurring with even
greater frequency. If, in addition, the piece belongs to a certain
period the listener is familiar with, there is more redundancy,
enabling the listener to predict even more; and if he can also
guess the composer, there is more redundancy still. Very much
the same is true of painting, dancing, and any other artistic
production. Usually, to enjoy any such work, we have to recognize it as belonging to an artistic school or style we are familiar
with, because that provides the necessary redundancy.

In short, some redundancy is essential to render anything
new pleasantly stimulating, and the degree or amount of redundancy has much to do with how pleasant it is. Just as perfect
originality or no redundancy is unpleasant because it is bewildering, so perfect banality or full redundancy is unpleasant because it is boring. The pleasant lies in between; and here too,
an inverted U-shaped Wundt curve seems to describe the way
in which pleasantness depends on redundancy.[30] The degree of
redundancy that is the most pleasing varies from person to person. Introverts, presumably, enjoy more redundancy, extroverts
less. Also, the very young and the very old seem to want very

much more redundancy than the rest of us do. Infants and young children seem, by grown-up standards, never to tire of repetition, and much the same is true of the very old, who not only repeat themselves, but seem to enjoy rereading old books and rehearing old stories. The explanation in both cases probably lies in the lesser retentive or absorptive capacity of their memories, but that is a subject on which little is known.

Unfortunately, the only quantitative estimates of redundancy which have been made so far deal with language, whose common vocabulary and universally observed rules create an objective redundancy which is more or less the same for all who know the language. From time to time there have been schools of painting and of musical composition with rules so rigid that the resulting redundancy ought to be amenable to estimation; usually, however, the redundancy of a picture, a piece of music, or any other source of stimulus enjoyment is very subjective, dependent on different people's widely divergent past experience and knowledge of artistic schools and traditions. For that reason it defies quantification.[31]

The experimental work of psychologists is usually couched in terms hard to quantify, but all of that work shows that novelty is the most stimulating and the most pleasant when it provides surprise, conflict, incongruity, "cognitive dissonance," deviation, or divergence between what is expected and what is experienced.[32] There can be no surprise, no conflict, no deviation whatever without the expectation of a norm: that is what redundancy provides. The subjectively novel contrasts with the redundant information, and their juxtaposition produces the conflict or surprise, which presumably is the greater, the larger the amount of subjective novelty. We have some notion of how much subjective novelty is the most pleasing, but we know nothing about how much redundancy is optimal. Many of the psychologists' experiments consist in exposing the same person repeatedly to the same sensation, so that increased familiarity increases redundancy and diminishes subjective novelty, while the amount of objective information, which is the sum of the two, remains constant. No one, as far as I know, has yet succeeded in devising an experiment which varies the amount of redundant information while keeping unchanged subjective novelty, although this or something like it will be necessary if we are ever to ascertain how stimulation and pleasantness vary with redundancy.

The need for conflict, for a combination of redundancy with subjective novelty as a condition of pleasant stimulation, is not only well documented, it is also quite obvious from our everyday experience. Everybody knows that what is unusual and contrary to expectation always makes the most interesting news, and that the scandalous and abnormal makes the best gossip. It was incongruity, the sudden realization that men in high office had been behaving like gangsters, which made Watergate and related scandals such highly arousing news and boosted the sales of daily newspapers and weekly news magazines.

In music, most pieces begin with the statement of a melody. Then that statement is varied, transposed, restated, and repeated by different instruments and in different forms. The initial statement provides an element of redundancy in all that comes after, and most of what comes after is deviation from what the first hearing of the melody has led us to expect. Moreover, in the case of music, the conflict between the new and the familiar comes on several planes, because the whole piece must also be viewed in relation to the musical tradition to which it belongs. For one thing, to be understood and enjoyed, the melody itself must provide some redundancy by belonging to a familiar musical style, though it must deviate from that style enough to avoid sounding hackneyed. For another, the subsequent development of the melody also has its own traditions which knowledgeable listeners are familiar with, and here again the development of the melody must, for maximum enjoyment, deviate not only from the melody but to some extent also from the traditional ways of deviating from the melody.[33]

As composers try to stay within the established style yet deviate, and deviate again, in ever new ways from it, the style gradually erodes and what once was deviation becomes the new style to replace it. Part of the development of music, therefore, consists in continual change aimed at maintaining a steady balance between the new and the familiar, in the face of the public's listening causing the new gradually to lose its novelty and become familiar. This is the old story of having to go forward in order not to fall behind. Another part of musical development is the discovery and perfection of new ways and dimensions in which to deviate and vary the melodic material, thus enabling the composer to provide enjoyment and hold the listener's attention longer. This part of musical development can be statistically documented. In western music, "As late as the sixteenth century very few instrumental compositions (i.e. single movements) lasted as long as five minutes." In the eighteenth century, the average length of a movement in Haydn's symphonies rose from five to 6.5 minutes over the half-century of his active life, while the average length of a Mozart symphony movement, also rising, reached 7.5 minutes. At the beginning of the nineteenth century, Beethoven's symphonic movements averaged ten minutes; fifty years later, Liszt was able to hold the listener's attention for an average of fifteen minutes; and by the turn of the century, the average length of movements in Mahler and Bruckner symphonies and Strauss tone poems had risen to twenty minutes.[34]

While a little redundancy is essential for the maximum pleasantness of a new sensation, some sources of stimulus enjoyment deliberately contain much more redundancy in order to provide only mild stimulation. The best example, again in the field of music, is what the Germans call *Gebrauchsmusik*, music to do things by. Such music is not meant to be arousing, interesting, and absorbing enough to be just listened to; it is merely meant to supplement the insufficient stimulus of some other activity so that the joint stimulation of the two together should be maximally pleasing. Dance music and some light music, including the light music written by serious composers, such as Telemann's table music, Handel's *Water Music,* and Mozart's *divertimenti,* are used for that purpose. Needless to say, any piece of music, however serious, loses subjective information content and gains subjective redundancy through repeated hearing and so becomes more suitable for background music. Similarly, the music which Musak pipes into department stores and offices to put customers into a better mood has been carefullly emasculated and its information content and arousing ability lowered lest it divert attention from the main business at hand.

Other examples of such deliberate provision of much redundancy and limited novelty are decorative objects as distinct from art objects—for instance, wallpaper as distinct from paintings. They are supposed to be mildly arousing, not to compete for center stage, but to keep their place as part of the background.

SIGNS AND SUPERSIGNS

One more obstacle to the quantitative measurement of the information content of a sensory input is the brain's tendency to encode what it perceives into signs and supersigns and to filter out the rest as irrelevant. We saw earlier how the brain focuses attention on a part of the environment and blocks out the rest; it is further selective in admitting and perceiving information even from the part attended to.

The almost limitless amount of information embodied in our environment makes this a necessity. A glance through a microscope gives us a glimpse of entire worlds the naked eye cannot see; and the naked eye in turn sees very much more than the brain can deal with. The eyes' information-transmitting capacity is variously estimated from 1.6 to three million bits per second,[35] many thousands of times greater than the brain's information-processing capacity, and the eyes are only one of our five senses. Hence our need to organize information into signs and supersigns and to blot out the rest.

For example, most readers of this page are likely to see only the letters (signs) and the words (supersigns), but not to see it at all as an abstract design whose pictorial quality depends on the shape and design of the type, the spacing of the letters and the lines, and the relation of the margins to the rectangle of lettering in the middle. Some of the brain's abstracting and organizing of information into signs and supersigns is automatic and involuntary. We hear the ticking of a watch or the sound of a train's wheels on the tracks as a rhythmic pattern of pairs, triplets, or larger groups of sounds, even when the spacing of the sounds and their loudness are completely even. The rhythm only exists in our minds; as the train speeds up, the rhythm often changes instead of becoming faster. The advantage of hearing the rhythmic groups (supersigns) instead of the individual sounds (signs) is that they come at a slower pace and so are easier to perceive. Similarly, in a sequence such as 00110011, we do not think of the 0's and 1's as the units, with each followed alternatively by one or the other; instead we instinctively simplify by forming the supersigns 00 and 11, and note their regular alternation.

Generally, the forming of signs and supersigns must be consciously learned. We learn to see only the letters and to disregard all else when we are taught to read. After we have learned to read rapidly, even the letters recede and we see only the words and groups of words, which further speeds up our reading by reducing the subjective information to be processed. Similarly, we reduce the subjective information content of a long number by thinking of it as a sequence of smaller groups of digits; this is why telephone and social security numbers are easier to remember if we break them down into pairs and triplets of digits.

To return now to the question of what makes the stimulus of novelty pleasant. Such organizing and filtering of information may equally well increase or diminish the pleasantness of its processing. For example, when I first listen to a complex piece of music with a large information flow, my brain automatically keeps the subjective information inflow within the limits of its capacity by blocking out part of the harmonic complexity. Only as repeated hearing reduces the subjective novelty of what I have already heard and so frees part of my brain's information-processing capacity do I begin to notice the complexity I have previously missed. This enables me to listen to the same piece of music repeatedly with undiminished or even increased enjoyment, because the increase in subjective redundancy does not diminish the flow of subjectively new information I perceive at successive hearings. Also, the more-than-manageable inflow of information which I receive on first hearing complex music creates a mild frustration or disorientation, whose resolution, and my expectation of whose resolution, is an important part of my enjoyment. Novelty creates a problem, and its enjoyment comes from the resolution of the problem. In order to enjoy information, I must understand it and make it my own, by doing so I reduce and, ultimately, eliminate its subjective novelty by incorporating it into the already familiar. The more difficult that is, the more enjoyable it becomes, provided it remains within the realm of the possible.

Here, then, are two more important differences between serious and light music. First, the greater complexity and information content of serious music often has the disturbing quality just mentioned, which is missing from light music. Second, the same higher information content renders serious music more durable than light music, for its information flow is large enough to cause the brain to ignore part of it at early hearings. Ultimately, enough repetition can exhaust the novelty even of the greatest music, but differences in degree can be large and are well documented. It is worth adding that in this respect true jazz is superior to both, because improvisation maintains its subjective novelty through repeated hearings.

The opposite case, that in which the brain's tendency to form supersigns diminishes rather than increases stimulus enjoyment, is probably more frequent and therefore more important. In a picture or sculpture which represents something, we often see only the thing represented and overlook all else. That

FIG. 2. My Wife and My Mother-in-Law

SOURCE: W. E. Hill, "My Wife and My Mother-in-law," *Puck* (New York), Nov. 6, 1915; see also E. G. Boring, "A New Ambiguous Figure," *American Journal of Psychology*, 42 (1930), pp. 444–45.

this is so is strikingly proved by trick pictures drawn to represent two things simultaneously. The moment we recognize either one of the things, the brain's tendency to block out all else keeps us from recognizing the other, because we are not used to summarizing the same information into two different supersigns. One of these pictures is reproduced in Fig. 2. It represents both the strong profile of an old woman and the pert face of a young one, but the prior recognition of either one makes it quite difficult to see the other.

The mind's habit of ignoring the irrelevant part of information is clearly efficient, in that it minimizes the burden on our information-processing capacity, but that is not always conducive to maximum enjoyment. Our tendency to see in a picture only what it represents and to appreciate only its success at representation makes us oblivious to all its other information content, the structure of shapes and volumes, and the combination of colors. Yet they could be important sources of stimulus enjoyment if we only noticed them. Some people never do notice them, and those people go through life deprived of that source of enjoyment. The reason may well be that the brain's tendency to form supersigns and ignore all else renders art appreciation especially difficult in the representational arts. In order to appreciate art we must overrule the brain's tendency to focus exclusively on supersigns and force it, so to speak, to look also at the information behind them. To a great extent that is an acquired skill, requiring deliberate effort and practice. Consider the difficulty we have in seeing the second picture in Fig. 2. We are very unlikely to discover it unless someone points it out to us, and even then we have to make an effort to find it.

Painters and sculptors often go out of their way to help us acquire that kind of skill; they do so by playing tricks with representation. Distortion, misrepresentation, non-representation, and abstraction in modern art are ways of making the observer look beyond the object represented and pay attention to the lines, shapes, volumes, colors, and their combinations. Sometimes, of course, the technique misfires. A person who is unused to abstract painting may need to recognize the representation of a familiar object to provide him with that minimum redundancy without which the information in the picture is too new and therefore too bewildering for him to enjoy.

UNCERTAINTY

So far in this chapter I have dealt almost entirely with novelty and its quantity, measurement, and ability to arouse by posing a threat. But if everything new and unexpected is arousing, then uncertainty, which is the expectation of the unexpected, must be arousing too. Indeed, everyday experience shows that uncertainty is not only arousing, it is usually so much so that it is unpleasant. People generally dislike most forms of uncertainty.

The explanation is simple. For the new and unexpected to be pleasantly stimulating, it must be sufficiently related to the familiar to be manageable and create a reasonable expectation of its manageability. Uncertainty, in most cases, precludes such expectation. We must have experienced the unexpected if we are to be reassured by its relatedness to the already known. When the unexpected still lies in the future, such reassurance is usually lacking, which is why the expectation of the unexpected is bewildering and frightening more often than it is enjoyable.

There is a "deep-seated human reluctance to wait an unnecessary moment for information about what the future holds, even when there is no way in which one could act on the information." [36] Children find it hard to wait for the surprises of birthday or Christmas; adults stay awake at night to learn election results a few hours sooner; and we all know that there is such a thing as "the comfort of knowing the worst." According to a psychologist's interview study of convicts, "one of the major sources of suffering in prison [is] uncertainty about how much time would have to be served. Those prisoners who had hopes of parole suffered much more than those who knew that they would never be released." [37]

But while uncertainty is mostly unpleasant and hard to bear, it can be pleasant and desirable when the impact of the expected unexpected event is under control and kept to a manageable level. Gamblers enjoy gambling because they have full control over the amount they risk, and they will not risk more than they enjoy risking. [38] In addition, they usually have control over the time dimension of the uncertainty involved. The arousing effect of uncertainty is usually unpleasant if it extends over a very long period or an indeterminate one; it may be pleasurable when we know in advance that it will end within minutes, as when the roulette wheel stops, or within days, as when the lottery has its drawing. Economists have occasionally been baffled by the rationale of the man who carries both an insurance policy and a lottery ticket, yet there is no contradiction between disliking the unpleasantness of prolonged uncertainty over large stakes and at the same time enjoying the excitement of a short- and fixed-term uncertainty with a freely chosen small risk.

Novelty is a major source of satisfaction, to judge by the large quantity we avidly consume every day and the high value we place on it. First love, the first taste of some special food, the first sight of a magnificent view, a beautiful building, or a naked body, together with many other firsts, are among our most cherished memories. We fill our bookshelves and photo albums with trophies of past novelty to serve as mementoes of our past enjoyment of them, and our most enduring enjoyment comes from husbands, wives, children, and friends because their spontaneity, imagination, or knowledge constitute large inventories of novelty we can draw upon for a long time. Since novelty, like food, is used up in the act of its enjoyment,[39] its enjoyment creates problems when the objects to which it is attached are durable and stay with us like more or less useless skeletons long after we have enjoyed and digested their novelty. Those problems are especially great in our affluent, mass-production economy, in which identical consumers' durable goods are churned out by the millions and occupy a prominent place in our lives, and they will be further discussed.

Another peculiarity of novelty, the fact that for maximum enjoyment it must come combined with the already familiar, implies that to enjoy it a person must first acquire related knowledge. In other words, the enjoyment of novelty requires learning; the consumption of novelty is skilled consumption. That again raises a host of important issues we will go into later. Before we do so, however, much preliminary ground has to be covered, and first we must complete our survey of the psychologist's view of behavior and its motivation by discussing yet another source of satisfaction, pleasure.

CHAPTER FOUR

Comfort Versus Pleasure

So far we have been concerned with behavior aimed at securing comfort or, what is the same thing, relieving or forestalling discomfort. That includes behavior which satisfies various bodily and mental needs and so lowers arousal that is too high; it also includes behavior which combats boredom and so raises arousal that is too low. Though somewhat different and of opposite sign, the two kinds of behavior are alike in that both aim at securing a negative good: freedom from pain, unpleasantness, or discomfort. The positive good is pleasure, and it is very different from comfort.

Twenty years ago, neurophysiologists who were mapping the brain discovered the brain centers for reward and punishment. Working with animals wired so that by pressing a bar they could give mild electric shocks to specific areas of their own brains, researchers located one area whose stimulation is avoided and gives every sign of being painful, and two other, separate areas whose stimulation is sought and therefore must be pleasant. The pain area is known as the punishment or aversion system, the other two as the primary and secondary pleasure systems or reward systems. The existence of separate pleasure and aversion systems confirms our introspective feeling that pleasure is something different from and more than the absence of pain or discomfort; it also explains why we occasionally feel pain and pleasure at the same time.

Mostly, however, pain excludes pleasure. "The primary reward and aversion systems are . . . closely connected, and at least partially identifiable with the brain structures controlling the manifestations of heightened arousal." [1] Experiments have shown that the mild stimulation of the primary reward system, which goes with increased arousal, is pleasant. As the level of arousal rises further, the punishment system, which seems to have a higher threshold, is also brought into action, and its activity, besides being unpleasant, inhibits the activity of the primary reward system and thereby eliminates the feeling of pleasure.

Experiments have also shown that the "secondary reward system . . . seems to be more or less identical with the . . . de-arousal system;" [2] that is, its activation goes hand in hand with the *lowering* of arousal. When stimulated, it closes out the aversion system and frees the primary pleasure system. The pain goes away and pleasure is restored. In this theory of the interplay of the three systems we have an explanation of why increasing arousal is pleasant at first (while it stimulates only the primary reward system), but becomes unpleasant beyond a certain point (the threshold of the aversion system), and why a decrease in arousal or release of tension both eliminates pain and gives pleasure. The theory also accounts for the fact that rats continue untiringly, for hours on end, to press a bar that delivers a mild electric shock to their primary reward system, while the apparent attraction to them of the similar self-stimulation of their secondary reward system diminishes with repetition and gradually comes to an end. [3] Such findings confirm the supposition that the primary reward system is directly involved in the feeling of pleasure, while the secondary reward system is involved only indirectly, and can only yield pleasure when its activation frees the primary reward system from suppression.[4]

The neurophysiologists' experimental findings and theories strikingly confirm an inspired guess made earlier by several psychologists—that feelings of comfort and discomfort have to do with the *level* of arousal and depend on whether arousal is or is not at its optimum level, whereas feelings of pleasure are created by *changes* in the arousal level, especially (but not exclusively) when these changes bring arousal either up from too low or down from too high a level, toward its optimum.[5] Put more simply, comfort and discomfort have to do with the speed, pleasure with the acceleration and deceleration of one's emotions.

That may be an oversimplification, too neat to be literally true, but it is close enough to experimental findings to be adopted here as a working hypothesis for our argument.

In accepting that hypothesis, we must abandon the old-fashioned notion that pain and pleasure are the negative and positive segments of a one-dimensional scale, something like a hedonic gauge, calibrated from utter misery to supreme bliss, on which a person's hedonic state registers the higher the better off he is. At least one experimental finding contradicts that notion. In a questionnaire survey of man's happiness, people were asked a number of questions about the frequency with which they experienced annoyances such as pain, worry, and unpleasantness on the one hand and elation, praise, good news, and various other pleasant sensations on the other. The two groups were called negative and positive affect, respectively, and a quantitative index was established for each. As we would expect, both the absence of negative affect and the presence of positive affect were correlated with people's self-rated happiness. But one totally unexpected result emerged from the study: there was a complete lack of correlation between positive and negative affect.[6] In other words, the frequency with which a person had pleasant feelings was quite independent of the frequency with which he had unpleasant feelings. That certainly does not jibe with the notion of a one-dimensional hedonic gauge, since it shows that absence of pain is no precondition for feeling pleasure and that a lot of pleasure is quite compatible with a lot of pain.

The theory that comfort depends upon the level of arousal and pleasure depends upon changes in that level fits in well with conventional wisdom and our introspective knowledge. To begin with, it explains the fleeting nature of pleasure. It also explains the closely related belief that, in man's striving for his various goals in life, being on the way to those goals and struggling to achieve them are more satisfying than is the actual attainment of the goals. The attainment of a goal seems, when the moment of triumph is over, almost like a let-down. Few sit back to enjoy it; in fact, most people seek a further goal to strive for, presumably because they prefer the process of striving toward a goal to the passive state of having achieved one.

If the pleasing changes in arousal are changes from a level associated with discomfort toward the level associated with comfort, then it logically follows that pleasure will always accompany the relief of discomfort and will seem the more intense the greater the discomfort that is being relieved. It also follows that for the level of arousal to move toward its optimum, it must first be at a non-optimal level. In familiar terms, discomfort must precede pleasure. This common-sense rule is a very old one—it was debated by the ancient Greeks. Psychiatrists call it the Law of Hedonic Contrast. An illuminating proposition follows from the rule: too much comfort may preclude pleasure. That proposition may contribute to an explanation of the widespread dissatisfaction with our standard of living. We shall return to this subject later.

First we must discuss another and much simpler aspect of this relation between comfort and pleasure. If comfort is the avoidance of discomfort and pleasure is the feeling associated with the relief of discomfort, then anything that ends a situation of discomfort will both give pleasure and leave comfort in its wake. That sequence of sensations is familiar to everyone, yet some of its implications are paradoxical enough to need further discussion.

THE SEDUCTION OF PLEASURE

Eating is motivated by our biological need for food. As we eat, our need for food declines, and that might be expected to reduce our urge to eat. In actual fact, the opposite usually happens. Our pleasure in eating reinforces our drive to eat; it tends to offset the reduction in our drive caused by our reduced biological need for food. Hence, eating increases the appetite—*l'appétit vient en mangeant*—a paradox. That is why the first course of a meal, or food served before it, is known as an appetizer, and why it is so much easier not to start eating than to stop once we have started. Here we have the origin of the psychologists' technical term, "the salted-nut syndrome," [7] which is also called the "mini-addiction." Some people overeat; that is, they continue eating for the pleasure of it after, sometimes long after, their physiological hunger is satisfied. An even more familiar case is the urge to continue scratching an itchy spot even though one knows that that will not stop the itch and may even prolong it.

Needless to say, the pleasure and the reinforcing effect of the pleasure of an ongoing activity is not confined to man. A variety of experiments have been made which show the same to be true of animals. The reward value of food and water is often used as an inducement to make laboratory animals perform various tasks, and experiments have shown that giving a thirsty or hungry animal part of his water or food reward *before* he starts on his task will *improve* his performance. Thirsty rats, especially, find their way to a goal box with water significantly faster and with fewer errors when they are given a little water to whet their thirst before they start.[8] Shipwrecked people and others restricted to a limited amount of drinking water find it very difficult to ration themselves in order to make their drinking water last for a maximum or desired number of days. The pleasure of quenching a severe thirst seems so great that some people cannot stop drinking even though they know that doing so will cost them a greater thirst in the future, or may even cost them their chance of survival.

Men and animals have many needs, but, because they cannot attend to all of them at once, they fill most needs intermittently, one at a time. As a particular need, say, hunger for food, builds up in intensity with the passage of time, a moment comes when that need begins to dominate all others. Then its satisfaction becomes the organism's highest priority. While it attends to this, hunger gradually diminishes, and, with other needs in the background building up in intensity, some other need soon becomes the strongest and so the organism's dominant preoccupation. If no pleasure accompanied eating, that is, if eating merely served to reduce hunger, we would expect the organism to stop eating and start attending to its new, now highest priority need before it has eaten its fill and completely satisfied its hunger.[9] But the opposite is true, because the process of satisfying a need is pleasurable in itself and strengthens the force of whatever activity is currently engaged in, causing the organism to continue whatever it is doing, often to the point of full satiation or even beyond. It is likely that that paradox in behavior and motivation is universal and generally governs want satisfaction and arousal reduction.

How can we reconcile such paradoxical behavior with the economist's theory of rational consumer behavior? Economists are concerned almost exclusively with a world of scarcity. They picture man as having many needs and desires, but not enough money, time, or energy to satisfy all of them completely. His typical problem, as economists see it, is the balancing of different discomforts, one against the other. To reduce the discomfort of hunger, he must put up with other discomforts, either by working or working harder and enduring the fatigue that entails, or by curtailing his spending and with it the relieving of his discomfort in other areas of consumption. If the economist's "ideal man" is not rich enough to fill all his needs to satiation, he will stop short of fully satisfying all of them, not just one or a few. And not only must he keep unsatisfied margins on all his needs and desires, but he also must see to it that any extra dollar he spends on one thing yields him as much satisfaction as that extra dollar would if he spent it on any other thing. If that were not so, a little rearrangement of his spending pattern could make him better off at no extra cost.

Economists not only consider this to be a faithful description of rational behavior; they also hold it to be one of the cornerstones of economic theory. On it is based their confident expectation that market sales at market prices correctly reflect what consumers want and provide the standard to which the structure of production must conform.[10]

But rational behavior as pictured by the economist and actual behavior as observed and explained in terms of the psychologist's motivating forces are not at all the same thing.

The economist assumes that the consumer with a limited budget will cut his food consumption short of full satiation; he ignores the fact that the consumer gains pleasure through the process of eating, and that the sheer joy of it is bound to make him go on eating. The conflict between economist and psychologist is there, but it is not as irreconcilable as it seems at first. Psychologists observe behavior directly related to the satisfaction of needs, while economists are concerned with budgeting and shopping, which precede that behavior. A person who economizes on food when he does his shopping can decide either to space his meals more than before or to eat less at each meal, and by doing the first rather than the second he can often resolve his problem. For by spacing his meals he can limit his food intake and yet eat to satiation or beyond whenever he does eat.

That trivial example is our first illustration of the potential conflict between the psychologist's interpretation of observed behavior and the economist's theory of rational behavior. It is comforting to find that the consumer resolves the conflict by using a kind of higher rationality which satisfies both psychologist and economist. For there is evidence which suggests that the spacing of meals is, indeed, the way most people resolve this conflict. In western Europe the number of meals a day eaten by the average population rose gradually over the centuries, from one or two meals in the early Middle Ages to three meals by the time of Queen Elizabeth I. The middle and upper classes of Europe progressed to four (and even to five) meals a day by the nineteenth century, although three meals are still the rule among the working classes of today.[11] By contrast, in very poor countries such as India, two meals a day are even now the most common. To judge by nutritional statistics, the Indians' two meals are often inadequate, while the three or more meals eaten by the bulk of the population in the industrial nations are more than adequate. People in advanced countries seem not to live up to the economist's ideal of rational budgeting: we eat to full satiation or beyond and economize on other things.

One of the things on which even people who do eat their fill economize is the quality of food—although the salted-nut syndrome seems to operate there too. Peasant communities the world over seem to opt for a routine of simple fare punctuated by great feasts produced on special occasions; then they stuff themselves with all the good things their table can provide. In very poor communities, families often plunge into debt for the sake of a funeral feast or a wedding celebration. Such behavior horrifies economists of the not-so-poor countries; their theory of rational consumer behavior postulates a judicious balancing of one discomfort against another and completely overlooks pleasure. Yet the very universality of the custom of feasting among the poor peoples of so many different cultures is evidence that the pleasures of a good meal for those who seldom taste one are very great and weigh heavily against the biological needs of survival. For the economist to condemn such behavior by the standards of the affluent consumer's rationality is presumptuous and wrong-headed. We must accept it as another example of conflict between psychological motivation and simple-minded rationality, one which is usually resolved by the very rarity of feasts. However, if the socially approved limitation of feasts to weddings and funerals fails to make them rare enough and overtaxes the budget of a poor man cursed with too many daughters or deaths in the family, he can hardly be blamed for not dealing better with a situation which chance has rendered impossibly difficult.

Here again, man's main response to increasing affluence seems to be an increase in the frequency of festive meals; he adds to the number of special occasions and holidays considered worthy of them and, ultimately, he makes them routine—in the form, say, of Sunday dinners.

Very much the same principles seem to govern the way in which men satisfy many of their other needs. The very act of satisfying a need often yields a pleasure strong enough to prompt the seeking of complete satisfaction, and when budgetary or other restraints militate against it, a compromise is sought and often found. The most important such compromise is probably the one already discussed: people arrange to have intermittent complete satisfaction, with the moments or periods of full satiation suitably spaced over time. Other forms of compromise, however, are also possible. For example, a man who is too poor to heat his home to the most agreeable temperature is much more likely to heat a part of it to that temperature rather than heat the whole of it to a suboptimal temperature.

All the above examples of the reinforcing effect of pleasure that accompanies need satisfaction have to do with biological or bodily needs. The choice of examples must not mislead us into supposing that the argument presented applies only to such cases. Many of our wants are not innate and biologically determined, but are acquired by learning. Once they *are* acquired, and once their ability to give satisfaction has been learned, they also become habitual and create drives to maintain or repeat the newly learned satisfactions. Moreover, the process of obtaining satisfaction is pleasurable here, too, and reinforces the primary drive. Acquired tastes motivate behavior in much the same way in which biological needs do, and my argument applies to both.

Up to now we have been concerned only with pleasure and its reinforcing effect on behavior during a reduction in arousal such as occurs when wants are satisfied or pain and discomfort eliminated. A rise in arousal, however, as with stimulating activity of some sort, also yields pleasure, and that pleasure also reinforces behavior.

In order to overcome boredom and raise arousal that is too low, we look for stimulating activity. Our need for that activity is brought to an end when our boredom is dispelled and our arousal raised to its optimum level. However, the pleasure that accompanies mounting arousal reinforces and sustains the stimulating activity once begun, causing it to raise arousal even further, beyond the optimum. A crime story or a crossword puzzle, started on to while away time and ward off boredom, often becomes so absorbing that we cannot stop until it is finished; we postpone other activities for its sake and readily accept both the tension our continued attention to it builds up to and the discomforts caused by postponing the other satisfactions. Children, too, often get carried away by the pleasure of the mounting excitement of a game, forgetting all else and going much further (by grown-up standards) than they should. Not only is the increase in arousal enjoyable, but the reinforcing effect of the enjoyment causes arousal to be temporarily raised above the optimum and gives rise to that later, often even greater, pleasure which accompanies the subsequent lowering of arousal and release of tension. The expectation of this later pleasure then becomes a secondary reward which yet further reinforces the activity.[12]

The simplest and most obvious example of the process is the sexual act, but sports, games, bodily exercise, the reading of a good book, and the pursuit of artistic activity, scientific inquiry, and a hobby all share this peculiarity of yielding first the pleasure of increasing tension and arousal, and then the further pleasure of the resolution of tension and diminishing arousal. Indeed, without these two rewards, the mounting excitement of grappling with a problem and the ultimate triumph of resolving it, we would hardly be willing to accept the anguish, the frustrations, and the difficulties which seem to accompany all major achievements in the arts, in the sciences, in exploration—perhaps in every form of human endeavor.

External circumstances can often introduce pleasure when the activities themselves seem unimportant or undesirable.

> On a holiday we may feel idle and averse to physical effort, but if, yielding to the exhortations of some more energetic companion, we start on a walk or expedition, after a little while we may begin to enjoy the muscular exertion itself and may even express our gratitude to the disturber of our rest by saying, "I'm glad you dragged me out." Similarly in intellectual work, there are many tasks which, approached at first with reluctance and distaste, soon become so interesting that we may be loath to break them off if some more urgent matter compels an interruption. In the sphere of sex, too, there are many persons (especially women) who may at first submit to the embraces of their lovers with indifference or even with a certain aversion, but whose desire and active participation are presently aroused. Indeed, the capacity to bring about this change, to overcome this initial frigidity, may be among the most valued characteristics of a "skillful" lover—just as a good cook is one whose dishes "tempt" the appetite when hunger is not present. Passing from single occasions to longer periods of time, we may recall that there are many activities which we were at first compelled to undertake against our wishes, but which gradually became so fascinating and absorbing that we returned to them, time and again, without any outer compulsion, or even in the face of other claims on our attention. Thus a good teacher may arouse a genuine and permanent interest in some subject that was at first repulsive; while it is generally recognized that a desire for riches or for power may obtain such a hold upon a person that it may continue to be the main driving force of his career, long after the goals to which it was at first incidental have been achieved.[13]

Animal experiments confirm that the process of increasing arousal has a reward value. Sex is the one biological need whose satisfaction requires an initial *increase* in arousal, and an experiment with male rats has shown the significant reward value and reinforcing effect of copulation even when ejaculation is not allowed and not expected to take place. In other words, the stimulus and increased tension of sexual play is rewarding, even without the release or the expectation of the release of such tension.[14] The reward value of arousal increase is also evident in the enjoyment which both men and women take in erotica.

Another type of experiment has shown that animals engaged in exploratory behavior will often persist in it even if a biological need has built up in the meantime and they are offered an opportunity to satisfy it. Monkeys, for example, when engaged in opening a padlock, will continue with what is for them a purely intellectual task long past their regular feeding time and despite the presence of food.[15]

The above examples of behavior are observable in man and reproducible at will in animal experiments. They cannot be described as rational, nor can they be explained solely by need satisfaction (drive reduction or boredom avoidance) without the additional motivating force of pleasure. Man's need for pleasure and its profound influence on his behavior are an essential part of his nature and must be taken into account by any theory of rational behavior.

THE SEDUCTION OF COMFORT

The customary economic conflict between our desire to satisfy our wants and the budgetary limitations on our expenditure is sharpened when our desires are reinforced by the pleasures that accompany their satisfaction. We would expect increased affluence and lesser budgetary limitations to lessen or resolve the conflict and eliminate the whole problem, but while this is true in a sense, such an expectation has a twist to it.

If the usual way of resolving the conflict is to space the occasions or restrict the areas of full satiation, then more income will naturally lead to less spacing and restriction. There is plenty of evidence that the rise in our standard of living takes the form of more occasions and larger areas of satiation, at least in part. We have already seen the secular rise in our number of meals a day and our festive meals a year; the trend still continues even in the United States, a very affluent country. In addition, of course, many other acts of consumption are also intermittent—the changing of linen, for instance—and their frequency, too, increases as incomes rise. The resulting increase in comfort is self-evident, but another likely consequence is a reduction in pleasure.

We saw that while comfort hinges on the level of arousal being *at or close to* its optimum, pleasure accompanies *changes* in the level of arousal toward the optimum. That is why the satisfaction of a need gives both pleasure and comfort. But the continuous maintenance of comfort would eliminate pleasure, because, with arousal continuously at its optimum level, there can be no change in arousal toward the optimum. In other words, incomplete and intermittent comfort is accompanied by pleasure, while complete and continuous comfort is incompatible with pleasure.

Here we have a dilemma: we must choose between pleasure at some sacrifice of comfort and more complete comfort at the sacrifice of pleasure. Many people are aware, more or less vaguely, of this. Most of us know that one must be tired to enjoy resting, cold to appreciate a warm fire, and hungry in order really to enjoy a good meal. We also make a clear distinction between spoiling an appetite and satisfying it, and some parents, aware of the difference, try to train their children not to eat between meals and so retain the ability to enjoy the pleasure of food.

By contrast, children in permissive families acquire the habit of raiding the refrigerator and having snacks more or less continuously throughout the day, complaining afterwards of their inability to enjoy food, and they retain the habit through life. Also, the rise in our standard of living has largely obliterated the difference in quality between festive and everyday meals, and again we often hear older people nostalgically recalling the poorer days of their youth, when a festive holiday meal was a great event, looked forward to and cherished, much prepared for and long remembered. In a similar vein, elderly immigrants to Southern California sometimes recall wistfully the pleasures of the changing seasons, even while they enjoy the comforts of eternal spring.

All these illustrate the same sequence: comfort gained, pleasure lost, awareness of the loss, and more or less regretful acquiescence in it. They may be examples of rational choice or of a half-involuntary drifting into behavior which may or may not have been adopted in full cognizance of the consequences.

The dilemma we are discussing marks the beginning of a new phase in the argument of this book. We have left behind us the realm of simple motivation and universal laws of behavior, where controlled experiments with rats can help us understand how humans behave and why they behave as they do. Pleasure and comfort have not only turned out to be very different motivating forces; they also seem to stand to each other in a peculiar relation, reminiscent of the relation between acceleration and speed, which renders conflict inevitable. To some extent, pleasure and comfort are mutually exclusive alternatives, confronting the individual with a conflict he must resolve one way or another, either unthinkingly, by following instinct, tradition, or habit, or rationally. Every resolution of the conflict is a compromise, and different people seek or reach different compromises, partly by chance, partly by choice. From now onward, therefore, we shall mostly be dealing with choice behavior, trying to understand what motivated choice.

Economists usually picture the consumer as rationally weighing the merits of the available alternatives before making a choice, much as a judge or jury weighs evidence and arguments of opposing counsel before passing judgment. Sometimes that is what happens, but sometimes it is not. In the examples just given, people may have weighed the gain in comfort against the loss of pleasure and opted for the change because the gain seemed to outweigh the loss. There is evidence, for example, that age changes many people's preferences, causing them increasingly to put comfort ahead of pleasure.[16] It is also possible, however, that with increased affluence, they were gradually lured into a new way of life by their love of comfort, unaware at first of the costs involved and finding themselves fully accustomed to their new ways by the time they realize the extent of the loss of pleasure suffered.

That is not at all an unlikely account of what may often happen. If the same action affects our well-being in contrary ways, these can easily differ also in their timing and predictability, and such differences may both influence our choice and make us regret it after it has been made. The gain in comfort is obvious and instantaneous; the loss of pleasure is almost certain to dawn upon us gradually, only later. It may even come as a surprise. What is more natural than that the first should outweigh the second more often than will seem rational afterwards, when we consider the choice with the benefit of hindsight? When a person finds he made an error in judgment, and the choice can be reversed or remade, he will correct the initial error and make a rational choice after all, but whether he can depends on how strong the new habit has already become and how much scope it leaves for rational choice at that stage.

For one of the most firmly established findings of psychology is that any act immediately followed by a reward (such as an increase in comfort) is reinforced; that is, the likelihood and frequency of its future performance are increased. Moreover, the reinforcement becomes the stronger, the more often the sequence—action immediately followed by reward—is repeated. The slower, therefore, the realization of the loss of pleasure, the stronger will become the habit, and the smaller the likelihood that the decision, once made, will be reconsidered and reversed.[17] Accordingly, it is reasonable to assume that the greater immediacy and clearer perception of the gain in comfort establish a bias in its favor with many people. At the same time, one can also find examples of the opposite preference. The

European upper-class tradition of limiting children's eating to mealtimes illustrates the forcible establishing of a habit that sets pleasure ahead of comfort; it also testifies, of course, to the parents' similar choice on rational grounds. The Law of Hedonic Contrast is known to consumers as well as to psychologists, and some know how to make good use of it.

There are people who are fully aware of the complex relation between comfort and pleasure; they are fully able, therefore, to arrange their lives rationally, whether their preferences go one way or the other. There are others who act on habits variously acquired, and still others who are lured into more comfort and who sacrifice more pleasure than they would have chosen to do had they known better. Some people seem to acquiesce in the overly comfortable life they drifted into, although sometimes they compensate for it by seeking pleasure elsewhere. For example, the idle rich born into that state or reaching it young are prone to take up dangerous sports and become involved in reckless adventures. Could it be that, deprived of the simple pleasures by too much comfort, they seek compensation in pleasures which accompany excitement and threat? Perhaps the increasing violence of our increasingly affluent society can be similarly explained.

If that is so, such a reaction to too little pleasure raises another set of questions. Are the pleasures of living dangerously greater than the pleasures of satisfying a biological need which has built up to high intensity? Or are those pleasures preferred merely because, once affluence has provided us with the comfort of never having to let a biological need build up to high intensity, we have become addicted to such comfort and are unable to recapture the pleasures of hedonic contrast?

There may be something to the idea of a hierarchy of pleasures. Many people look upon some comforts—for example, those of an even and agreeable climate—as a necessary condition of the better enjoyment of the other pleasures in life, and those people consider the loss of a pleasurable contrast of seasons a minor loss by comparison. Even the peculiarly American lack of interest in the enjoyment of food may be so explained. It is as though we would cheerfully sacrifice the delights of food for the enjoyment of some more important pleasure or pleasures.

The other explanation—that too much comfort, by eliminating the simple pleasures, forces us to seek those of excitement instead—seems plausible, but might not a steady diet of excitement share the fate of a steady diet of steak and also lose its attraction? That brings us to an important difference between the two sources of pleasure.

FREE CHOICE BETWEEN COMFORT AND PLEASURE

We have been mainly concerned with the pleasures and comforts that come from satisfying a need or eliminating a disturbance, and we have seen that when people use their increased affluence for the more complete and more continuous satisfaction of their needs they dampen or eliminate their pleasures. But there is comfort in escaping boredom, too. Could the pursuit of that comfort also be inimical to pleasure? That it can be reinforced by pleasure we have already seen. Most stimuli not only eliminate boredom, but also yield pleasure, whose reinforcing effect causes arousal to overshoot its optimum level, thus providing the occasion for a subsequent release of tension and its attending pleasures. Are the twin pleasures of first building up and then relieving tension more persistent, more immune to being crowded out by comfort? Could they therefore be those more important pleasures for whose sake the simpler, biological pleasures seem, to most people, worth sacrificing?

The answer is obvious in the case of people who have one overwhelming passion in life—their work or their hobby—to which they subordinate all else: they clearly opt for comfort in everything other than their one, single passion. But what about the many people who are less single-minded, those who seek their stimulation in a variety of things? Different activities vary greatly in their ability to stimulate, depending on their chal-

lenge and the amount of novelty and surprisingness they contain. A dull book, a banal play with a predictable happy ending, a piece of too-familiar music routinely played, and a game
of cards against much weaker players are not very stimulating.
They while away time and keep boredom at bay, but they yield
little if any pleasure in the process.

By contrast, some books, plays, works of art, and other
sources of stimulation are gripping, exciting; they are able to
shake us up and heighten our consciousness. They do much
more than merely keep off boredom, but they do so at the cost
of that temporary raising of arousal beyond its optimum, whose
strain is the price we must pay for the pleasures of mounting
tension and its subsequent release. Some people will accept that
as an inevitable cost, one well worth paying for the experience
of pleasure; others, less tolerant of discomfort, will rather have
less tension and less pleasure, and so opt for more sedate stimulation. The psychologist's term for a person's seeking such sedate stimulation is "diversive exploration." He contrasts the
term against specific exploration, the seeking of stronger stimulation which yields the twin pleasures of mounting tension and
its subsequent release, but with the temporary disorientation of
above-optimal arousal. [18]

The same distinction can be found in some recent work in experimental aesthetics, where subjects are asked to rate the aesthetic qualities of works of art and various shapes and patterns
while their psycho-physiological reactions are measured. It appears that people value two distinct qualities in art, the pleasing
and the interesting. The simpler patterns, with more symmetry
and other forms of redundancy, are the ones rated pleasing; the
more complex patterns, with higher information content, are
rated interesting. The two qualities partly overlap: people's
preference between them varies, and even the same person's
preference for one or the other, as revealed by the length of time
he spends viewing them, depends in part on how aroused or
how bored he was at the start of the experiment. It seems that
in art, people use the word "pleasing" to describe whatever

gives them sedate stimulation and the word "interesting" to describe disturbingly arousing sensations.[19] The distinction corresponds to the one we made between fully arousing and mildly arousing novelty.

It seems, therefore, that the dilemma of choosing between comfort and pleasure is much the same whether they accompany stimulation or want satisfaction. There is no way of having a full measure of both comfort and pleasure. Too much seeking for comfort will reduce or eliminate pleasure in any and every activity. One, perhaps the only, exception to this rule is the male's sexual pleasure. For physiological reasons, the male must raise his arousal above its optimum level to complete the sexual act, thus it is always accompanied by pleasure—the twin pleasures of mounting tension and its subsequent relief. The sexual act is one in which the individual's choice between comfort and pleasure is strictly limited: nature itself keeps him from relinquishing too much pleasure for the sake of too complete an avoidance of excitement and tension. It is not surprising that the very symbol of pleasure, for most men, is sexual pleasure.

We have seen the similarities between want satisfaction and stimulation; now we must deal with an important difference between them. The satisfaction of wants eliminates a discomfort whose initial presence is a necessary condition of pleasure. We eat to appease hunger, but we must be hungry to *enjoy* eating. And too much stilling of hunger can destroy our pleasure in food. By contrast, stimulation eliminates the discomfort of boredom, but the condition of deriving pleasure from stimulation is the discomfort not of the boredom it relieves, but of the temporary strain it creates. To be enjoyable, a play or a film must build up tensions which are resolved before the end, but the audience does not have to be bored on its arrival at the theater (although it helps if it is). While the seeker of stimulation can choose between more and less strenuous forms of stimulation and accordingly get more or less pleasure out of it, he is in no danger of missing the fun because he is too avid in his quest for stimulation. The pleasures of stimulation, unlike those of want satisfaction, are *not* eliminated by their too persistent and too continuous pursuit.

There lies the answer to the question, are the pleasures of stimulation more persistent, more likely to survive the competition with comfort, than are the pleasures of want satisfaction? The answer is yes. Not because they are more important; that we cannot tell. Rather, because the scope for free and rational choice is much greater in their case. We are free to choose rationally between more comfort and more pleasure. There is no danger of a bias in our perception of the two, and no danger of rising affluence luring us into putting comfort ahead of pleasure, as was the case with drive reduction. Indeed, there is plenty of evidence that people will often actively seek disturbances for the sake of the pleasure that accompanies their relief.[20] In other words, we cannot assume, as with drive reduction, that some people miss their chance of choosing between comfort and pleasure because they have unthinkingly drifted into the habit of continuously satisfying their every want and are unable to kick the habit. When it comes to stimulation, man is much more a free agent to choose between its comforts and pleasures. Those are his main, if not his only, choices.

COMFORT AND STIMULATION

Drives to relieve discomfort, stimulation to relieve boredom, and the pleasures that can accompany and reinforce both—those are the three motive forces of behavior distinguished by psychologists today. David Hume, in the middle of the eighteenth century, had almost the same three motivations in mind when he said in one of his essays that "Human happiness, according to the most received notions, seems to consist in three ingredients: action, pleasure, and indolence." [21] It is a simple framework, but not simple enough for the modern economist, for he has thrown the insights of his predecessors to the winds and recognizes only one motivation of behavior: desire for satisfaction.

I propose to simplify the psychologist's threefold classification into a twofold one. We shall henceforth be concerned with choice, especially with choice in economically advanced and affluent societies, where the main scope for choosing between pleasure and comfort lies in the area of stimulation, because affluence crowds out, for many people, the pleasures of want satisfaction. In such societies want satisfaction can be more or less equated with comfort. Most pleasures of most people come from stimulation in such a society, though, again, some stimulation may not be very stimulating and may yield little or no pleasure at all. Thus we get a twofold classification which is much less rigorous and much less general than the psychologist's careful distinctions but fits in better with ordinary usage and is also easier to reconcile with the economist's categories.

CHAPTER FIVE

Enter Economics

We have looked at the psychologist's broad canvas of human satisfactions, and though we have made next to no mention so far of economic activity, it should be clear that it is only one of many sources of satisfaction, perhaps not a very important one. Why is it that some satisfactions depend on economic activity while others do not and are kept out of the market altogether?

The economy's contribution to human welfare—its magnitude, nature, and components—is well known, well measured, and much discussed. What we lack, however, is an understanding of the economy's place in the total scheme of human satisfactions. Only by comparing the economy's contribution with that of all other sources can we attain a balanced perspective, and to do that we must understand better what all the other contributions are. We also need to reclassify satisfactions according to some principle which will separate the economic from the non-economic and help us identify the factors that distinguish them.

SELF-SUFFICIENCY

Economics is a social science, and it deals only with services rendered and products sold by one person to another. Some human satisfactions, however, are obtained or best obtained without help from others, while some services we customarily render to ourselves, and none of these figures in economic accounting. Most people feel the need, occasionally, to be left alone with nature or their thoughts; a fair part of bodily and mental exercise is performed alone; and, while we devote some economic resources to facilitating all these when we provide privacy and maintain parks and playgrounds, such satisfactions are mostly outside the realm of economics. So are the services we perform for ourselves. We wash, dress, and do quite a few household chores ourselves, and all of those activities are beyond the range of the economic accounts, although economics has much to do with where the dividing line lies between services we perform for ourselves and those we have performed for us by others.[1]

Most satisfactions, however, stem from personal contact with others and from the use, consumption, or contemplation of goods and services to whose production others have contributed. These, again, may or may not be economic satisfactions, depending on whether or not they go through the market and acquire a market value in the process. Passage through the market is the criterion: whatever passes through the market belongs in the realm of economics. For the need to pay a market price makes the recipient of a satisfaction perform a service in exchange or otherwise contribute to the satisfactions of others, and assuring and regulating reciprocity in the rendering and receiving of satisfactions is the main function of the economic system.

It is apparent that self-sufficient satisfactions and services rendered to ourselves have always been outside of economics. Satisfactions that depend upon a division of labor or upon different people's interaction are also often outside of economics, because they may, for a variety of reasons, not be subject to market exchange. Sometimes reciprocity cannot be enforced or is not worth enforcing. Sometimes it is automatic and instantaneous, and there is no need to enforce it. Sometimes it is easily assured by tradition and informal social pressure, which renders unnecessary the formality of market contracts. Also, to complicate matters, the same activity, even the same product, can yield an economic and a non-economic satisfaction at the same time. A worker may get satisfaction out of making the goods he sells in the market; a garden may give pleasure to passers-by as well as to its owner, who pays for its upkeep. We must appreciate these distinctions and categories in order to get a feel of the relative importance of economic and non-economic satisfactions, considering that the measurement of that importance is not possible.

Quantifiability is another of the distinguishing characteristics of economic satisfactions. The market prices which emerge from market transactions are our only index of the value people place on the satisfactions they receive and the services they render. With their aid we construct national product and income estimates, and those estimates capture the value of satisfactions that go through the market, but *only* of those satisfactions. To ascertain the relative importance of economic and non-economic satisfactions, therefore, is to ascertain the relative importance of measurable and non-measurable ones, and this, clearly, cannot be quantified in any rigorous way.

MUTUAL STIMULATION

One of the main forms of human satisfaction is stimulus enjoyment, most of which comes from mutual stimulation and as such is usually outside the realm of economics. The reasons for this are simple enough. Stimulation comes from change, variety, surprise, novelty—and most of these originate in human action and imagination. Moreover, we are most stimulating to others when we are stimulated by them. Think of the innumerable direct personal contacts we have with others, whether they come naturally, through our work and various other activities, or are actively sought for the stimulation they yield: discussion, argument, conversation, and gossip; making love and playing tennis; cooperation in any work or joint venture; social games and activities. The stimulation comes from the infinite variety, unpredictability, and challenge of human contact, especially when we take the trouble to provoke and stimulate the other person. After all, the matching of wits and skills is our main challenge, and other people's information, knowledge, experience, behavior, accomplishment, response to situations, solving of problems, and speculation about unresolved problems are our main sources of novelty.

We can, if we want to, think of each person's contribution to the others' satisfactions as payment for the satisfaction he receives. It is obvious that no economic exchange, no formal guarantee of reciprocity, is needed to assure participation in such contact.

Also, the satisfactions of all are likely to be the greater the more evenly the participants are matched. Stimulation is the most pleasant when it calls for the fullest use of our skills and mental powers, and this is most likely to happen when we are facing an equal adversary. Games, conversation, and argument become dull and unchallenging when we have a weaker partner; they may overtax our capacity and become too tiring when we have a much stronger one. Too unequal matching may eliminate altogether the satisfaction of one or more of the participants and so remove their incentive for such contact. In such cases, however, participants with nothing to offer and something to gain may provide a monetary inducement, which, if sufficient, will turn the activity into an economic one. Hence such professions as tennis pro, master of ceremonies, prostitute, gigolo. Society tends to look down upon those and similar professions, perhaps because the commercializing of a normally non-economic activity is taken as a sign of mismatched partners and consequent loss of satisfaction, or perhaps because people disapprove of the performance as a chore of what for most others is a source of satisfaction. Whatever the reason, when money is paid for what normally would be mutual stimulation and so brings the transaction into the national product, that is often a sign of inferior or diminished satisfaction. Luckily, those activities are relatively unimportant, both as sources of mutual stimulation and as forms of economic activity.

While mutual stimulation is outside the realm of economics as a rule, economic resources are often required to provide opportunity, the necessary tools, the premises, and the environment. One function of the market is that of transmitting information and helping the partners to any transaction—economic or non-economic—to sort themselves out and find each other. Since mutual stimulation is greatest when the partners are well matched, matchmaking is a valuable service, often sold for money. That is what marriage counselors and computer dating companies do. Tennis and bridge clubs perform similar services in their respective areas, and they also provide the tools. It is hard to play tennis without a court, or bridge without a card table, and even conversation is more enjoyable over a drink. The value of those activities and amenities enters, of course, into economic accountancy, but their contribution to satisfaction is negligible compared with the mutual stimulation the participants provide for each other.

MARKET GOODS AND SERVICES

The other large category of human interaction besides mutual stimulation is the provision of services and the making of products. Each person could perform at least part of such work for himself, but the economies of scale and of the division of labor render it more efficient and mutually beneficial for people to specialize and to produce goods and services mainly for the benefit of others. Hence the reciprocal nature of such activity. Here, however, the reciprocity of services and satisfactions is neither automatic nor simultaneous; for that reason it must be guaranteed by some form of compulsion if the benefits are to be truly mutual. The exchange relations of market transactions are the usual form such compulsion takes; the size of the national product gives an idea of their importance, since it measures the value of the goods and services that go through the market. Both the production and the distribution of private goods and services is organized through the market; in the case of public goods, only production is organized by the market, while distribution is usually free, paid for through taxation. Consumer expenditure reflects the valuation of the satisfaction consumers get from private goods and services bought; government expenditure on public goods and services reflects only cost, but that cost is used, for want of anything better, as a crude index of their value to those benefited.

When the market value of goods and services is used as an estimate of the value people put on the satisfaction they get from consuming them, it must be recognized as being always an underestimate. The consumer gets more satisfaction out of anything he buys than out of the money he pays for it, otherwise he would not buy it. That additional satisfaction is his consumer's surplus, whose value cannot be estimated, although it can be gauged by finding out what he would pay, if necessary, for continued access to a particular good at its present price rather than go altogether without it.[2]

EXTERNAL BENEFITS AND EXTERNAL NUISANCES

While the national product provides an estimate of the worth of market goods and services to those who buy them, those goods and services often yield satisfaction or give pain to third parties as well. The sight of my house may please every neighbor and passer-by who sees it; on the other hand, the noise, dirt, and dust its construction generated may have pained many people. Those so-called external economies and diseconomies are not considered part of the economic product because the people affected neither pay nor are compensated for them, but they clearly add to and detract from human satisfaction. Since external economies and diseconomies are an important by-product of economic activity, they ought to be taken into account when economic activities are decided upon. How to do the accounting is one of the unsolved problems of economics.

Most externalities, good and bad ones alike, are sensory stimulants, and the good ones are almost always the by-products of those goods and services, or of those features of goods and services, which aim at providing entertainment, amusement, aesthetic pleasure, and other forms of stimulation. The reason is obvious. Sounds and sights, the main sources of sensory stimulation, are not easy to confine, and what is pleasing to one person's ears and eyes is often also pleasing to other people's. The enjoyment of the person who pays for the stimulation need not be abridged and may even be enhanced by other people's sharing it. In short, stimulation is, typically, a non-exclusive or shared source of satisfaction. By contrast, comforts and want satisfaction usually lack these spill-over effects. Since many comforts come from the substitution of mechanical power for man's muscular power, they often have unpleasant side effects, such as noise and air pollution.

NON-MARKET GOODS AND SERVICES

In addition to market goods and services, there are many others that do not go through the market, but are rendered free, their reciprocity and equitable distribution being assured by custom, tradition, social pressure, family discipline, or law. Some of the public services so rendered are compulsory military service and such compulsory citizens' services as fire fighting in emergencies and jury duty. Private non-market goods and services range all the way from the food produced and consumed on the spot by farm households to that advice which parents and in-laws used to give and which in today's world more often goes through the market, being dispensed by social workers and psychoanalysts. Increased specialization, increased mobility, and the change from the extended to the nuclear family have greatly diminished the importance of such non-market goods and services, but they are far from negligible, and one form of them, household chores and personal services performed and rendered within the family and among friends, may even be on the increase.

Household chores and personal services are not easy to define. They certainly include housekeeping proper—cooking, cleaning, bed-making, tidying up, mending, and looking after the children. They include minor, and sometimes major, repair and maintenance of household appliances and other consumers' durables, as well as what goes under the name of do-it-yourself activities. And they also include personal services, help, and advice which otherwise would have to be bought and paid for.

Compared with many other non-market and non-economic satisfactions of man, those derived from the housekeeping and similar services family members perform for each other are probably minor. But since these are similar to corresponding market services, their worth to recipients can be estimated and compared to the value of the economic product, and even partial comparisons between the worth of market and non-market satisfactions are helpful for assessing the contribution of the economic product to all satisfactions.

Time budgets showing average weekly hours of regular housework, volunteer work, and free help rendered to and received from others are available; the time so spent can be valued either at the wage rate of the person performing such unpaid work or at the going market wage for such activity. The estimates show that the non-market activities people perform within and for their families add almost one-half to the family's money *income* (48 per cent on the one, 42 per cent on the other method of reckoning), or about two-thirds to their *expenditure* on market goods and services.[3] The estimates in Table 4 (p. 102), which show national totals, are even higher, presumably because they include the non-market work of the retired and the unemployed. If the value of non-market family tasks is indeed minor compared with other non-economic satisfactions, yet not much smaller than the value attached to the economic satisfactions derived from market goods and services, then the value of the economic product must be minor compared with man's non-economic satisfactions taken as a whole.

If so much that contributes to man's satisfaction is left out of the national product, why do we attach so much importance to its size? One reason is that the GNP seems more easily influenced by policy; another is the belief, or hope, that changes in the national product are positively correlated with changes in man's general welfare, because they leave unaffected man's non-economic satisfactions or at least cause no offsetting changes in them. We cannot here deal properly and exhaustively with that issue, but a counterexample, where a change in the national product leaves total welfare unchanged, is worth discussing.

That change occurs when the dividing line between market and non-market goods moves so that the measured change in the national product is exactly offset by the unmeasured contrary change in the volume of non-market goods and services. I have already mentioned the change from the extended to the nuclear family and the increased scope for specialization and economies of scale as two factors which brought to the market much that existed previously but was outside it. Since those changes typically go hand in hand with development, measures of the marketed product and the income derived from it are bound to overstate the pace of development, since they measure not true development, but the sum of that development and the bringing into the market what before was outside it.

At the same time, the two factors just mentioned have not much to do with where the dividing line lies between householding activities that go and do not go through the market. Most domestic chores and personal services are simple enough for everybody to learn, sufficiently so for differences in innate ability to count for little. Moreover, since they usually have to be performed on the person or in the home, they also offer little scope for exploiting the economies of scale and specialization. If the wealthy of one hundred years ago had domestic servants to perform chores that today's wealthy perform for themselves, the reason is not that they were less good than their servants at performing those chores, but that the disparity between the incomes of the wealthy and those of the servants was great enough that the former would pay for having such services performed and the latter would perform them for that pay. Specialization depends not only on differences in ability and economies of scale, but also on differences in income, and differences of income are the main cause as far as the division of labor of domestic chores and personal services is concerned.

Differences in income may be due to the unequal distribution of power, wealth, job opportunities, educational opportunities; they may also be due to differences in ability. Only in this indirect way, by creating income inequalities, do differences in ability reduce the self-sufficiency of the individual person and household as far as household work is concerned. The wealthy find it economical to have the poor do for them chores they could just as competently do for themselves, because this frees their time for more pleasant or more lucrative pursuits. The proportional difference between the time the wealthy spend at household work versus the time the poor do is almost as great as the proportional difference in their income. The implication for society as a whole is that the greater the inequalities of income, the larger the number of domestic servants and the less the amount of household work performed by family members for themselves and each other. The many domestic servants in the well-to-do households of a poor country are a sign not of the country's poverty, but of its great inequalities.

WORK AS SELF-STIMULATION

Up to now we have discussed goods and services as they relate to the satisfaction of the recipients. Yet the welfare of the producers of goods and services is also affected—and not only by the pay they receive in exchange. Work can be pleasant or unpleasant, and its pleasures, comforts, and discomforts play an important role in our lives. Those effects of work are completely missing from the economist's numerical index of economic welfare: the net national income or net national product is *not* net of the disutility of the labor that went into producing it, nor does it include the satisfactions of labor, if this is what work gives rise to. The reason is simple. Work which produces market goods may be an economic activity, but the satisfaction the worker himself gets out of his work is not an economic good because it does not go through the market and its value is not measurable. It may be very important, nevertheless.

The Protestant, or Puritan, ethic considered work the main source of worldly satisfaction and the only one to receive its blessing. Karl Marx shared that view. "Only in being productively active can man make sense of his life." Work is the "act of man's self creation," "not only a means to an end—the product—but an end in itself, the meaningful expression of human energy." [4] Marx not only believed that work should be enjoyable; he was convinced that it was the most important source of human enjoyment. He criticized other economists for "commodity fetishism," their habit of focusing their attention on the product to the neglect of the activity creating it. He criticized even more the factory system and capitalist organization for changing the nature, conditions, and organization of work in a way that takes the satisfaction out of it and renders it unpleasant instead. He blamed specialization and the subjection of workers to discipline imposed by others for this change, which he called alienation, and he believed that capitalists as well as workers would suffer from it. Work could be either a pleasure or a burden, depending on economic institutions and property relations. One of the main aims of communism, in Marx's view, was to render work enjoyable by eliminating the compulsion of economic necessity, so that "each can become accomplished in any branch he wishes. . . , [making] it possible for me to do one thing today and another tomorrow, to hunt in the morning, fish in the afternoon, rear cattle in the evening, criticize after dinner, just as I have a mind."

Modern economists have nothing to say on whether work is pleasant or unpleasant. They believe that its burden increases (or pleasantness diminishes) with the quantity of work performed and that work on the margin—that is, the last increment of work performed—is unpleasant and only performed for the sake of the income it yields. In this marginal sense therefore, they seem to accept Marx's sweeping generalization and pessimism. Yet, the economists' conclusion can be derived neither from economic data nor from economic theorizing, and even less can it be established through the psychologists' approach.

To the psychologists, work is a source of stimulation, and so it is potentially pleasant. Physical work is not very different from physical exercise; it is or ought to be pleasantly stimulating if taken in the right dose with the proper intensity, duration, and timing. Mental work can also be pleasantly stimulating, as long as it provides novelty and the challenge of learning; and variety or increasing difficulty can maintain its challenge and stimulation for a long time. Exploration, research, and artistic and scientific creation probably provide the most satisfying stimulation known to man, and many other forms of mental work are stimulating and enjoyable, too. The most striking experimental evidence to prove that work can be enjoyable is probably that produced in a celebrated Canadian experiment. The 600-odd pupils of a Montreal primary school were suddenly told that they no longer had to attend classes unless they wanted to, and that punishment for misbehavior would henceforth consist in being sent to the playground to play. All of the children dashed out of the school, but within two days they were all back in class, on a somewhat less regular schedule than before, but doing no less, and sometimes better, work.[5]

Of course, there is some work which is unpleasant because it is too stimulating and therefore tiring, even exhausting, and other work which is insufficiently stimulating and therefore dull, monotonous, fatiguing. Throughout most of history, the biblical image of man's having to earn his bread by the sweat of his brow remained appropriate. The unpleasantness of work consisted in its requiring greater or more prolonged exertion of a man's physical powers than he would exert just for the fun of it, and to induce people to make greater or additional exertion necessitated reward, compulsion, or both. The Industrial Revolution added monotony, mechanical discipline, and the speed of factory routine, and while it lessened the physical exertion required, it more than made up for it by the greatly lengthened working week. That is the picture Marx painted.[6] Since his day, mechanization, automation, and the division of labor have been pushed to new heights, and the working week has been shortened, all of which has relieved man of his backbreaking physical exertion without, however, taking the unpleasantness out of work. Only the nature and causes of the unpleasantness have changed.

Few people in the advanced industrial countries still perform work that is too taxing, yet workers still find their work unpleasant. A number of questionnaire studies have been made of working conditions in the United States and in other industrial countries. They fully confirm the modern objection to work.[7] Most work today is too easy—it is dull, monotonous, mechanical, undemanding, demeaning in its lack of challenge, and unpleasant mainly because it fails to stimulate the worker yet prevents him from seeking stimulation elsewhere. That information is of great practical importance, because the unpleasantness of work is much easier and less costly to remedy when it stems from insufficient challenge and stimulation than when it is caused by exhaustion due to excessive stimulation.

However, my concern here is with the difference between pleasant work and unpleasant work, whatever the cause. Marx was unduly pessimistic when he said that the capitalist system was taking the fun out of work for workers and capitalists alike. There seem to be plenty of pleasant and enjoyable jobs around. The assumption that all work is unpleasant is disproved by the many people who engage in unpaid volunteer work,[8] by the many retired workers who continue doing some work even without pay, and by the professionals of all sorts who readily admit to liking their work.[9]

The same work can, of course, be pleasant to one person and unpleasant to another; it can be pleasant at times and unpleasant at others even to the same person. There is a daily variation in our attitudes to work as fatigue builds up; there may also be long-run change, when work which is at first too difficult becomes interesting and challenging as we master the difficulties and ultimately becomes humdrum and boring as repetition exhausts its challenge and novelty.

The stimulus satisfaction of work is no different from the satisfaction we get from any other source of stimulation. When work is challenging, the reinforcing effect of rising arousal usually carries one beyond the point of optimum comfort, often creating tension and an inner compulsion to continue until the challenge is met. Then one experiences that final release of tension which is perhaps the main component of stimulus satisfaction. The sequence—pleasant stimulation, followed by an obsessive drive to continue, despite fatigue and tension, to a satisfactory completion, leading to the triumph of a problem solved or a task accomplished—is the familiar accompaniment of all strong stimulation (specific exploration), be it work or play. It does not fit the economist's simple notion of the monotonically diminishing pleasantness or increasing unpleasantness of work, although that may still be a realistic picture of the effects of monotonous, mechanical work which is devoid of challenge. The question is, how can we tell the two kinds of work apart?

Empirical evidence reveals great differences in different people's evaluation of their work. Independent people work much longer hours than employees whose tasks and work routine are prescribed by employers and whose hours, once negotiated and agreed upon, are also prescribed. The United States Census distinguishes very few occupational groups, but it does show, for

1960, the actual weekly hours worked to be 58.4 for farm managers, 53.5 for self-employed managers and proprietors other than farmers, and 57.3 for physicians and surgeons, as contrasted to 43.2 for all male employees.[10] West German data contrast all independents against all employees, and the 1970 Austrian Microcensus shows the difference between independents and employees separately for each occupational group that contains both. In Austria, over-all, there was a 50 per cent longer workweek for those able to set their own pace.

TABLE 1

Average Length of Workweek of Independent and Employed Workers in Western Germany (in hours)

	1957	1960	1963	1966	1969	1971
Independents	58.5	56.9	57.5	57.8	57.1	57.3
Employees (office workers)	46.6	46.1	45.3	44.5	44.1	43.5
Employees (production workers)	45.3	45.0	44.1	43.2	42.8	42.5

SOURCE: *Statistiken für die Arbeits- und Sozialpolitik 1973*, Bonn: Bundesministerium für Arbeit und Sozialordnung, 1973, Table 4.6.

We *cannot* interpret these great disparities to mean that employers keep their employees from working (and earning) as much as they would like to: hours worked are among the main issues in every union contract, and the shortening of the working week is one of the proudest achievements of the labor movement. The simplest explanation to account for differences so great and so universal, and found in so many occupations and countries, seems to be the one here stressed. People who do not have to work according to rules and discipline imposed by others and who are free to vary their tasks and routine sufficiently to avoid boredom and keep up their interest seem to get more personally involved in their work and to find it more challenging and enjoyable. They are as likely to experience periods of tension and strain as anyone else, but their way of

TABLE 2

Average Length of Workweek of Independent and
Employed Workers by Industry in Austria 1970

Industry Groups	Independents	Employees
	(IN HOURS)	
Agriculture and Forestry	65.2	48.3
Energy and Water Supply		40.8
Mining		39.6
Food, Beverages, and Tobacco	58.7	41.8
Textiles (excluding clothes and bed linen)		40.1
Clothing, Bed Linen and Shoes	49.5	39.9
Leather, Leather products (Shoes excepted)		40.4
Toys and Wooden Musical Instruments	51.8	41.0
Paper and Cardboard		40.4
Printing and Duplicating		40.8
Chemicals, Rubber, Oil		39.8
Stone and Glassware		41.0
Metal, Metalwork	51.7	40.6
Construction	52.1	40.5
Distributive Trades and Storage	54.4	40.9
Lodging, Hotels, Restaurants	66.9	44.9
Transportation, Communication	57.3	41.5
Banking, Private Insurance		40.5
Real Estate, Legal and Financial Services	52.1	40.3
Hygiene, Cleaning, Undertaking	48.2	39.5
Art, Entertainment, Sports	45.4	40.9
Health Care		40.8
Teaching and Research		34.5
Local Administration, Social Insurance		41.1
Domestic Work		36.1
Average of All Industries	61.5	40.8

SOURCE: Österreichishes Statistisches Zentralamt, *Mikrocensus 1970*, pp. 51–64.

relieving such strain is not to stop working, but, on the contrary, to keep at it until their sense of accomplishment brings
relief. Differences in working hours therefore testify to differences in people's personal involvement in their work. Those
who are most involved almost certainly also get the most satisfaction out of work, but the data do not and cannot prove this.

Questionnaire studies of cross sections of the working population show that the higher the hourly earnings, the longer the hours worked.[11] Considering that people in the higher income groups are usually those who have more discretion and freedom of action in their work, this finding does little more than duplicate and confirm those cited above.

Yet another confirmation comes from urban transportation studies, which occasionally yield estimates of the value people implicitly attach to the time they spend commuting. A 1963 study of London civil servants commuting by car or underground and separated into three income groups has shown that the higher civil servants value the time they spend in commuting at a very much higher proportion of their salaries than lower civil servants do.[12] Such conclusions are drawn by regarding the additional cost of the faster transportation as the price of the time it saves and inferring people's valuation of their time according to their willingness or unwillingness to pay that price for time so saved. Differences between the various groups' choice of a mode of transportation are then explained by their different valuations of the time commuting encroaches upon. Similar studies made in the United States have occasionally shown the same result.[13]

The evidence so far cited merely indicates a greater involvement, and possibly greater liking or lesser dislike for their work, of those who have more control over what they do and over when and how they do it, either because they are their own masters or because, being higher up in an organizational hierarchy, they are allowed more discretion. Nothing so far has shown whether the value or marginal value attached to work by a particular group of people is positive or negative, and empirical data seldom throw light on that issue.

The existence of unpaid volunteer work is one of the few pieces of evidence we have of people's attaching a positive value to work. Most such work is done by housewives and by retired people who enjoy going back to their old routine at their previous place of work, but it is also done by people who are in the labor force. It is worth noting that most such volunteer work is performed by people in the higher income groups, who spend more time also at their paid work.[14]

Another piece of evidence which shows that many people enjoy their work is the great importance of philanthropy. In the United States, philanthropic donations made by individuals during their lifetime (as distinguished from philanthropic bequests) average slightly below 30 per cent of total net personal savings.[15] Subtracting the estimated value of what is given under the social pressure of United Fund drives, church collections, and so on still leaves truly voluntary donations equal to about one-quarter of net personal savings. They represent a very large sum of money, and people's willingness to give that sum away while they are still alive shows that such funds are in excess of what their owners need and can use for their own purposes and wish to leave to their families and beloved. Most philanthropists are active people, who have themselves earned what they give away, but it is hard to imagine their making an extra effort, working longer hours or for more years, for the sole purpose of accumulating more money to give away. It is much more likely that they enjoy their work for itself, as well as the act of making money or the exercise of their skill at making it, and that it is the satisfaction of their work which keeps them at it long after all their needs for money and for all the things that money will buy are fully satisfied. It is worth adding that this argument and the previous one establish the positive satisfaction a man gets out of his work, not only in total, but also on the margin, where he makes his decisions between longer and shorter hours and between a longer and a shorter working life.

Further evidence which suggests that even on the margin some people like and others dislike the work they do is provided by the divergent *trends* in the length of the working week. Much has been made of the secular shortening of the working week in industry. United States data show a fall from about seventy hours in 1850 to around forty hours today; [16] the trend was much the same also in most other developed countries. An ever shorter working week seems a natural accompaniment to the rise in the standard of living and a sign of the worker's desire to enjoy his rising income partly in the form of more leisure. In terms of the economist's formal model, the rise in wages raises the price of leisure (that is, the earnings lost by taking leisure), so pushing people into buying less leisure and more goods; at the same time, the wage increase also raises real income, making people better off, more able to afford all of the good things of life, including leisure. The rise in the price of leisure and the rise in real income are just two aspects of the same wage increase, known in the economist's language as its substitution and income effects, respectively. They push the person who got the wage increase in opposite directions. The economist visualizes the actual change in the worker's demand for leisure as the net balance of the two opposing influences. Since a change in the relative prices of leisure and goods seems to have little impact on people's expenditure pattern, the income effect prevails, causing the demand for leisure to increase and the length of the work week to diminish as wages rise.

The model explains pretty well the observed shortening of the work week in manufacturing, if we assume that leisure is pleasant and work unpleasant. How would the same model perform if leisure and work were both assumed to be pleasant? Unchanged would be the substitution effect of a rise in earnings, but very different or absent would be the income effect. When work and leisure are considered the only uses of time, and both are assumed to be pleasant, there can be no income effect, because money cannot buy more time. The substitution effect, therefore, would be the only effect of the rise in earnings, which would then necessarily lead to a *lengthening* of the work week.

That result, which is the opposite of what the assumption that work is unpleasant leads to, is also obtained in a more realistic model, which, in addition to pleasant leisure and pleasant work, also distinguishes an unpleasant third use of time, that required for the daily chores of ordinary living.[17] A rise in income in such a model does have an income effect: it frees time for both leisure and work by causing people to save time on housekeeping through additional expenditure on household services, household appliances, and labor-saving goods. Here, therefore, substitution and income effects both pull in the direction of lengthening the work week as incomes rise.

The above is a typical example of the economist's customary reasoning. If work were pleasant, a rise in wages would make one work longer. Then, if statistics showed that some people's working week did get longer as their rates of earnings rose, that would not prove that such people's work was pleasant, but it would certainly make such a conclusion plausible.

There are few statistics which show such a relation between wage or salary rates and hours worked, but those few do pertain to people who are likely to enjoy their work. Most discussions of the declining work week of wage- and salary-earners stress the absence of a corresponding trend in the professions and among independent businessmen. Data on the latter's present-day working hours show these to be so long that it is hard to imagine them to have been longer in the past.[18] In fact, they seem to have been shorter, to judge by the few scattered data we have. In the United States, the only data on professionals' working hours that go back in time relate to university professors and instructors. These have been assembled in Table 3. While they are not strictly comparable since they refer to different schools at different dates, they nevertheless show an unmistakable upward trend. It is significant that the time spent on instruction and instruction-connected activities and on administration and student affairs remained virtually unchanged between 1917 and 1968; whereas time spent on research, which is what academic people enjoy the most, more than quadrupled.

The same upward trend is also evident in the working hours of higher civil servants in England. One hundred years ago, higher civil servants in Great Britain had office hours from ten a.m. until four p.m., six days a week, "with but an hour or two to spend at luncheon with a City friend"—a net total of 30 hours or less a week and considerably shorter than the office hours of lower civil servants and clerks in the same offices.[19] Annual vacations ranged from 32 to 52 working days. Today, the annual vacations of the same higher civil servants range from 18 to 30 working days and their workweek net of lunch periods is 36 hours in London, 37 hours elsewhere—the same as the lower ranks.[20] It hardly needs adding that these hours are more likely to be minima than averages, but that does not change the argument.

Another set of data comes from a detailed study of changes in the work and leisure time of workers and independent businessmen in the City of Hamburg between 1750 and the present. This shows, first of all, that the merchant's workday in the eighteenth and nineteenth centuries was hours shorter than the worker's, while the disparity is the other way around today. As to trends, while the worker's workweek reached its greatest length, 72 hours, in the mid-nineteenth century, at the height of the Industrial Revolution, and has since shrunk to almost 40 hours, the merchant's has been steadily getting longer, having risen from between 39 and 51 hours a week in 1750 to an average of 50 hours or more in 1850;[21] whereas an official 1972 questionnaire survey of West Germany puts the length of the average workweek of top executives in large corporations at almost 60 (59.4) hours.[22]

One more piece of evidence, though indirect, is worth mentioning; it comes from studies of the effect of progressive taxation and consequent high marginal tax rates on the incentive to work. These studies naturally concentrate on the free professions, where people are free to vary the amount of work they do, and almost all of them show no or negligible impairment of the incentive to work.[23] This result seems surprising or inconclusive, given the assumption that work is a chore or a bore; it is the natural result to expect if we take the opposite assumption.

TABLE 3 Length of Workweek of University Faculty Members (in hours)

	1917 Univ. of Washington	1924 North Colorado Univ.	1930 Rochester Inst. of Technology	1940 Univ. of Minnesota	1941 Ohio State Univ.	1960 Univ. of Calif.	1967 Univ. of Colo.	1968 Univ. of Calif.	1969 Univ. of Minn.
Total Hours	46.5	49.2	47.3	59	58	58	56.2	60.9	58.1
Standard Deviation of Total Hours [a]	(12.4)	(11.5)						(10.9)	(18)
Instruction	33.2			29.0		31	32.1	31.3	27.0
Research	4.0			7.5		17	14.0	18.4	11.4
Administration	9.4 [b]			5.9		6	6.7	6.2	7.7
Other				16.6		4	3.4	5.0	12.0

[a] See note 20 to Chapter 2 for an explanation of standard deviation.
[b] Includes other.

SOURCES:

Fisk, Martin, University of Minnesota Faculty Activities Report for Fall Quarter, 1968.

Heilman, J. D., "Methods of Reporting the College Teacher's Load and Administrative Efficiency." Educational Administration and Supervision, 11 (March, 1925), pp. 167–87.

Morecock, E. M., "How the Faculty of a Technical Institute Divides its Time," Educational Research Bulletin, 13 (April, 1935), pp. 88–91.

University of California Survey of Faculty Effort and Output, 1968–69.

Chartes, W. W., "How Much Do Professors Work?" Journal of Higher Education, 13 (June, 1942), pp. 298–301.

Koos, L. F., "The Adjustment of the Teaching Load in a University," Washington D.C.: U.S. Dept. of Interior, Bureau of Education, Bulletin, 1919, No. 15.

THE IMPORTANCE OF THE ECONOMIC PRODUCT

Now we have distinguished six categories of sources of satisfaction, of which only one is economic and measurable. The value of one other category, that of non-market goods and services, can at least be estimated. Not even that is possible for the remaining four: self-sufficient satisfactions, mutual stimulation, externalities, and work satisfaction. Some economists have tried to estimate the value of leisure time, and since we enjoy all but one of the non-economic satisfactions during our leisure time (the exception, of course, is work), such estimates ought to give at least a rough index of the value people attach to these other satisfactions. One such set of estimates is shown in Table 4. Unfortunately, the leisure estimates are not only crude, they are conceptually dubious as well; [24] even so, they might be good enough to indicate rough orders of magnitude. They show the value of leisure time to be a multiple, usually a twofold to three-

TABLE 4

National Income, Non-market Work, and Leisure
(Billions of Dollars in 1958 prices)

	1929	1935	1945	1947	1954	1958	1965
National Income	131.1	110.8	176.5	227.9	306.9	367.8	454.7
Value of Non-market Work	85.7	109.2	152.4	159.6	211.5	239.7	295.4
Value of Market and Non-market Work (sum of the first two rows)	216.8	220.0	328.9	387.5	518.4	607.5	750.1
Estimated Value of Leisure	339.5	401.3	450.7	466.9	523.2	554.9	626.9

SOURCES:
Row 1, U.S. Department of Commerce, Office of Business Economics, *The National Income and Product Accounts of the United States, 1929–65, Statistical Tables.*
All other data from Nordhaus, W., and J. Tobin, "Is Growth Obsolete?" National Bureau of Economic Research, General Series 96, *Fiftieth Anniversary Colloquium V*, Table A.16, p. 53.

fold multiple, of the national income. When we bear it in mind that the satisfaction of work is additional to this, then we find that the contribution of the economic product to human welfare turns out to be small indeed.

Why, then, do most of us attach so much importance to money income and the things money will buy? Of course, the fact that the size and distribution of the national income or national product can be influenced by public policy is important from society's point of view. But why is the individual so greatly concerned with his personal income? The question has many answers. The simplest and most obvious, of course, is that survival in our economy depends on things we need money to buy. The average person, however, devotes a rather small part of his income to mere survival, which suggests that this is a relatively small part of the answer. Another and probably more important part of the answer is that economic satisfactions are usually accompanied by many other, non-economic satisfactions. My income, besides giving access to economic satisfactions, also serves as an index of some of my other satisfactions, and this second function of income may be no less important than the first.

We know that people in the higher income groups typically have more pleasant work and enjoy that work more than those who are low on the income scale, and some evidence suggests that the high-income people enjoy even the last hour of the day's work, while low-income people consider it a drag. In a society which attaches great importance to work and its satisfactions—such as ours—the difference between liking and disliking one's work may well be more important than the differences in economic satisfaction that the disparities in our income lead to. Moreover, people with some control over how they divide their time between work and leisure will carry over differences in their work satisfactions into their leisure satisfactions as well. For they will try to allocate their time so that, on the margin, the satisfaction of leisure equals the satisfaction (positive or negative) they get from an hour's work together with the satisfaction they get from the earnings of an hour's work. This means that the value also of leisure will be greater to those who enjoy their work than to those who do not.

To say that people allocate their time that way may look like a theoretical deduction from the assumption of rational behavior, but it need not be unrealistic. Those who work with gusto tend to bring the same spirit also to their leisure; those who are disgruntled in their work are usually not much less disgruntled after work. If such differences in attitude are due to the nature of the work and correlated with income, then inequalities of income clearly mean much more and go much deeper than the mere differences in money expenditure they lead to. This is especially worth stressing in affluent economies, where almost no one stays cold or hungry any more and where much of the difference in expenditures goes into buying the same collection of goods at different prices and in only slightly different qualities.

External economies are also non-economic satisfactions that go hand in hand with economic ones and add to their worth. The satisfactions the public gets from the beauty of Europe's Gothic churches and Romanesque palaces or from the excitement of New York's skyline and cosmopolitan atmosphere are the external benefits of whatever uses their builders originally built them for. Because of the commercial exploitation of the tourists they attract, we can even form an idea of what these externalities are worth in terms of money and how their capitalized value might compare to the original cost of the buildings that give them off. Externalities are important, and people's vague awareness of this fact might well explain their attaching more weight to measures of economic satisfactions than such satisfactions by themselves would justify.

On the other hand, not all economic satisfactions give off external benefits; some, as we have seen, even inflict external nuisances. It does not go without saying, therefore, that economic satisfactions go hand in hand with non-economic ones and that changes in the one are accompanied by changes in the other. Whether and to what extent they do depends on many factors, and these factors, therefore, are important determinants of welfare. That is why the performance of the economy cannot be judged by the size, growth, and distribution of the national product alone. As important, or perhaps more important, is the economy's ability to produce the economic product with a maximum of beneficial and minimum of harmful accompanying side effects.

CHAPTER SIX

Necessities and Comforts

We have made a first step toward closing the gap between the psychologist's and the economist's approaches by looking at human satisfactions and their sources as psychologists see them and trying to decide where, when, and how economic ramifications fit into the picture. Now let us reverse the procedure, starting with the economist's classification of economic goods and services and relating them to the psychologist's categories.

Economists view consumer satisfaction as the goal of all economic activity. They measure economic efficiency by the economy's success in satisfying consumers' desires, economic progress by the higher and higher levels of consumers' satisfaction that progress makes possible. By so doing they tacitly assume either that consumers' wants are immutable, so that economic performance is measured against an unchanging scale of aspirations, or, if higher achievement raises aspiration, that such a raising of sights will not diminish the consumer's satisfaction with what he has already achieved. Only recently have doubts been voiced about the validity of these assumptions.

NECESSITIES AND LUXURIES

The very variety of goods and services that surround us demands that they be classified in some way. The simplest classification divides them into necessities and luxuries. The division seems to combine a rigorous economic definition with an important psychological distinction. Economists define necessities as goods and services for which consumer's demand either does not rise with their income or rises in lesser proportion than income. Luxuries are all those goods and services for which demand rises either in proportion with income or in greater proportion than income. Put in the economist's language, the income elasticity of demand is less than one (inelastic) for necessities, equal to or greater than one (elastic) for luxuries.

The distinction as just drawn seems to correspond to the psychologist's distinction between biological needs and all others. Necessities serve man's biological functions, which is why the demand for them is urgent at first, but limited and quickly saturated. Luxuries is the catch-all category for everything else. There is also a hierarchical difference between the two categories. Most people feel that necessities have or should have priority over luxuries, and that only as the need for necessities gets saturated should the desire for luxuries be catered to. The dividing line between the poor and the not-poor used to be drawn according to whether a person could afford anything beyond the necessities of existence. Poor relief used to provide necessities alone, or just enough money to buy them.

Unfortunately, the distinction is not as clear-cut and unambiguous as it first seems. A smoker's demand for cigarettes, for example, is no less inelastic than his demand for food; are cigarettes therefore a necessity? Also, there are no biological standards to establish the necessary minimum of clothing, housing, heating, lighting, kitchen and bathroom facilities. Having a toilet and bathroom in the building you live in has come to be considered a necessity in modern America even by the poor and by those providing and administering relief for the poor. Yet this American necessity is still a luxury, and an unattainable one, for many millions, even billions, of the world's population.

The dividing line, therefore, between necessities and luxuries turns out to be not objective and immutable, but socially determined and ever changing, very differently drawn in different societies, by different people, and at different times by the same people. One cannot unequivocally separate commodities according to whether consumers' demand for them is elastic or inelastic. Demand for the same commodity may be nil, it may be increasing more or less than proportionately with income, it may even have reached a stable level of complete satiation, depending on a person's standard of living or a society's level of economic development. That detracts greatly from the usefulness of the categories mentioned and also raises the questions of whether and how one might predict the tendency of a luxury to become a necessity. Those questions lead us to consider another little-known commodity classification, one which is, seemingly, quite different from the one we have been discussing, yet related because one of its categories will turn out to be something of a generalization of the concept of necessities.

DEFENSIVE AND CREATIVE PRODUCTS

"It will be convenient to distinguish two broad classes of objects of consumption: on the one hand those products which are intended to prevent or remedy pains, injuries or distresses, and on the other those which are intended to supply some positive gratification or satisfaction. They may be conveniently named defensive products and creative products. . . . The same product often fulfills purposes of both kinds. Food, for example, is needed to guard against hunger, weakness, and ultimately death by starvation, but at the same time different kinds of food are designed to give the consumer positive satisfaction. This duality does not invalidate the distinction. . . . [Also,] it is not easy to draw the line between products which prevent pain and

those which promote physical pleasure, because it is characteristic of any physical need, which causes distress while it is still
unsatisfied, to cause positive physical pleasure as soon as it is
in the course of being satisfied. We have all heard of the man
who had a thirst he would not sell for ten dollars. The pleasure
that arises *merely* from the removal of distress cannot be
regarded as constituting the product that occasions it a creative
product. But it is often possible by a suitable adaptation or
elaboration of the product to procure much more pleasure than
the satisfaction of the need alone would yield. Then the product
will become creative." [1]

The categories described in the quotation above were proposed half a century ago by Sir Ralph Hawtrey, one of the most
distinguished economists of the time. They come close to the
psychologist's concepts, which they anticipated by several decades; and they are almost identical to our simplified two-fold
distinction between comfort and stimulation. [2] The only difference is that Hawtrey deals with products, I with forms of satisfaction; and it is better to stick to the latter, because what
seemed the exception to Hawtrey is probably the rule: most
products are not just defensive or just creative, but yield both
comfort and stimulus. The distinction, therefore, is clearer and
easier to make with satisfactions than with products. We shall
find the distinction very useful, but since it has been available
to economists for almost two generations, the question naturally
arises: why, if it is really so useful, has it been left in limbo all
this time?

The probable reason is that economists could not use and felt
no need for the distinction. Their central concept, the consumer's satisfaction, does not distinguish between the avoidance of pain and the seeking of pleasure, and when the consumer's preferences are inferred from his market behavior, we
cannot tell whether he chose what he chose for the lesser pain
or the greater pleasure it gives rise to. We encountered this
problem in our discussion of work, where we found plenty of
evidence of great differences in the marginal satisfaction work

gives to different people, but had difficulty in proving that there were differences in sign, with some people getting positive, others negative, marginal satisfaction from their work. Yet on the basis of intuition, man has made the distinction since time immemorial, and neurophysiology confirmed its objective reality when it identified separate pain and pleasure centers in the brain.

The distinction, then, is valid, even if economists have gotten along quite well without it all this time. But today, economic progress has created a new situation. As long as there was plenty of room for both avoiding pain and seeking pleasure, it was not too interesting to find out which of the two was our main source of satisfaction, which we strove for with more energy or greater success. To distinguish between them has become interesting and relevant only now, as the satiation of one of them has, at least in a few countries, come into sight.

It seems obvious that the avoidance of pain is a satiable desire, and this also fits in with the neurophysiologist's finding that pain is caused by stimulation of the pain center in the brain and ceases when such stimulation ceases. By contrast, the desire for pleasure seems insatiable; this again is confirmed by the untiring persistence with which laboratory animals seek to stimulate the primary pleasure centers of their brains. This difference between satiable and insatiable desires acquires practical relevance as technical, chemical, medical, and economic progress bring complete pain avoidance within practical reach.

In a few fortunate countries, the pain of hunger has already been eliminated for virtually the entire population, and the same may also be said of the pain of exposure to cold, and perhaps of a few other pains as well. Can one generalize from these to all forms of pain, and from food and shelter to all defensive products? The desire to avoid hunger and cold is clearly satiable, and so is the demand for the defensive products, or the defensive aspects of products that cater to these desires. Does it not follow that all pain avoidance is a satiable desire; and does it not also follow that as these desires near satiation, consumers' demand for the products that cater to them should also become satiable—inelastic with respect to income and ultimately approaching an upper limit? In other words, can we not conclude that all defensive products or comforts are like either necessities or potential necessities, things that will become necessities as increasing affluence renders them more accessible?

Hawtrey himself may well have reached the same conclusion. He seems to have introduced the distinction between defensive and creative products, because he believed that society around him spent too much on the first and too little on the second. He gave two reasons for his belief. The first had to do with externalities. "The protection given by clothes is exclusive to those who use them. But when people are not satisfied with a mere covering and provide themselves with fine clothing pleasing to the eye, the enjoyment is shared by all who meet them." [3] He also gave a few other examples to illustrate the same point. This is not accidental, but an inherent characteristic of creative products or stimulations. I also mentioned a parallel point which reinforces Hawtrey's, the tendency of many defensive products to contribute to pollution and so inflict a burden on the general public. This means that creative products are more valuable and defensive products less valuable for society than they appear to the individual when he takes a selfish attitude and when he also neglects the impact of other people's selfish attitudes on himself.

The second reason for Hawtrey's belief was the one at issue here.

> It is possible for a rich man to incur heavy expenditure without any assignable purpose beyond securing the minimum of discomfort and the maximum of leisure. . . . But the whole yields no *positive* good; it merely brings him to the zero point, at which he is suffering from no avoidable harm. He has weeded his garden and still has to choose what he will plant in it before he can be said to have made anything at all of his life. [4]

Defensive consumption can do no more than to prevent harm; therefore, Hawtrey seems to imply, people should not spend so much money on it.

Hawtrey's advice is good if his premise is right. But is it really true that our need for *all* defensive products or comforts is strictly limited and satiable? Before accepting so sweeping a generalization, let us examine it more carefully, taking some of the main forms of comfort one by one.

SOME OF THE COMFORTS

Is the need for comforts limited and the demand for the goods that provide them satiable? These are the questions we must investigate in detail, and one difficulty is best faced at the outset. Conceptually, it is easy enough to distinguish the consumer's demand for a defensive product from his desire to avoid the pain that motivates it, but it is hard to observe or measure them separately. One can *observe* a person's market demand and changes in his demand; one can only *infer* the presence of pain and the desire to avoid it from the behavior it motivates—and all too often market demand is the *only* behavior it motivates. When that is the case, the difficulty of ascertaining the intensity of pain otherwise than by the urgency of demand for the pain killer is insurmountable. Sometimes, however, conflicting actions, or the several actions motivated by the same desire, or different people's different actions motivated by the same desires enable one to distinguish the two.

To start out with the simplest case, it is a well-established fact that consumers' demand for almost all the narrowly defined biological necessities is satiable,[5] in the sense of having a low income elasticity of demand and, presumably, an upper limit. From this one can always infer that the biological needs to which these necessities cater are also satiable. The desire to escape physical pain stops when the pain stops; and the pain stops when the biologically determined need is satisfied.

Very similar to the comforts that relieve physical pain are those that relieve fatigue, eliminate bother, or save time. To use Hawtrey's words once again, "a special class of defensive product is the kind of expenditure which is intended to provide leisure. . . . Leisure, like money, is a form of power, which people covet without necessarily having any clear idea of what use they wish to make of it. To avoid some encroachment on one's time seems to be clear gain" [6]—and most people would so regard also the saving of effort, bother, and skill. A large part of our economy's output of goods and services is designed to save some of the time, energy, attention, and skill required by the routine of daily living, and it does seem correct to classify as comfort the outcome of consuming this output. The question is, is man's desire for such comfort also limited and satiable?

Each of us has around sixteen waking hours a day to dispose of, a certain fund of energy and attention to use up, and a variety of skills to exercise and show off. Work, routine living, and the enjoyment of life constitute the claims on his supply of all these. To save time and energy in all uses but one is rational and adds to one's satisfaction if, but *only* if, the time and energy so saved can be put to better purpose in that one use. If one's ability to do that is limited, one's need for the comfort derived from saving time and energy in all the other uses is equally limited. That can create a quandary, and it almost certainly does in modern America, where the average person's not getting enough exercise and not knowing what to do with his leisure time are becoming universally recognized as increasingly serious social problems. We may tentatively conclude at this point that the need for this source of comfort is also satiable.

What about anguish or mental pain? Most mental pain consists in the expectation and fear of future physical pain, and since the uncertainties of the future can seldom be perfectly eliminated or fully insured against, we might expect the demand for this category of comforts not to be fully satiable. Indeed, there are anxious people whom no amount of security and reassurance can rid of their anxiety and who have an unlimited and insatiable demand for the comfort of reassurance. Such people, however, are generally considered ill and exceptional. Society usually develops a standard of what it considers normal safeguards against uncertainty and regards as unreasonable anyone's desire for much greater or better safeguards. These generally accepted social standards may change over time, of course, but a given standard, however vaguely defined, usually exists at any given time. It sets a limit, if not to all demand, at least to reasonable demand for relief from mental pain.

A simple example is financial security, reassurance that one's future biological and other needs will continue to be met to the degree to which one is accustomed to meet them. Savings are the economic good that provides this comfort. Of course there are misers, unreasonable people whose demand for financial security is insatiable, but there is plenty of evidence that most people's demand for assurance against future contingencies is not only satiable but of a fairly low priority. Some of this evidence will be cited later. For the time being, let us assume that the demand for the comfort of savings is also satiable.

THE COMFORT OF BELONGING

The comfort of belonging, up to a point, is a biological necessity in a very real and literal sense of the word. Man as an individual cannot survive in isolation; he must defend himself by the concerted action of an organized group. The individual's survival therefore depends on his being accepted as a member of the group, and he must behave in a way that will assure his acceptance and assert his membership. In species that must live in groups, such behavior is no less necessary for physical survival than the obtaining of food. The need for group membership is manifest in many animal societies, and its nature and urgency are most apparent in the young, who feel least secure in their acceptance by the group.[7]

The young of these species—and man is only one such—are greatly disturbed and agitated when left alone or excluded from the activities of the group; they spend much of their time imitating the actions of peers and adults, and their imitative behavior is clearly aimed at gaining and maintaining acceptance and membership in the group. Most people are aware of the strength of this drive in their children, though they are much less aware of it in themselves. Yet the power of precedent, custom, fashion, mass movements all testify to the great strength in man of the desire to imitate and conform to the behavior of the group he belongs or wants to belong to.

My concern with imitative behavior is confined to status consumption, the part of the consumer's purchases motivated by his desire to gain and assert his membership in the society around him. The desire "to live up to the Joneses" is often criticized and its rationality called into question. This is absurd and unfortunate. Status seeking, the wish to belong, the asserting and cementing of one's membership in the group is a deep-seated and very natural drive whose origin and universality go beyond man and are explained by that most basic of drives, the desire to survive. On the other hand, status can be sought in many different ways, some better, some worse in their usefulness for society as a whole. Accordingly, it makes sense to approve of some ways and disapprove of other ways of seeking status. We must beware, however, of a wholesale condemnation of status seeking and status consumption.

The strength of man's desire for status is best shown by his great concern with poverty. One thinks of poverty as insufficient means to buy the biological necessities of life. But the minimum real income below which a person is considered poor, considers himself poor, and qualifies for public support is vastly different in different times and places; and it varies between different countries as those countries' average standards of living vary. In Table 5 the index of the standard of living given in the first column shows a more than thirtyfold differential between the poorest and the richest country listed; the poverty norms, given in the second column, show even greater differentials. If Egypt's poverty norm is a true survival minimum, then Switzerland's or the United States', which are so very much higher, cannot possibly be that. They must be something altogether different. It is true that the Egyptians' life expectancy is quite a bit lower than that of the Swiss or the Americans, so that their physiological survival minimum is also likely to be more sparingly defined; but this can hardly account for more than a small part of the more than thirtyfold difference in their poverty norms. Most of the difference can be explained by the fact that in the advanced countries, the poverty norm has long ago ceased to reflect a physiological minimum necessary for survival and has become instead a "minimal social standard of decency," the life-style that a particular society considers the minimum qualification for membership. The explanation is confirmed by the custom, in many countries, systematically to revise the poverty norm upward in response to rises in the average standard of living.[8] However arbitrary or even frivolous may be the life-style with which a society identifies itself, to be able to adopt that life-style is, for the individual member or would-be member of that society, a necessary condition of his membership. If such membership is, in turn, a necessary condition of his survival, then we are justified in considering this part of status consumption, which removes the stigma of poverty, a biological necessity. The desire for membership and the demand for the list of goods that cater to this desire are clearly satiable, at least in the short run, with the poverty norm expressing their cost in money terms.

More complex is the situation in the long run. In a progressive economy, where the average standard of living is rising, the poverty norm is also likely to rise, clearly raising the cost of membership in society for each successive generation. Not quite so clear is the situation of the old who have not been poor in the past and whose standard of living has not fallen, but who find themselves bypassed by the rising poverty norm, pushed, so to speak, into poverty, through no fault of their own and without change in their own way of living. Many of them are probably unaffected, secure in their acceptance by society, pleased with their ability to maintain undiminished a way of life they got used to and found satisfactory in their youth and

TABLE 5

Gross Domestic Product Per Capita and Poverty Norm (excluding rent)
Selected Countries for Selected Years

	GDP/cap. US $	Single Person poverty norm as % of GDP/cap.
United States (1965)	3,240	25.8 [a]
Switzerland (1966)	2,265	30.3
Canada (1965)	2,156	23.3 [b]
Denmark (1965)	2,070	24.4
Finland (1967)	1,801	24.1
France (1965)	1,626	22.4
United Kingdom (1963)	1,395	32.8
West Germany (1962)	1,321	25.4
Japan (1964)	717	30.3
Ireland (1962)	639	24.3
Singapore (1958)	435	14.0
Hong Kong (1958)	257	6.1
Ceylon (1963)	136	18.5
Egypt (1953)	92	21.0

[a] The general assistance standard of Santa Clara County, Calif.

[b] The general assistance standard of the Province of Ontario.

SOURCE: Taira, Koji, "Consumer Preferences, Poverty Norms and Extent of Poverty," *Quarterly Journal of Economics and Business* (July 1969), Table 1, p. 37.

paying no heed to the new generation's new ways and new standards. On the other hand, there must also be others who, seeing the rise in other people's standards, resent having their own eclipsed and left behind. Their unchanged desire for respectability must be translated therefore into an ever-rising expenditure on the tokens of respectability.

We do not know the relative importance of these two groups, but the total number of people affected is quite large. Almost 10 per cent of the U.S. population is old—sixty-five years or older—and even more are old if we include in our definition all members of households headed by the old; 47 per cent of those who are old are poor, while among the rest of the population only 17 per cent are poor.[9] Some of this excess incidence of poverty among the old must be due to inflation, some to improvidence, some to people's underestimation of their life expectancy. But much of it can be explained by the secular rise in the poverty norm.

For, if everybody, at age thirty-three, tried to adopt for life a fixed standard of living, saving enough for his old age while he is active and contenting himself with the highest standard he could hope to maintain undiminished till death, there would result the same disparity in the incidence of poverty between young and old as we have today. The old would have decided on their standard of living thirty-seven years ahead of their old age (assuming their average age to be seventy), the rise in the standard of living and presumably also in the poverty norm over such a period is approximately 94 per cent, and, given the shape of the income distribution in the United States, such a rise in the poverty norm is enough to raise the percentage of people falling below it from 17 to 47 per cent.[10]

Clearly, thirty-three is too early an age for deciding upon, and its income too low for determining, one's level of living for a lifetime. Most people's consumption habits and standards probably jell and get rigid only when they are in their forties, or even later. To that extent, therefore, this explanation is insufficient by itself to account for an incidence of poverty among the old, which, in the United States, is almost three times that among the young. Even so, this factor probably explains half or more of the excess incidence of poverty among the aged, leaving the rest to be explained by inflation and profligacy due to people's yielding to pressure to live up to what society considers a minimal standard of decency.

So far I have been concerned with only that part of status consumption which assures membership in society at large. Many people's desire for status, however, goes far beyond. They want to rank within society, and they seek acceptance or distinction within a certain social class or a narrower group of colleagues, co-professionals, or neighbors. The demand for the comfort this yields may or may not be satiable, depending on how it is sought. It is satiable when people seek recognition for excellence in their job or profession, in a sport, game, or hobby, or in their expert appreciation of food, wine, music, painting, or any other of the many good things of life. Thanks to the great multiplicity possible in such aims and the standards set for them, full status satisfaction in such form is within many people's reach. By contrast, when people seek status not in other people's recognition of their specific accomplishments, but in a general token, like income, which is supposed to express the value society places on their services, then status becomes a matter of ranking on a one-dimensional scale, and the seeking of status becomes a zero-sum game. This means that one person's gain in status is automatically matched by an equal loss of status suffered by those he now outranks. A gain in status by anyone becomes merely a change in ranking, which changes only the distribution of status satisfaction but leaves unchanged the sum total of such satisfactions if we attach equal weight to the satisfaction different people get from their ranking in society.

Such limitation of the supply of status satisfaction, however, imposes no limits on people's demand for status, nor on the amount of money they may spend in seeking it. Money income as a measure of one's success in life has the drawback that knowledge of it is seldom in the public domain. Therefore, to enjoy not only one's high income, but also the esteem it can secure, one must make it known through appropriate spending behavior. Part of this consists in buying what the rich buy. Not performing personal services and household chores for oneself used to imply a division of labor based on differences of income rather than of skill, and it has become a symbol of high income. The number of a man's servants has been, rightly, considered a measure of his rank and riches throughout most of history; and although domestic appliances rather than domestic servants provide most of our freedom from household chores today, such freedom remains nevertheless a symbol of high income. The other and perhaps more important symbol of high income is conspicuous consumption. A large income is best advertised by largesse in spending, by not pinching pennies, by not counting too finely the cost of consumption, and by buying conspicuous objects because of their high cost rather than in spite of it.

There clearly is no limit to such spending, and, since the supply of status satisfaction so obtained is limited, that satisfaction is one of insatiable demand. As I spend more on prestige goods, I gain in status but cause others to lose; as others spend more to regain their lost status, they inflict a corresponding loss of status on me, and there need be neither an end to such competitive increase in conspicuous consumption nor any gain to the players engaged in this competitive game taken as a whole.

THE COMFORT OF BEING USEFUL

The above discussion of status satisfaction is one-sided; it contains only part of the story. It deals only with the status that comes from conformity and living up to the Joneses, not at all with that derived from outdoing them and being different. Yet this is no less important; it is itself only part of a larger and more general source of satisfaction: the status to be had by being useful.

It seems self-evident that a simple way for an individual to gain acceptance by and membership in a group is to be useful to its members. One can be useful to others by providing them with either comfort or stimulus. The former is especially important within the family circle and among close friends. Husbands and wives provide many material and physical comforts to each other; so do parents and children and so do friends. I have stressed the reciprocal nature of these non-market comforts and the fact that social customs and family discipline are sufficient to assure their reciprocity. Let me now add that reciprocity, and the assurance of reciprocity, while desirable, is not very important.

I buy my daughter birthday presents not in the hope of reciprocity, but because I enjoy giving them to her and witnessing or imagining her pleasure. One can call this love or altruism, but it is also the assertion and strengthening of the ties of my membership in the family, or of my status as father, for the satisfaction this gives me. Perhaps all these are just different names for the same thing.

Beyond the circle of family and close friends this form of altruism or status seeking is rarer, but it is by no means absent in our society. Philanthropy, donating blood, treating kids with candy at Halloween, many of the everyday gestures of ordinary politeness, helping a stranger in need are all examples. Giving gifts to individuals or families beyond one's own family circle is frequent and important in many other societies (for instance, in Japan) as a form of status seeking, but it is rare among Americans.[11] Since most gifts have a commercial value, the giving of gifts would to us, smack too much of "buying acceptance," especially in view of our singular ineptness at shopping and finding things of high value but low commercial cost.[12]

Among us, the customary way of seeking status by making oneself useful is to provide stimulation to others—presumably because most stimulation is in any case provided free in our economy and outside of the formal contractual framework of the market.

This kind of status seeking is again easiest to observe in children, whose need for acceptance is strongest. Children like to clown, to show off, to dress up, to do anything that will entertain, surprise, or provide a spectacle to their peer group or to grown-ups. They seem early to recognize stimulation for the important source of satisfaction that it is and to seek acceptance by providing it.

Adults obtain the comfort of status in much the same way when, to stimulate others, they tell jokes, spread gossip, bring news, make witty or erudite conversation, dress well, and furnish their homes and entertain in an elegant, beautiful, or striking fashion.

A stimulus, of course, must be not only stimulating, but pleasantly so, and, as we know, pleasant stimulation calls for an intermediate degree of novelty, a judicious blend of the reassuringly conventional and the titillatingly eccentric. Thus there is no conflict, really, between seeking status through dull conformity and seeking it by offering something stimulatingly different. On the contrary, optimal stimulation and maximum success in being accepted as one of the boys require their combination.

Why, then, does all the world equate status consumption with dull imitation and boring conformity? And why, for that matter, did I adopt the same interpretation in the previous section? The answer to those questions has much to do with the success or failure of stimulation to stimulate.

Different people have very different notions of what is the most pleasantly stimulating behavior, what the most pleasing style of dress, and what the most pleasant way of furnishing one's home and entertaining one's guests. After all, what they themselves find the most pleasing also varies, and varies greatly, with temperament (average arousal level), education, cultural tradition, past experience, etc., and one's own taste as a consumer of stimulation is bound greatly to influence one's choice of the stimulus one offers others to win their favor.

Also, there are great differences in people's ability to stimulate others. Novelty is the essential element in all stimulation, and to provide, and keep providing, novelty—especially novelty of the right degree—in one's conversation, behavior, appearance, etc., takes skill and imagination; not to mention the need for a good repertory of such raw materials as news, gossip, information, jokes, clothes, recipes, etc. People differ widely in the skill and imagination they possess, depending on their innate ability, training, practice, and, not least, their own ability to enjoy stimulation. One cannot be a good cook if one does not enjoy good food, and a woman's attempt to stimulate and impress others with her elegance is doomed to failure if she cannot appreciate and enjoy other women's ability to dress and wear their clothes well. In short, anyone who is a stimulating member of society has a skill, one which few attain and to which not all aspire. Many of us set our sights humbly and realistically much below the optimum and usually find it easiest to stay well on the reassuringly conventional side of it rather than on the daringly eccentric. In addition, it generally seems safer to be boring than to be objectionable, and this is yet another reason why the picture of status-seeking behavior presented in the last section seemed quite so true to life.

So far I have tacitly assumed a close correspondence between people's ability to stimulate others and the comfort of status they get out of doing so. In reality, there is no need for such correspondence, and often it is missing. Many people misjudge the figure they cut in the world, believing themselves to be impressive or stimulating and deriving satisfaction from that belief, although in other people's eyes they are conventional at best, insufferable bores at worst.

We can make three distinctions in terms of which the different ways of status seeking can be classified. One of these is the distinction between self-esteem and society's esteem. My membership and good standing in society is a matter partly of my own opinion of myself, partly of what I believe other people's opinion of me to be. Either or both can be important sources of satisfaction. A philanthropist may want his name to be remembered or to remain anonymous, a blood donor may choose to wear or not to wear the badge, a worker may insist on working well to earn other people's praise and appreciation, or he may do so irrespective of it, merely to live up to his own high standards. The behavior of these people yields comfort, the comfort of status, in each case.

A second distinction hinges on whether or not status seeking benefits society. When people seek status by being useful to others and succeed in this, they clearly benefit society, quite apart from and in addition to the satisfaction they obtain themselves. It is helpful to distinguish such status seeking from its other forms.

The third distinction relates to the satisfaction of the status seekers themselves; it separates cases where my gain in status is a net gain to society from those where it is not, because my gain from an advance in ranking is matched by an equivalent loss to those I have outranked. This and previous distinction overlap to some extent, but they are by no means identical. For example, conspicuous consumption as evidence of income that betokens one's value to society is, as I have said, a zero-sum game, but it may or may not confer benefits on others, depending on the form it takes. Riding a Cadillac confers no such external benefits, but the magnificent palaces built and works of art made to glorify the rich of past ages have done so.

THE COMFORT OF STICKING TO OUR HABITS

The last and perhaps the largest category of comforts we will consider contains those many little comforts of our everyday existence in modern society which most of us easily get used to and soon consider necessary for civilized living. Most people in our society take them for granted and notice them only when they feel the discomfort of being forced to do without them. Presumably, we adopted some of these because they contributed to our well-being, others we may have first tried by imitating other people's consumption habits or out of idle curiosity and then gotten used to; we continue with them all not so much for the satisfaction they yield, as to avoid the pain of relinquishing or interrupting a habit.

People will seldom acknowledge or even be aware of the extent to which their consumption behavior is governed by habit; when pressed to explain a particular consumption expenditure, they are likely to justify it on grounds of health, hygiene, proper nutrition, and the like. Annual physical checkups, weekly changes of bed linen, daily baths, daily changes of underwear, daily consumption of meat, daily intake of vitamins are some of the activities most of us would probably justify on such grounds, yet no conclusive evidence exists that any of them improve health or prolong life.[13] Of all nations, we have the reputation of being the most anxious about health, hygiene, and proper nutrition,[14] yet we have little to show for it. Europeans take a much more casual attitude to these things, yet most of them live longer than we do and their mortality and infant mortality rates are lower than ours (see Table 7, p. 166).

The discomforts, therefore, that we feel when we are deprived of our accustomed routine cannot, as a rule, be explained in terms of legitimate concern over increased dangers to health, but is, more properly, more generally, and more simply explained by our difficulty of relinquishing habits we have become used to.

Habit-forming, better known as conditioning or learning, is one of the most studied and best documented subjects in psychology; experiments have clearly established that all organisms with a central nervous system are creatures of habit. Any act immediately followed by a reward which reduces arousal, and which can be either a desired event (positive reward) or the omission of a feared one (negative reward), is thereby reinforced; that is, the likelihood of its future recurrence is increased. Repeated pairing of the act with the reward reinforces the former yet further and so strengthens the habit. The strength of a habit as a function of the number of reinforcements characteristically increases by diminishing increments and converges to an upper limit.[15]

In addition to the primary reinforcement of an act through its pairing with a rewarding event or the omission of a punishing one, there is also a reinforcement which takes place when an act is paired with an event or the omission of an event which, though not itself rewarding or punishing, has, through previous pairing with a rewarding or punishing event, become capable of arousing the hope or fear of such an event in the subject's mind. Such so-called secondary reinforcement is no less important in explaining consumption habits; and the two together seem to be the origin of all habits, good and bad, reasonable and unreasonable.[16]

One reason for the persistence of habits is that once they are established, they become painful to stop. Experimental evidence shows that acts frequently reinforced by reward create the expectation of future reinforcement of similar acts, and the disappointment of this expectation is frustrating, whether that frustration is caused by the omission of the expected reward or by inability to carry out the act itself.[17] Frustration so caused has been found to raise arousal and to have all the other earmarks of pain and punishment as well.[18]

A habit is extinguished by so-called extinction trials, the nonrewarding of an act whose previous rewarding reinforced it and made it into a habit, but it usually takes many more extinction trials to extinguish a habit than it took reinforcements to establish it. For example, experiments with rats have shown that animals rewarded for pressing a lever by a pellet of food only once will continue pressing that lever an additional fifty or more times even though they are never again rewarded for doing so.[19] Psychologists explain the belief in superstitions in those terms. Indeed, if one were to generalize to man from the above experiment, it would explain why a single piece of bad luck on a Friday the thirteenth can establish that particular superstition for life—after all, it takes thirty years for another fifty Fridays to fall on a thirteenth day of a month and so provide the occasion for fifty extinction trials to extinguish the superstition.

The resistance of habits to extinction is one of the many measures developed to gauge their strength; a particularly simple form of it is the extinction ratio, the number of extinction trials needed to extinguish a habit divided by the number of reinforcements that established it. The rat experiment with its extinction ratio of fifty to one well illustrates the great persistence even of a habit established by a single reinforcement, but such simple measures can be misleading and are little used, because neither reinforcement nor extinction is a simple matter of numbers alone. Habits that seem fully extinguished through repeated non-reward in the short run usually recover spontaneously with the passage of time; also, habits once established and then seemingly extinguished can easily and quickly be reinstated. Similarly, the strength of a habit depends not only on the number of reinforcements, but, even more, on their pattern. Intermittent reinforcement, with reinforced acts alternating with non-reinforced ones in a given ratio or at given time intervals, forms stronger habits than continuous reinforcement does, and the habits most resistant to extinction are those formed by intermittent reinforcement on a random (unpredictable) schedule. This is well worth noting, because the great majority of consumption habits probably originate in such random intermittent reinforcement. No less important than the persistence of habits is their tendency to change the hedonic tone of whatever has become habitual. Things one enjoys and enjoys repeatedly tend to become less enjoyable by repetition, yet one often continues to seek them because their oft-repeated enjoyment has turned them into necessities one can no longer do without.

The obvious example is drug addiction. The repeated taking of drugs increases a person's tolerance and so diminishes the euphoric effects of the drug. By the time he has become an addict, he gets little or no positive satisfaction from the drug, and his main, often his sole, motivation for continued use of the drug is the desire for relief from the pain of withdrawal symptoms, which can be very severe.

Most people consider addiction as something atypical and exceptional, peculiar to the unique, physiologically addictive, action of a few chemical substances. Yet psychologists increasingly look upon addiction as a psychological phenomenon which is pretty nearly universal, one which is certainly much more common than generally realized. Their explanation so far is little more than a theory, but in view of its increasing acceptance it is well worth summarizing in its most recent, most convincing version.[20]

Many feelings of pain and pleasure seem to be followed by a contrary after effect: pain by a pleasant feeling of relief, pleasure by an unpleasant feeling of letdown or emptiness. When the stimulus is repeated its initial effect seems to become weaker, its after effect stronger and longer lasting. Objective physiological indices confirm this observation. The heartbeat of a dog which has been subjected to electric shock accelerates; on termination of the shock it not only drops, it drops below normal and stays there for a while before returning to normal. As the experiment is repeated the heartbeat rises much less, and, ultimately, not at all, but on cessation of the shock it falls much more and stays much longer below normal.

The theory which explains such succession of contrary feelings postulates that every stimulus, in addition to leading to a primary pleasant or unpleasant reaction, also initiates a secondary, so-called opponent process whose hedonic sign is opposite to that of the primary reaction and which is sluggish both in making itself felt and in dying out. This opponent process explains the after effects of relief or letdown, and it presumably has the function of helping to restore the organism's hedonic equilibrium. "Any significant departure from hedonic or affective neutrality should have correlates in increased autonomic and central nervous system activity aimed at reducing that departure." [21]

As the stimulus is repeated, the primary reaction remains unchanged, but the opponent process recruits more promptly, becomes stronger, and lasts longer. By becoming prompter and stronger, it weakens or even offsets the primary reaction; its greater strength and longer duration explain the enhanced after effect. When the after effect becomes so unpleasant and so long-lasting that repeating the stimulus seems the best (though only temporary) way of eliminating it, addiction is established.

That, in bare outline, is the theory which well explains drug addiction and has also been used to explain many other things most of us do not think of as addiction—such as falling in love. The initial reaction, here called state A, "is characterized by pleasurable excitement, frequent sexual feelings, a prevailing mood of ecstasy, happiness, and good feelings. When the lovers . . . are separated from each other, they will feel lonely, sad, and depressed." That is the after effect, here called state B. "Even with anticipations of reunion (symbolic, conditioned arousers of state A) loneliness may prevail. Actual reunion will simultaneously erase B and reinstate A just as in . . . addiction to opiates. After several years of repeated mutual stimulation, the qualitative and quantitative changes in A and B are a matter of public lore. [The changed A and B are denoted A' and B'.] State A' is characterized (if all has gone well) as contentment, normalcy, and comfort. But State B' is now potentially of high intensity and long duration. If it should occur, it is often called grief or . . . 'separation syndrome.' It requires a lot of time for this B' state to decay. The partners have become addicted to one another, and when separated they experience withdrawal symptoms." [22]

I chose to quote this example because the public's reaction to it is so very different from its reaction to drug addiction. Both are the result of decisions which are habit-forming yet are entered into lightly and usually without full awareness of this fact. One is seduced, and that is why many people consider drug taking irrational and justify its prohibition. Yet the same people accept, even revere, a person's addiction to his or her mate, and they approve of falling in love all the more because it can lead to life-long addiction.

There are very many habits whose persistence is similarly explained, though one never thinks of them as addictions. The theory of addiction just stated is very incomplete, of course, since it has not yet explained why some habits are more addictive than others and why some people get addicted while others do not. But it performs the useful function of stressing the generality of habit-forming and explaining the change in motivation from the seeking of pleasure to the avoidance of pain (frustration) as habits get established.

One is too easily tempted to dismiss drug addiction as an exceptional and untypical case of consumer irrationality, on the ground that the number of addictive chemical substances is small. But the drug user's desire for his drug is not qualitatively different from the average person's desire to continue consuming whatever he habitually consumes. A drug addict's withdrawal symptoms are clinically observable and occasionally very severe; the withdrawal symptoms of a man deprived of his accustomed morning paper or bacon and eggs for breakfast we tend to treat lightly, although his frustration and anger can occasionally also be loud and easily observable. The drug addict's frustration can be painful enough to make him break the law for the sake of getting his daily dose, but all drinkers broke the law during Prohibition, and only an estimated 10 per cent of them were alcoholics. The other 90 per cent were merely adhering to a habit.

It is also worth bearing in mind that as long as a habit or addiction is satisfied, its strength is seldom realized. Caffeine, for example, is an addictive drug, with physiological withdrawal symptoms,[23] but most coffee drinkers neither know nor care if they are addicts and would be quite unable to predict which they would miss the most, their daily cups of coffee or their daily bath. The dividing line between physiological addiction and psychological addiction is often blurred, sometimes unknown, and probably never very sharp. Drug addiction, therefore, is an extreme but not atypical example of how consumers' habits are formed, motivated, and clung to.

One more form of addiction, a form worth mentioning separately in view of its importance, is people's addiction to their status and to the regard others have for them. We know that being considered and considering oneself a member of society is a basic necessity, or something close to it; people can suffer from losing such status even more than from lacking it. We also know that the comfort of ranking—being regarded more highly than others or belonging to a smaller, more specialized, more distinguished group within society—yields further satisfaction, though it could hardly be called a basic necessity. Once acquired, however, such higher rank and more distinguished place in society often has all the earmarks of an addiction. It ceases to give satisfaction after a while because it is taken for granted, but its loss can give much pain. People's striving to maintain their status seems better explained by their desire to avoid the pain of withdrawal symptoms than by their desire for any positive gratification.

WHAT IT MEANS TO BECOME SPOILED

Having discussed some of our comforts in detail, let us now return briefly to the question I started with. Is our need to avoid pain limited and our desire for comfort satiable? The answer was yes, but with important exceptions. One of these had to do with man's tendency to form habits. The issue was not that the enjoyment of some satisfactions is an acquired taste, but rather that, by forming any kind of habit, we acquire a *dis*taste for breaking that habit. In fact, we become spoiled. Whatever we get used to doing (or consuming, or avoiding to do), for whatever reason, becomes, by that act alone, something indispensable; it becomes a comfort, in the sense that doing without it has become uncomfortable. This means that not only can we enlarge our capacity to enjoy life, we can also enlarge our capacity to suffer discomforts. We can add to our enjoyments by learning new skills of consumption, but we also add to the costs of being comfortable by acquiring new habits or to our discomforts if we are unable to stick to our new habits. Whether such new habits, while maintained, also add to our satisfactions is an altogether different question, to which the answer may be yes or no, depending on the particular habit. In other words, it may or may not be worth it for us to get spoiled.

Another exception to the rule of limited needs and satiable comforts has to do with status consumption. Not only can the individual enhance his own capacity for discomfort, he may have an enhanced capacity thrust upon him by society. When the average standard of expenditure rises, society gets spoiled, but the individual has to pay for it—in money if he can afford it, in discomfort if he cannot. Whether anyone benefits depends on whether higher expenditure by everybody yields higher satisfaction to anybody. Only slightly different in nature is the satisfaction from ranking in society, as distinct from belonging to it. The difference lies in the much more limited scope we have for satisfying our desire to rank than for satisfying our desire to belong, especially for those of us who want to rank high in terms of income or wealth. For such people, the desire to advance in rank may well be insatiable, or close to it. The similarity lies in the fact that here, too, other people's advance in rank can cause me misery. Take the example of a prize or award. Designed to give satisfaction to the recipient, it can also cause agony for a non-recipient who, rightly or wrongly, considers himself more deserving than the recipient. If he gets the prize a year later, his satisfaction is more a relief of pain than a feeling of pleasure.

A third exception, perhaps the most important one, is the combination of the two just mentioned. Status and rank are themselves habit-forming: losing status and losing rank can be a source of suffering and the fear of losing them a source of anxiety. Indeed, competitive pressures, the tensions of modern society, usually refer to the anxiety due to the ever-present dangers of such loss.

Now we have brought together the economist's classification of products and (a simplified version of) the psychologist's classification of satisfactions. That was not too difficult, because defensive products turn out to be both the source of comfort and a second cousin to necessities. Since the demand for necessities is satiable, the question arose whether the demand for the sources of comfort is also satiable. To answer that question led us to consider status and addiction, the first a source of comfort, the second a psychological process which can turn almost anything into a comfort, and both exceptions or sources of exceptions to the rule that the demand for defensive products is satiable. Such exceptions disrupt the obvious relation between money expenditure and satisfaction.

CHAPTER SEVEN

Income and Happiness

After all this discussion of the psychologist's concepts and constructs, it will be useful to stop for a moment and take stock before proceeding to the more practical and interesting task of applying them.

At the center of the economist's stage is the market, with its wheeling and dealing, and its central act in which two parties make an exchange because each prefers what he gets to what he gives in return. That act of exchanging is the source and proof of all economic gain, which explains the economist's preoccupation with it. Yet market exchange is neither necessary nor sufficient for mutual gain. It is not necessary because innumerable exchanges occur without benefit of the market and because many unreciprocated acts also yield satisfaction to both giver and recipient. It is not sufficient because market exchanges often create not only satisfactions, but also the needs they satisfy, and anything that gives rise to both a need and its satisfaction is of little or no use to anyone.

These are simple and obvious observations, but they clash head on with an equally simple and seemingly obvious principle that is basic to much of the economist's work—that the higher one's income, the more one can spend, and the more one spends, the most satisfied one should be. If correction for change in the value of money is kept in mind, that principle can be said to be an important part of the economist's creed. But does the principle survive the evidence which the psychologists have given us? The question is interesting in its own right, and in trying to answer it we shall see the differences between the economist's world view and the ideas expressed in this book.

What, to begin with, is the evidence? Data on income and expenditure are plentiful and generally available; satisfaction or happiness cannot be measured, of course, but data do exist on how people rate their own happiness. In carefully conducted surveys of random samples of the population, people were asked if they were "very happy," "fairly happy," or "not very happy"—in a few of the surveys, the questions were "very happy," "pretty happy," and "not too happy," or just "not happy"—and the answers were then tabulated to show the percentage of people at each level of satisfaction, both for separate income groups and for the population as a whole. Ten such surveys were conducted in the United States at fairly regular intervals between 1946 and 1970. Their results are summarized in Table 6a. Table 6b shows the dependence of self-rated happiness on people's ranking in the income scale in one of the surveys at the middle of the period covered.

"RANKHAPPINESS"

As might be expected, the surveys showed that the proportion of people not too satisfied diminished and the proportion of very satisfied people increased with their ranking on the income scale.[1] Our confidence in the data and the significance of what they show should be strengthened by the fact that the distributions in the different surveys are fairly similar. Actually, they are too similar. Over this period, almost twenty-five years, per capita real income rose by 62 per cent, yet the proportion of people who consider themselves very happy, fairly happy, and

TABLE 6A

Percent Distribution of Population by Happiness, United States, 1946–1970

A. AIPO POLLS

Date	Very happy	Fairly happy	Not very happy	Other	Number polled
Apr. 1946	39	50	10	1	3151
Dec. 1947	42	47	10	1	1434
Aug. 1948	43	43	11	2	1596
Nov. 1952	47	43	9	1	3003
Sept. 1956	53	41	5	1	1979
Sept. 1956	52	42	5	1	2207
Mar. 1957	53	43	3	1	1627
July 1963	47	48	5 *	1	3668
Oct. 1966	49	46	4 *	2	3531
Dec. 1970	43	48	6 *	3	1517

B. NORC POLLS

Date	Very happy	Pretty happy	Not too happy	Number polled
Spring 1957	35	54	11	2460
Dec. 1963	32	51	16	1501
June 1965	30	53	17	1469

* The question read "not happy," rather than "not very happy."

SOURCE: R. A. Easterlin, "Does Economic Growth Improve the Human Lot?" in P. A. David and M. W. Reder (eds.), *Nations and Households in Economic Growth. Essays in Honor of Moses Abramovitz*, New York: Academic Press, 1974, p. 109, Table 8. The first set of surveys was made by the American Institute of Public Opinion, the second by the National Opinion Research Center.

not too happy has hardly changed at all. Our economic welfare is forever rising, but we are no happier as a result. The puzzle is that rising in rank on the income scale seems to improve one's chances of happiness, but a rise in one's income when everybody's income is rising does not. The obvious explanation would be that one's happiness depends on where one stands in relation to the Joneses and not at all on one's absolute standard of living—and, indeed, we have seen the importance of status

TABLE 6B

Per Cent Distribution of Happiness by Size of Income

Annual Income in Dollars	Very happy	Pretty happy	Not too happy	Number polled
Under $1,000	20	52	27	200
1,000– 1,999	22	57	20	207
2,000– 2,999	23	62	15	259
3,000– 3,999	31	55	14	290
4,000– 4,999	36	57	7	390
5,000– 5,999	37	54	9	322
6,000– 6,999	46	50	4	237
7,000– 7,999	48	48	4	141
8,000– 9,999	43	51	6	148
10,000– 14,999	48	48	3	120
15,000 or over	53	38	8	66

SOURCE: J. L. Simon, "Interpersonal Welfare Comparisons Can Be Made—And Used for Redistribution Decisions," Kyklos, 27 (1974), p. 86, Table 2.

and rank. But surely that cannot be the main basis of happiness.

Another, and possibly a more important, source of satisfaction is work, both the stimulation that work provides and the self-respect that well-accomplished work gives. The evidence we have suggests that work satisfaction is positively correlated with one's ranking in the social and income hierarchy. Here we have a second explanation of the fact that people's self-rated happiness rises with their position in the income scale.

Work satisfaction and status satisfaction together are clearly more important than status satisfaction alone, but even so it would be surprising if they counted for everything and all else for nothing or next to nothing. At this stage, addiction becomes relevant. Many comforts are satisfying at first, but soon become routine and taken for granted. Consumer demand for them remains undiminished, but the original motivation, the desire for additional satisfaction, is replaced by the new and very different motivation of wishing to avoid the pain and frustration of giving up a habit to which one has grown accustomed. Inference from observed market behavior will never reveal such a change in motivation, but the juxtaposition of a substantial rise in material welfare with little change in people's self-rated happiness suggests that some such factor may be at work.

People presumably rate their happiness on the basis of what they remember having felt in the past, and it is quite possible that they should only remember the highlights; the pleasure of stimulation and the pain of discomfort, taking for granted and forgetting what I have called comfort, that is, the absence of both pain and pleasure. That would not only explain the surprising lack of correlation between happiness and the secular rise in real incomes; it would also help explain the dependence of people's happiness on their rank in the income scale. For the higher income groups are certain to contain a higher proportion of people whose income has recently risen and who still enjoy, therefore, the novelty of their higher income. Accordingly, one would expect the higher income groups to contain a higher than average proportion of well-satisfied people.

This brings me back to the subject of novelty. It is important as a source of stimulus satisfaction, but it has had no place so far in the economist's world. Considering that most of our stimulation comes from other people, and in ways and situations that have little or nothing to do with economics, this would seem excusable enough; on the other hand, some of the stimulus of novelty and variety comes from the rise in our standard of living and the additions to our comforts that a rise in income makes possible. In other words, there is novelty in the *change* from a lower to a higher level of living, and the satisfactions such novelty yields are not only additional to those derived from a stable level of living, they are also likely to be much more important and more vividly remembered. A rising income, therefore, may be worth much more than a high income, however high, and especially when it is already high.

But if a rise in the standard of living provides stimulating and satisfying novelty, why is not a fall, which also provides change and novelty, equally stimulating and satisfying? Sometimes it is, because change is pleasant whichever way it goes. One of the pleasures of camping and vacationing stems from the drastic change and reduction in our accustomed standards of comfort. Similarly, most of the young enjoy getting away from the comforts and luxury of the family home to the much simpler and poorer amenities of their own apartment or college room. In short, change is pleasant and there is pleasure in roughing it for a change.

Yet people seem to enjoy roughing it only when it is voluntary and temporary. The pleasures we get from camping and vacationing may well hinge on our certain expectation that we will soon return to our accustomed comforts. When a reduction in our standard of living is imposed by economic necessity, it usually seems quite painful. Even the threat of it can be painful—perhaps even more so than materialization of the threat. The main reason, probably, is the loss of status and rank that such a reduction symbolizes. Most people find losing status to be painful, and if they believe that their status depends on the money they make or spend, then a reduction or threat of reduction in their earnings or spendings becomes painful, whether or not such belief is justified. In short, status and rank are addictive. To acquire them gives satisfaction, but we soon take them for granted, and thereafter we cling to them not for the satisfaction they yield, but to avoid the pain their loss would inflict.

The altogether separate and different addiction to our accustomed level of living can also nullify the pleasant novelty of a downward change. Whatever comfort we get addicted to, be it cigarettes or bathrooms, becomes hard to do without, and the pain of withdrawal symptoms is almost certain to swamp the pleasantness of change. What we get addicted to, why, when, and with what probability, are questions to which we do not yet know the answers, but such detail is not necessary to establish the general proposition that a rise in one's level of living is more likely to yield satisfaction than is a fall. Accordingly, we would expect more "highly satisfied" people among those whose standard of living is rising and more "not too satisfied" people among those whose falling incomes force them to abandon accustomed comforts and suffer the frustrations and withdrawal symptoms that accompany such retrenchment. There are no data that would correlate happiness ratings with income changes, but the high income groups are certain to contain a higher than average proportion of people whose incomes have recently risen, and, by the same argument, the low income groups are bound to contain a disproportionately large number of people whose incomes have recently fallen. This implies that one would find a positive correlation between people's satisfaction and their ranking in the income scale even if status and work satisfaction counted for nothing and only the stimulus of novelty counted for something.

I have proposed four different explanations to reconcile the secular rise in our material standard of living with the peculiar behavior of the self-rated happiness surveys. One was the satisfaction of status, another the satisfaction of work, the third the enjoyment of novelty, the fourth addiction, with all it implies. Taken together, they well explain why happiness should depend so much on one's ranking in society and so little on the absolute level of one's income. Those four need not be the only explanations, nor can I appraise their relative importance, but they illustrate pretty well most of the features that distinguish the approach taken in this book from the economist's traditional approach.

WHATEVER MADE US BELIEVE THAT INCOME YIELDS HAPPINESS?

So far, I have taken it for granted that income is good and more income better. Starting with that premise, I have tried to explain why a rise in income may fail to increase happiness. But, since we have found so many explanations for what at first looked like a paradox, we should also question perhaps the very premise itself. What makes us think that income is good and more income better?

After all, income is often payment for doing something unpleasant, and more income, occasionally, is payment for doing something even more unpleasant. Why, then, should we believe that, on the contrary, more income is a token, if not of more happiness, at least of more sources of satisfaction?

The reason for that belief is that although income often is compensation for the pain of labor, that labor creates an output of goods or services which the consumers of them find satisfying; and the gain from having this output is assumed always to exceed the pain of producing it. Whoever voluntarily performs services for income implies by his action that his gain from that income exceeds the pain of what he does to earn it; similarly, the person who buys those services implies by *his* action that the services he receives are worth more to him than the money he pays to get them. Such reasoning justifies the assumptions that the gain exceeds the pain and that the *net* gain is shared between the person who performs the work and the person who enjoys its fruit. In short, the existence of economic output and income earned for producing it prove the existence of mutual net benefit.

Unfortunately, there is no way of ascertaining the value of

this net benefit. A $1000 income in the national accounts shows that someone performed work whose discomfort, if any, he valued at less than $1000, and that the services he rendered were worth more than $1000 to someone else. But the sum of the worker's and the consumer's net gains could equally well be a small fraction or a large multiple of the $1000 that changed hands, and there is no way to tell which it is. The size of the national income or national product gives no indication of the size of the net benefit, even if the existence of that income proves that there is a net benefit.

How about a rise in income and output? Does it signify an increase in net benefits? It does if the rise in income comes from new transactions having been added to preexisting ones which they leave unchanged, considering that every economic transaction is a token of a net benefit to each of the transacting parties. Often, however, the rise in income results from the replacement of a smaller by a larger transaction. If the worker can choose between more work for more pay and less work for less pay, and his employer between paying more for greater services and less for lesser services, then their agreement on more work, more pay, and greater output is again proof of greater mutual net benefit. To proceed, however, from this conclusion, which concerns agreement between two people, to the general statement that a higher national income or larger national product means greater mutual net benefit to an economy made up of hundreds of markets with millions of members is a very big logical step, one which can only be taken when there is competition, nondiscrimination, and a free flow of information within and between all the markets. These are conditions customarily assumed by economists, but they are by no means always fulfilled in reality.

Another crucial but questionable assumption underlying economic reasoning is that all other things remain unchanged. The assumption is customarily made, believed by no one to be literally true, yet seldom questioned. Why? Probably because economists believe other things to be not so much unchanged, as unimportant and uninfluenced by economic changes. If they were indeed unimportant, changes in them would matter little; if they were really uninfluenced by economic changes, then economic argument and policy could be conducted with little or no regard for them.

Unfortunately, many of the arguments I have presented here throw doubt on both those propositions. Our economic sources of satisfaction are just some among very many, with the dividing line between them and the non-economic sources thin and easily shifting in response to economic and other factors; some economic satisfactions go hand in hand with non-economic costs and benefits to others, and the main economic activity, work, creates economic satisfaction for others and non-economic pains or benefits for the worker himself. In short, the economic and non-economic factors are closely interwoven; therefore, to ignore one while considering the other is inadmissible. Two examples can illustrate that fact.

Let me deal first with the non-economic satisfactions of an economic activity, work. With some work unpleasant, performed only for the income it earns, and some work enjoyable, a $1000 income can stand for very much less or very much more benefit, depending on the kind of work that earned it—but the data never show which is which. Therefore, a rise in national income, accompanied by an increased proportion of unpleasant work, might well stand for a much less steep rise in the sum total of society's satisfactions—in an extreme case it might hide a *fall* in satisfactions. This is important, because most of the rise in national income comes from increases in productivity created by increases in specialization, which usually mean increased monotony of work.

The general proposition is obvious enough, but the question remains: how might the extreme case come about? The more work/more pay/more output argument of p. 141, above, seems to have ruled it out; but that was based on an oversimplified model, which envisaged a change in methods of production to come about by agreement between the *same* employer and employees on the new methods, new conditions of work, and new wage rates corresponding to them.

That however, is not the typical way in which such changes occur. Usually, the new methods of production are introduced by *new* businessmen, employing a *new* breed of workers, and they displace the old methods by outcompeting the old, established manufacturers with their old methods and old workers, throwing these workers out of their jobs. An early but not atypical example is England's Industrial Revolution, in which a new class of manufacturers, employing unskilled female and child labor, displaced skilled, male, grown craftsmen. For such a change not merely to appear in the statistics as an improvement, but to represent a true increase in economic and noneconomic satisfactions, the labor market would have to fulfill the competitive conditions mentioned on p. 141, above; that is, transmit information and assure non-discriminatory competition to a degree that now, when we are beginning to understand the way markets function, we can no longer take for granted.[2] In the nineteenth century, the female and child labor of England's sweatshops did not constitute part of the same competitive labor market to which the skilled men belonged; that is why one cannot take it for granted that the shift in production from handicrafts to sweatshops constituted a net gain to society and a net gain to labor. Also, since then the most unpleasant work and the most alienated labor has usually been performed by recent immigrants, minority groups, foreign workers—in short, by a part of the labor force which is not in competition with the rest of labor. It may be rare for an increase in the dollar value of income and output to stand for a *fall* in satisfactions, but it certainly is not impossible.

Economists usually admit, if somewhat grudgingly, the existence of external benefits and nuisances, but then they proceed to argue as if those benefits and nuisances did not exist. Let me break this tradition. We have seen that an important difference between comfort and stimulus is that many stimuli carry with them external benefits. All stimuli, to be pleasant, must titillate either the senses or the mind, and those that titillate my senses usually titillate other people's senses too, often at no extra cost and even with extra benefit, since my enjoyment is often enhanced by my sharing it with others. (The argument is slightly different, but not very much so, with respect to stimuli that titillate the mind.)

By contrast, comforts not only fail, typically, to carry external benefits, many of them generate external nuisances as well. This is certainly true of many of those that substitute mechanical power for human effort, because they often generate noise, chemical air pollution, or both. It is also true of many of the comforts that consist in being free from insects, from garden and house pests, since they, too, worsen the environment, and it is true, too, of those comforts provided by appliances, packaged products, and throwaway but durable (i.e. non-biodegradable) objects whose containers and carcasses cover our beaches and countryside in ever-increasing density.

The individual consumer's choice, therefore, between comfort and stimulus has a social significance that transcends his personal welfare. When he can buy two commodities at the same price, he is presumed to allocate his expenditures between them so that they should, on the margin, give him the same satisfaction. That is the justification the economist uses when he gives equally priced commodities equal weights in estimating the national product. But if one of these commodities provides comfort and the other, at the same market price, provides stimulus, then they may give the consumer the same satisfaction, but the total satisfaction they provide for society as a whole is likely to be very different. If the stimulus is shared by people other than the consumer, then their satisfaction is additional to his; if the source of comfort to the consumer is a source of annoyance or pollution to others, then their pain must be subtracted from his benefit; and if either or both of these are true, then the stimulus is certainly worth more than the comfort from society's point of view, however equal their market price. Here is an important reason for my preoccupation with people's choice between comfort and stimulus. It provides another warning against taking a rise in income at face value as a sign of a rise in human welfare.

I have given the two examples above in order to inspire the reader to caution when he interprets the economist's figures. The economist's valuation of national income and national product has many uses, but it is inappropriate as an index of human welfare. The better we understand the complexity of human satisfaction and human behavior, and grasp the fact that economic goods and services are only two among several sources of satisfaction, the more clearly we realize, or should realize, the inappropriateness of the economist's valuation.

Numbers are a wonderful aid to clear thinking, but they defeat their purpose if we read more into them than what, in fact, they contain. Our preoccupation with economic problems and economic indicators of welfare is partly explained by their quantitative and quantifiable nature. Economic quantification is attractive and useful, but we must not let it seduce us into attaching more significance to the measure of quantity and to what is quantified than they deserve. The national income is, at the very best, an index of economic welfare, and economic welfare is a very small part and often a very poor indicator of human welfare.

PART II

The American Way of Life

CHAPTER EIGHT

Is Our Life Too Good?

We now have the framework and elements of a theory of consumer behavior. To build them into a formal, theoretical model would be out of place in this book; I shall try instead to apply them. What better application could there be of the ideas so far presented than to try to explain why our affluence leaves so many of us unsatisfied?

The economist's traditional picture of the economy resembles nothing so much as a Chinese restaurant with its long menu. Customers choose from what is on the menu and are assumed always to have chosen what most pleases them. That assumption is unrealistic, not only of the economy, but of Chinese restaurants. Most of us are unfamiliar with nine-tenths of the entrées listed; we seem invariably to order either the wrong dishes or the same old ones. Only on occasions when an expert does the ordering do we realize how badly we do on our own and what good things we miss.

The trouble we have with the economy's menu stems not only from our lack of skill in ordering, but also from our lack of skill in consuming, from the impossibility of making substitutions, and from the fact that our enjoyment of what we have depends on what others at other tables are having. The traditional theory of the consumer's behavior fails to recognize his need for novelty and variety, his need of consumption skills to enjoy certain forms of consumption, and habit as a force which can prevent satisfaction or rational choice. It recognizes interdependence or externalities but slurs over them as unimportant.

I am setting out to illustrate all those factors, especially the first. The discovery that man needs stimulation as well as comfort is not new. After all, the ancient Romans clamored for bread *and* circuses. The economist, in his model of the consumer, does not include that part of the consumer's needs. And, more important, the consumer himself, at least in America, also seems reluctant to recognize his need for stimulus. That is reflected in the bias of our consumption pattern. Our American life-style provides much comfort, but little stimulation. That statement is so simple and so sweeping that one might hold it suspect, but it can be documented and explained.

In the first place, comfort and stimulation do not come pure and undiluted. The consumption of most commodities gives rise to both effects, but simple statistics of output or sales seldom lend themselves to separating the two and showing how much comfort and how much stimulation we consume.

In the second place, people's behavior, as reflected in their purchases, necessarily results from the interaction of demand and supply, the preferences they have, and the market opportunities they face. If their buying choices lead more to comfort and less to stimulation, then either they are seeking comfort or they are victims of a biased market in which the availability of goods and services leans in that direction. What looks like comfort-seeking behavior may merely be a response to what is available. A felt desire for comfort and the pull of comfort-producing things may both be present, but the forces of demand and supply can seldom be disentangled. Economic data show what the public buys; they do not show whether it buys what it wants or only what it can get.

In addition, demand and supply are themselves subject to the influence of cultural traditions and economic forces. One of our prominent traditions is the so-called Puritan ethic, which influences both what we want and what we can get. Economic forces also affect both demand and supply. Most people are, in one way or another, producers as well as consumers, and their two roles are not mutually exclusive. To do well as producers, they must economize labor time and effort; the same concerns carried over into consumption strengthen their demand for comfort and for goods that provide comfort. On the supply side, economic forces determine costs and availabilities, and they too load the scales in favor of comfort.

To establish the presence of a bias in someone's consumption pattern, it would seem necessary to contrast it with someone else's consumption pattern, one which can be considered the norm. Occasionally I shall compare American behavior with European behavior, especially western European behavior, for which alone adequate and comparable information is available. But let us beware of regarding Europe's consumption pattern as a norm. After all, who is to say what is the norm, what the deviation from the norm? Besides, people's consumption patterns change, the Europeans' almost certainly in the direction of ours, ours perhaps in the direction of theirs. That could mean that the true norm lies somewhere in between; it could also mean that while their rising affluence makes them approach our expenditure pattern, the meager pickings of affluence makes us branch out in their direction. Indeed, what I call American behavior for short is, strictly speaking, the behavior only of our Establishment, and perhaps also that of the newly affluent elsewhere. The behavior of our counterculture is much closer to that of average Europeans, from their shedding bras, wearing their grandparents' clothes, and sewing individualistic patches on the seats of their pants to their interest in cooking and preparing food from scratch. It is too soon, however, for their tastes to show up in the statistics, and I have ignored them for the most part. I have to oversimplify to keep what I have to say simple; in any case, I know of no norm to start out with.

Instead, I shall adopt a much simpler and more eclectic approach. Our real income in the United States is higher than that of most western European countries; we could be expected, therefore, to spend more on everything than they do. On most things we do spend more; on a few we do so to an extent that seems to go beyond the bounds of reason, as will be shown presently. On some other things we spend very much less than do others who are poorer than we are. That is surprising and significant; its documentation and, even more, its explanation will take up much of the remainder of this book.

That our American standard of living is higher than that of any other country has been taken for granted for many years. But, strangely enough, such differences are very difficult to document. International comparisons of real income which would show by how much, if at all, one country's average income is worth more than another's are rare, rough, and notoriously unreliable. It is easy enough to tell how many francs a dollar will buy, but going beyond that is made difficult by international differences in the pattern of prices, the pattern of expenditures, and people's consumption habits.

Many international comparisons circumvent the difficulty by comparing not incomes, but levels of living, using some average of a miscellaneous collection of indices of the level of living such as the number of telephones, radios, road vehicles, bathrooms per capita, and the per capita consumption of meat, newsprint, steel, cement, electric power, etc.[1] Noteworthy about the choice of such indices is that most have to do with comfort, few with pleasure. We have unwittingly fallen into the habit of identifying a high standard of living with a high level of comfort, neglecting stimulation or pleasure as a source of satisfaction and assuming that the more comfort we have the better off we must be. That might well be true, but we should not prejudge the issue. It would be less misleading to choose indices that try expressly to measure comfort as distinguished from the standard of living, such as, say, the amount of insurance held by households [2] or the volume of solid waste they generate.[3] We are far ahead of other nations in the number of life insurance policies we hold and the quantity of garbage we throw away, but those facts do not tempt one quite so much into assuming that we must be better off than others as a result. We probably have more comfort than others, but how are we to decide whether we have too much or they have too little? The question is wide open, and it calls for an answer.

Many comforts are purely subjective, and that subjectivity renders the person experiencing them their only judge. The indoor temperature people consider the most comfortable is subjective. Some like it cold, some like it hot; each person must be considered the final arbiter of what best suits him, however absurd or exaggerated his tastes may seem by one's own, different standards. The actual temperature, therefore, to which another person heats his home I must accept as optimal by *his* standards—either as the best suited to his tastes or the best compromise between his tastes and the limitations which his income and the market conditions he faces impose upon him.

Some comforts, however, can also be judged by objective tests, and if the person experiencing such comforts accepts those tests as valid, they become objective and subjective tests at the same time. Clearly, if we are to find evidence of consumer irrationality, we should focus on such testable comforts.

Rational spending requires that no need be filled to the point of satiation as long as some others of the same consumer's needs and desires go unsatiated (p. 65). That rule provides a simple test for deciding what spending or consumption is excessive. It is true that the rule is not quite as simple as it once seemed to economists. In Chapter Four I discussed a case in which the pleasure of continuing a satisfying activity once begun can lure the consumer off what once seemed the straight path of economic rationality into pushing to satiation or beyond the filling of a particular need. But there only a minor modification of our notions of rational behavior was needed. There are other instances where the need or desire for comfort is being filled to excess for altogether different reasons, instances which definitely seem to be violations of the principle of rationality.

THE ECONOMY OF EFFORT [4]

A good example of excessive comfort is the economy of effort, and the extent to which we economize effort is a striking case of irrational behavior. To save labor in work and in the many other activities of daily living has been the supreme aim and proud achievement of modern civilization. We are justly proud of our many technical and economic advances, most of which have to do with the substitution of mechanical power and mechanical ingenuity for human effort. Throughout most of history, every step in this direction has been considered a clear and unmistakable gain in human welfare, and quite rightly so; no wonder we still retain the habit of considering every economy of effort desirable, whether or not we can still put further increments of human energy so saved to good use. The body of a man or of any animal can be looked upon as a machine which converts food into energy. Within a broad range which lies between well-defined lower and upper limits, appetite and the body's food intake rise with the level of physical activity, while body weight stays constant or falls slightly. The stable, monotonic relation [5] between activity and appetite breaks down beyond the limits at both extremes. Beyond the upper limit, further increases in the level of physical activity tax the organism beyond its capacity and *reduce* its appetite, which lead to progressive weight loss, exhaustion, and ultimate death. Below the lower limit, a further reduction of physical activity *increases* appetite and food intake and leads to a progressive gain in body weight, with almost as bad ultimate consequences for life and health. The consequences are not always recognized, but every farmer knows that restricting an animal's freedom of movement and level of activity will increase its food intake and lead to a quick gain in its weight; this, after all, is the way we fatten

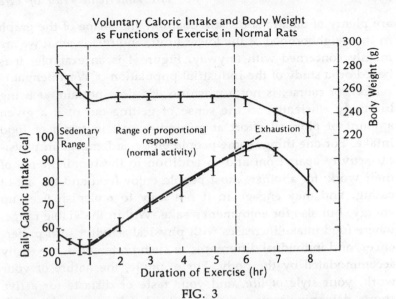

Voluntary Caloric Intake and Body Weight
as Functions of Exercise in Normal Rats

FIG. 3

SOURCE: Jean Mayer, *Overweight: Causes, Costs, and Control*, Englewood Cliffs, N.J.: Prentice-Hall, 1968, p. 73.

chickens, steers, and all other livestock for slaughter. The prescription for fattening up man is no different. In the story of Hänsel and Gretel, the old witch locks Hänsel into a cage to prevent his exercising and so fatten him for the table. Modern civilization does much the same thing for all men, although the women's liberation movement may end discrimination in this respect.

Figure 3, derived from an experiment with rats, is a graphic representation of the relation just described. The lowest and the highest points of the lower graph show the two limits between which appetite and food intake move with activity and the body can be considered a viable energy-producing machine; the upper graph shows the dependence of weight on exercise. The same relations seem to hold also for man. Empirical data to locate for man the position of the upper limit to the viable range cannot be collected in the civilized twentieth century, but there are plenty of data to show the position and shape of the graph in the neighborhood of the lower limit; and this is what we are mainly concerned with anyway. Figure 4 is an example; it is based on a study of the industrial population of West Bengal.

Man, of course, is not a machine. He does not aim at using his body efficiently, in the sense of getting out of it a given amount of physical effort at minimum cost in terms of food intake. For one thing, some people enjoy and engage in physical activity apart from and in addition to the requirements of their work; for another, most people enjoy food and the act of eating, and they engage in it not only to replenish used-up energy, but also for enjoyment's sake. Within the viable range, where food intake increases with physical activity, such preferences, and individual differences in such preferences, are easily accommodated by the body. For example, the nature of your work, your style of life, and your taste or distaste for active sports determine your activity level. That level, together with your body weight, determines the rate at which you burn up calories. If your enjoyment of the pleasures of food makes you consume more calories than you need to replenish what is burned up, you gain weight until the increased calorie requirements of engaging in the same activity level with a now heavier body equal your calorie intake. Man's energy consumption is a multiplicative function of body weight and activity level; this means that a suitable adjustment of his body weight will equate his energy consumption to his preferred intake of calories for any preferred activity level.

This simple, self-equilibrating process provides some of that freedom of consumer's choice we so greatly cherish, but, unfortunately, it does not seem to work for sedentary people, whose activity level is below the normal range. If a sedentary person overeats, he will gain weight, all right, but it will not help him much if his physical activity is minimal, because the additional energy required to perform such minimal activity with a heavier body will not be sufficient to use up his excess calories and stabilize his weight at a reasonable level. Instead, his weight

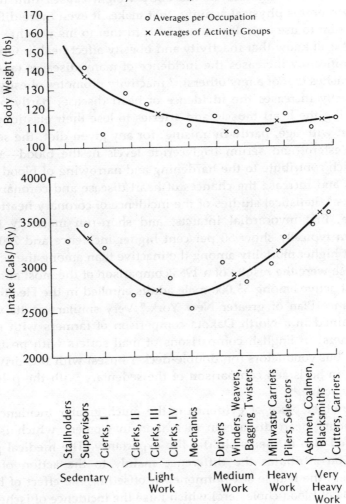

FIG. 4

SOURCE: Jean Mayer, *Overweight: Causes, Costs, and Control*, Englewood Cliffs, N.J.: Prentice-Hall, 1968, p. 74.

will continue rising, often rising too much and creating health problems.[6] If the rise in his body weight causes him to cut down on his physical activity, that makes it even more difficult for him to use up calories and adds further to his weight.

We all know that inactivity and obesity affect health. Obesity significantly increases the incidence of many diseases (and diminishes that of a few others);[7] inactivity promotes obesity and directly increases the incidence of heart disease, partly by allowing the heart muscle and arteries to lose their elasticity too soon with age, partly by raising, for any given diet, the serum cholesterol and serum triglyceride levels in the blood—all of which contribute to the hardening and narrowing of blood vessels and increase the chances of heart disease and coronary attacks.[8] Statistical studies of the incidence of coronary heart disease, first myocardial infarcts, and short-run mortality from them typically show 50 per cent higher incidence and 200 per cent higher mortality among the inactive than among the active. These were the results of a 1965 comparison of the most and the least active among 55,000 male adults enrolled in the Health Insurance Plan of greater New York.[9] Very similar results were obtained in a North Dakota comparison of farmers with non-farmers, in English comparisons of mail sorters with postmen and bus conductors (on double-decker buses) with bus drivers, and in an Israeli comparison of the sedentary with the pshysically active.[10]

Another piece of evidence is the much greater incidence of coronary heart disease in men than in women, which is reflected also in men's shorter life expectancy. The medical profession attributes the difference mainly to the action of estrogen, the female sex hormone, in offsetting the effect of high levels of blood cholesterol which raise the incidence of ischemic heart disease, but the explanatory power of this theory has not yet been tested statistically, and it is probably not the whole story. Triglycerides, like cholesterol, are forms of fatty blood lipids which are clearly implicated in ischemic heart disease, and every statistical study shows them to be in significantly higher concentration in the blood plasma of men than in women at all ages.[11] Experiments have repeatedly shown that even moderate physical activity of short duration has dramatic effects on the plasma triglyceride level of the blood, lowering it almost immediately and keeping it low for several days.[12] At the same time, the 1966 United States time-budget study shows that the daily average amount of time spent weekdays on housekeeping, gardening, running errands, hiking, and active sports is 51 minutes for employed men, 164 minutes for employed women, and 387 minutes for housewives—an enormous disparity.[13] Other questionnaire survey studies, which deal with household chores only, confirm this finding, and they show even greater disparities.[14] We have here an important explanation, additional to the hormonal one, to account for the greater incidence of heart disease in men than in women.

According to nutritionists, a large proportion of the United States population today is below the minimal activity level, in the range where equilibrium between the preferred calorie intake and preferred activity level cannot be assured by minor adjustments in body weight. What is known from time-budget studies about our reluctance to walk and engage in physical exercise fully supports this view. According to the 1966 UNESCO comparison of time budgets in twelve countries, American adults devote, on average, less than eight minutes a day to physical exercise (active sports or walking) as compared with the almost twenty minutes a day that the people of eleven nations of western and eastern Europe devote to it.[15]

No less important than the observable and testable behavior is the individual's own subjective view of it. When a person spends his day surrounded by power-driven equipment and vehicles to help him save effort on his every move, at work, at home and at play, and he then proceeds on doctor's orders to squander the energy he has so carefully saved on jogging around the block or riding his exercycle in the bathroom, he gives clear evidence that he realizes the irrationality, if not of his personal behavior, at least of the pattern of behavior society imposes, the pressure of which he is not strong enough to resist. The same is also true of those who diet, instead of exercising (presumably because they find it less painful) [16] and it is estimated that approximately seventy million Americans are on a diet.

But is it really irrational for us to save effort to the point where doing so either affects our health or forces us to engage in unwanted exercise or restrict our diet below that preferred? We must not accuse man of irrationality lightly, especially if an alternative explanation is possible.

One such alternative explanation might be the following. The saving of effort usually goes hand in hand with the saving of time. If we overdo the saving of effort, might this not be the inevitable accompaniment of a perfectly rational desire to save time? Modern man's high labor productivity and high hourly earnings render his time precious, and he may well be prompted to save time whenever and however he can. If in the act of saving time he cannot help saving effort as well, and saves that to excess, what could be more rational than to balance the gain from saving time against the loss from conserving excess energy, and to eliminate the latter through diet or exercise, whichever is the less painful?

The argument is plausible, but it is contradicted by people's observed behavior. Modern, urban man spends a part of almost every day riding escalators—in airports, subway stations, department stores, offices, etc.—and on each occasion he can decide whether to stand on the escalator and so spend time on saving effort or to walk and so devote a little effort to saving time. We would expect some people to do the one, others the other, and again others to pursue now one, now the other course of action, depending on the time, the place, and on how much in a hurry they happen to be in. In most countries, notices or loudspeakers ask the public to stand on the right and let those in a hurry pass to the left when escalators are wide enough to carry two people abreast; the crowd is usually divided into the leisurely, who stand, and the hurrying, who walk or run on the escalator. In the United States, escalators are as wide and as popular as they are anywhere else, but one almost never sees Americans walking on escalators, either up or down. We have never developed rules of escalator traffic; and we have never had to.[17] The conclusion is inescapable that most of us, most of the time, want to save effort, not time. Accordingly, we face the issue of consumer irrationality.

We have been conditioned for generations to regard all saving of effort as desirable. Saving labor in production increases labor productivity and reduces costs, thus raising employers' profits and, usually, employees' wages as well. Housekeeping is another area with great scope for labor-saving innovation. Not having to perform household chores has been a status symbol throughout history, and it persists in our age, though domestic appliances rather than domestic servants free us from housekeeping. In the two main areas of human activity, therefore, society considers it desirable to save labor, and it is not easy for the individual to go against such long-established and universally accepted conventional wisdom, just because it happens in his case to be wrong. Public opinion is hard to defy in such matters, and it cannot be expected to make an about-face in so short a time. It was less than twenty-five years ago that a medical journal first printed a letter asking if inactivity, rather than tension, might not be the main cause of heart disease in the modern world, and conclusive statistical studies which tested and confirmed this inspired guess are more recent still.[18] It will take some time yet for this newly won wisdom to displace the old.

THE ECONOMY OF TIME

Having failed to explain the excessive saving of effort by its complementarity with the saving of time, we may well ask whether in that case the too-great economy of effort, due to other factors, may not, in its turn, carry with it a too-great economy of time as well. After all, time and effort are usually

spent or saved together, and although I cited evidence to show
that most people seem more anxious to save effort than to save
time, they might nevertheless overdo the saving of time. We
would expect wage- and salary-earners to be the most likely to
save too much time, considering that their workweek is by far
the shortest and forever getting shorter.

The danger of irrationally budgeting our time seems much
smaller than that of badly husbanding our energy. A person can
continue to spend too little energy for a very long time without
becoming aware of the harm to his health, and by the time he
realizes it, his excessive economy of effort may have become an
ingrained habit, harder to relinquish than to offset by dieting.
By contrast, we have a fixed daily ration of time, with very limited scope for varying the period of sleep. Boredom reminds us
within the day of any excesses committed in the saving of time.

But let me concentrate on the inducements to save time, other
than its going hand in hand with the saving of effort. We are
here dealing with a paradoxical situation. The rise in labor productivity is forever raising the value of time, as reflected in
wage rates and the hourly cost of personal services, and we instinctively budget carefully and use sparingly whatever is valuable. That is why we try the harder to save time through the use
of time-saving innovations, the more highly the market values
an hour of our labor. Yet the rising market price of time does
not signify its increasing scarcity. The length of the day is
unchanged, and that majority of people whose workweek is getting shorter (and who can also afford an increasing number of
time-saving products) are left with ever more free time to do
with as they please. In other words, the amount of their free
time increases as its value, in terms of the products the hourly
wage will buy, goes up. We would expect rational men to have
contrary responses to these two changes, but how do we actually behave under their combined impact?

The question is a difficult one to answer because we are dealing here only with the masses, the low- and middle-income
wage- and salary-earners, who alone benefit from the short and

shrinking workweek, but whose behavior is bound to be influenced by the example set by the hard- and long-working elite, the professionals, independents, and executives.

Much has been written recently of the paradox in our society of *The Harried Leisure Class*,[19] whose high hourly earnings make their time so precious that they cannot afford the time it takes to enjoy life and are forced to eat their meals on the run, cut short the foreplay in lovemaking, attend abbreviated religious services, buy books to glance at, not to read, and have no time to look at the beauty spots of the world to which their conferences take them. Such is the life-style of today's elite. The paradox lies not in their behavior, but in the use of the term, "leisure class," to refer to people with no interest in leisure and with work their only passion.

The average man, the wage- or salary-earner, has followed that lead. Time-budget data on the way he husbands his time show that between 1934 and 1966 he drastically reduced the time he spent at meals (from 107 to 70 minutes a day), walking for pleasure (22 to 1), at the movies (22 to 3), listening to the radio (26 to 4), playing cards (9 to 4), watching sports events (7 to 2), reading books (22 to 9), and purposeful traveling (129 to 76). Of the almost three hours he saved, half went into watching television (almost 90 minutes) the other half being divided between more time spent on shopping (34 as against the earlier 16 minutes), visiting (46 against 26), doing housework (140 against 95) and correspondence (6 against 3).[20]

The switch from radio to TV is obviously explained by technical progress, but most of the other changes go from planned and structured activities to unplanned, unstructured, residual ones, and they are the sorts of changes one would expect to occur when the high cost of time makes people anxious to save it, leaving them with more time on their hands than they know what to do with. It is natural to save time on activities that have to be decided upon, prepared for, or planned in advance; it is also natural to waste time on those one can take up at a moment's notice, linger over at will, or drift into unwittingly.

Watching television is the prime residual activity; and everything shows that it is often used as such. Experiments with pay
television have demonstrated that the public is unwilling to pay
even a modest hourly fee of the magnitude of one-tenth of an
hour's wage for better entertainment (e.g. newer films, more
important sports events) and fewer or no interruptions,[21] which
clearly shows how little people value the time they spend in
front of the TV screen. At the same time, questionnaire surveys
of viewers of commercial television indicate how bored they are
with what they get. According to the author of one of them,
about two-fifths of the people watching television can be described as "compulsive viewers." They were asked, "When
you're watching TV do you ever feel you'd rather do something
else but just can't tear yourself away?" and, "About how often
do you feel that way?" Twenty-four per cent answered, "Occasionally," another 12.5 per cent, "Almost always." Yet they
continue watching. Is it by force of habit (addiction), or because
they have no better use for their time? [22]

The large increase in the time spent in housekeeping, shown
above, is surprising, in view of the many labor-saving household appliances introduced and sold during the period. Yet the
trend is reliably documented by a comparison of all the time
budgets available, and it strikingly confirms our argument. We
buy time-saving gadgets to save time, but, having no better use
for the time saved, we unwittingly waste it on more of the same
activity.

One more residual activity worth a careful look is shopping.
An important reason why we spend so much more time on it
today is that we have supermarkets and other self-service retail
distributors, which save on costs by making the customer perform much of the work clerks used to do and making him wait
in line at the check-out counter rather than having more clerks
to wait on him. Part of the resulting savings are passed on to
the customer, who—to judge by the popularity of such stores—
seems quite willing to spend the additional time if he can
thereby save money. Indeed, self-service is so popular that even

manufacturers can save on costs by letting the customer do the assembling of certain toys, furniture, hi-fi equipment, and so on. The sellers' motivation is easily explained by the rise of labor costs, but the same rise in wages and salaries also raises the value of the buyers' time, which ought to make the buyers increasingly reluctant to spend time on shopping. It clearly does nothing of the sort. The question is, why doesn't it? One explanation is that we have had a continuing rise in income-tax rates, which renders a dollar not spent increasingly more valuable than a dollar earned—of which a large part is taxed away. The other explanation is that time is becoming not only more valuable, but also more plentiful, and that shopping, so easy to decide on at a moment's notice, is becoming a favored way of passing residual time.

THE PURCHASE OF HEALTH

One more comfort whose consumption we seem to have pushed too far, even to the point of satiation or beyond, is medical care. Our per capita expenditure on medical care is the highest in the world; as a percentage of our income it is the second highest. But the benefits we receive are not commensurate. Our mortality and infant mortality rates are certainly not the lowest, nor is our life expectancy the highest; most western and eastern Europeans, and the Japanese, are better off in such respects than we are. (See Table 7.) All these rates have ceased improving with time; our life expectancy actually declined between 1960 and 1970, both absolutely and in relation to other countries. Moreover, cross-section studies show that differences in medical care expenditures have insignificant effects on mortality and life expectancy, implying that the marginal contribution of medical care to health is zero.[23] If we regard longevity as the main aim of medical care, then we must accept the conclusion that our expenditure on it has reached or passed the point of satiation. The desire to live longer may be insatiable, but to spend more money on health is not the way to its fulfillment.

TABLE 7

Life Expectancy and Infant Mortality in Developed Countries

Country	Life Expectancy at Birth		Infant Mortality	
	1971	1988	1971	1988
Sweden	74.1	77.3	11.1	6
Netherlands	73.9	77.1	12.1	8
Norway	73.5	76.3	12.8	8
Denmark	73.3	75.3	14.2	7
France	72.4	75.7	17.1	9
Switzerland	72.1	78.0	14.4	6
Canada	72.0	77.1	17.6	7
United Kingdom	72.0	75.1	17.5	9
U.S.A. (white)	72.0	75.5	16.8	9
German Democratic Rep.	71.8	72.7	18.0	11
U.S.A. (total)	71.1	75.3	19.2	11
Bulgaria	70.8	70.8	19.6	18
Italy	70.7	76.7	28.3	8
Japan	70.6	77.8	12.4	6
Belgium	70.6	75.4	19.9	8
West Germany	70.6	75.8	23.3	8

SOURCES: U.N. *Demographic Yearbooks* supplemented from the *Statistical Abstract of the United States* and some other countries' *Yearbooks of Statistics*.

What we have here are summary conclusions based on aggregative data, but they seem to be fully corroborated by more detailed and specialized studies, of which those that deal with the demand for surgery are the most worth quoting, for surgery and hospital stay are the most expensive items in the medical-care budget. If we can document and explain our excessive demand for surgery, we can account for much of our excessive spending on health.

Ideally, the incidence of surgery would be determined by informed medical opinion and the prevalence of disease, with the limited availability of surgeons and hospital beds keeping its actual incidence below the ideal. We are shocked, therefore, to learn of the high proportion of surgical operations which cannot be so explained. The extreme examples are circumcision, tonsillectomy, and adenoidectomy. Circumcision on other than religious grounds can hardly be justified: it "seems to be performed in quest of hygiene and purity, somewhat in emulation of Jews and Arabs"; but at least it does as little harm as it does good. Not so the other two, which have a death rate of 1 per 1000, serious complications in 15.6 cases per 1000, and an even higher incidence of long-lasting emotional effect.

No more than 2 to 3 per cent of the entire pediatric population should require tonsillectomy and adenoidectomy. . . . Despite its [tonsillectomy's] meager scientific justification . . . approximately 20 to 30 per cent of the children of most communities still undergo this procedure. Parental pressure may be a major determinant of a physician's decision to perform the operation, although the great legacy of misinformation from the past may condition his attitude or help him rationalize his . . . willingness to comply with parental demand. . . . Tonsillectomy tends to be performed much more often in the children of wealth, whose parents are in the professional and managerial classes. This may simply reflect economic ability to pay for the procedure. It may also tend to equate tonsillectomy and adenoidectomy with social status. Furthermore, circumcised boys, [in the United States] are seven times more likely to have undergone tonsillectomy in early childhood than uncircumcised boys.[24]

Unfortunately, these three surgical procedures are not the only ones whose incidence is greater than what would seem indicated on medical grounds. The incidence of all types of surgery shows very great variation between different countries and even between different regions of the same country. Whether that is proof of too much surgery in the one place or too little in the other is not easy to tell, but various pieces of evidence of various degrees of persuasiveness strongly suggest that tonsils, adenoids, and foreskins are not the only parts of their anatomy people get rid of without good reason.

International studies comparing the incidence of surgery in

the United States, Canada, England and Wales, and Sweden show it to be about twice as great in the North American countries as it is in the European countries. When the raw data are adjusted for differences in the age and sex distributions of the different populations, the disparities become greater still, and a comparison of them with the incidence of and mortality from diseases for which the surgeries are the cure shows that it is we who have too many operations, not they who have too few.[25]

An econometric study of the incidence of surgery among the Blue Cross insured population of Kansas showed that there is a more than threefold variation among the ten different regions of the state (other than Greater Kansas City), and that that variation is highly correlated with regional differences in the capacity of hospitals and availability of surgeons and physicians. The authors of this study regarded as self-evident the absence of regional differences in need or income level sufficient to account for such great differences in incidence.

> The reasons for threefold variations in common surgical procedures seem difficult to explain on the basis of differences in the prevalence or incidence of disease in the population or their illness behavior [although] the most comforting explanation would be to assume that hospital beds are built and surgeons aggregate in areas that have the greater number of people prone to appendicitis or gall-bladder disease. . . . The results presented might be interpreted as supporting a medical variation of Parkinson's Law: patient admissions for surgery expand to fill beds, operating suites and surgeons' time.[26]

These studies show, convincingly, that we have too many surgical operations, but they fail to account for this superfluity. The high correlation between number of operations and surgeons in both the Kansas study and the U.S.–U.K. comparison suggests that the surgeons are to blame, but the authors of most of the studies put more blame on the patient.

> The surgeon may be influenced by a wish to sell his services, but a more important factor may be the patient's wish to buy a cure.

The American patient, particularly if he is educated, has high expectations of what medicine, and particularly surgery, can accomplish. With an impatience in proportion with his affluence, he demands active therapy, whether it is an operation for his ulcer, or an antibiotic for his infant's fever. . . . The medical profession has oversold its product, exaggerating its success and at the same time minimizing its limitations, with the inevitable result that patients' demands far exceed their needs. It is difficult for a physician to resist the patient's demands. If the patient prefers a gastrectomy—with the expectation of instant cure—to the effort and inconvenience of medical management, he will go from the surgeon who is reluctant to another who is willing. The same principle holds throughout medicine, of course; another obvious example is that of the pediatrician who most readily accedes to the mother's demand for antibiotic treatment and inevitably has a bigger practice than his therapeutically more cautious colleague in the next office.[27]

That brings me to another extreme example of our excessive expenditure on health—the overuse and overprescribing of drugs. In 1972, we spent $6 billion on prescription drugs. What proportion of that expenditure was unnecessary and harmful no one knows at this stage, but of the $1.3 billion spent on antibiotics, which are among the most dangerous of the prescription drugs, well over half is believed to have been unnecessary. According to the Bureau of Drugs of the Food and Drug Administration, half of the antibiotics prescribed in hospitals are unnecessary;[28] as to their total consumption by adults in and out of hospitals, according to the Health Research Group (Washington, D.C.), "we appear to have a fivefold excess of antibiotics made in this country [net of exports] in terms of what the real need is."[29] The annual cost of adverse reactions to these drugs is estimated at 30,000 deaths and $2.25 billion spent on treatment; at least half, maybe well over half, of the deaths (and, presumably, also of the treatment) are deemed preventable.[30] "These examples [and many more] document instances of overprescribing and misprescribing which lead to billions of wasted dollars and thousands of wasted lives," to quote from the testimony of the director of the Health Research Group before a Congressional subcommittee.[31] How to apportion the blame between pharmaceutical companies, physicians and patients is a matter of controversy; but there is no doubt that all are to blame in some measure, including the patient himself, who foots the bill.

THE ECONOMY OF CARE AND BOTHER

So far I have discussed three cases in which consumers' preferences for a comfort were not only excessive by objective standards but, once they recognized the validity of those standards, appeared irrational by their own subjective standards as well. Let us now proceed to a case in which a comfort is once again being used to excess, but which is very different, nevertheless, because irrationality, at least in the narrow, individualistic sense of the word, is not involved.

Time and effort are not the only inputs of our daily existence which require economizing and on which we tend to economize too much. Another one is care, or bother. It is not always easy to distinguish care from time and physical effort, with which it is highly complementary. But care consists in the expenditure of the mental effort of thinking, planning, remembering, judging, deciding, and taking responsibility. It is unlike time, whose supply is fixed, and unlike physical effort, of which a minimum quantity must be spent for health's sake, but it is like them in that our capacity to care is limited. Moreover, the good life is not only leisurely, but also care-free, which is why we also try to economize on caring.

I have argued that the individual overdoes the budgeting of his time and energy and so creates an excess supply, which then is wasted. And I have presented these as instances of irrational behavior, however naturally they may result from the conflict of present forces and past traditions impinging on the consumer. With care, the problem is very different. The conflict here lies not between obsolete modes of thought and greatly changed circumstances, but between what appears to be rational to the individual and what is in fact good for society. Accordingly, I shall not question the rationality of the individual's budgeting, but argue that in this case even rational budgeting can be at fault and lead to too much freedom from care. Such freedom is bad, not because we have an irreducible minimum supply of care which gets under-utilized, but because we obtain our excessive freedom from care at an excessive cost.

Most of us cannot be bothered to turn the lights out and the radio or TV off when we leave a room, perhaps because we want to save ourselves the effort of trying to remember to do so, or perhaps because we want to avoid the momentary distress of fumbling for the switch in the dark on our return. Many suburbanites do not bother to lock the front door when they leave the house. We use food lavishly and throw away remnants rather than save them for later use in another dish or to feed to pets, which are more conveniently fed out of can or carton; we sooner replace than repair our durable belongings, again to avoid the bother which repair involves. I have already mentioned a good index of our enjoyment of these and related comforts—the high rate at which we generate garbage. Further examples of a similar nature are the many services consumers buy in order to relieve themselves of the bother of planning vacations, preparing for parties, furnishing and arranging the interior of their homes, matching accessories to their clothes, and so on and on.

A slightly different kind of example is our careless shopping. We hardly bother to look out for our own interests, hardly try to get good value for money by shopping around for the best quality or the lowest price. Also, we seldom bother to complain about a badly prepared dish at a restaurant; we rather swallow our anger or disappointment along with the bad food, in silence. Finally, we seem occasionally—which is all too often—not to notice when someone is in need of help, having a heart attack in the street, lying hurt in the roadway, or being assaulted on a busy intersection.[32] An increasing number of such incidents are being reported in the press. A recent experiment in San Francisco showed that when a young person was left gagged, tied, and splattered with "blood" in a public place in broad daylight, almost no one stopped to help or even to investigate. Here again, not wanting to be bothered or to get involved seems to be the explanation, although fear undoubtedly plays a role too.

Not to be bothered is clearly an advantage, but it is only to be had at a cost. The question is, how much of it is worth the cost? The cost can be monetary, non-monetary, or both; it can weigh on the consumer, on others, or on both him and others. As a general rule, the consumer can be fully trusted to do a good job of weighing the costs against the benefits only when he alone is affected and money cost is the only cost. In most other cases, their rational behavior leads people into overindulging the freedom from bother because, as individuals, they underestimate its true and full cost.

Many people believe, for example, that the extra time needed for careful comparison shopping is usually worth more than the gain in quality or saving in price this might yield; and that it is rational, therefore, to save on shopping time and accept the money cost of such saving, at least as far as minor, everyday purchases are concerned. Such reasoning hinges on the assumption that the consumer's free time is as scarce and valuable to him as is his worktime to his employer—but I have just finished casting doubt on this very assumption. Even so, let me grant it for argument's sake; let me accept the rationality of a time allocation which allows too little time for careful shopping on the ground that the actuarial value of the savings to be had is not worth the bother.

Such a decision on the consumer's part, however rational, ignores the external benefits to others from his, and to him from other people's, careful shopping. For, in addition to his immediate benefit from careful shopping, it also contributes, in the long run, to keeping producers on their toes, merchants honest, and the market competitive. Unfortunately, the impact of one buyer's market behavior on the market behavior of the sellers facing him is usually too small to be noticed. The individual is probably right, therefore, in ignoring as negligible his own benefit from the tiny impact his own action has on the market's competitiveness. He would benefit from careful shopping by the public at large, which alone can force producers and sellers into doing their best to earn the consumer's dollar.

To be more precise, the individual would be best off if he could benefit from a market rendered competitive by other people's careful shopping while at the same time letting his own market behavior be governed by time-saving considerations. It is true that the extra time of his own careful shopping would be a price well worth paying for an assurance of everybody's else's careful shopping, but such assurances cannot be bought and sold, and the individual usually doubts—and is probably right in doubting—that the example he sets would be followed by enough people to make a difference. In other words, the consumer finds himself in a situation where his own action's direct impact on competitiveness and its impact via the example he sets for others are both negligible. His most rational course of action, therefore, is to save time on shopping, whether or not other people's more careful shopping provides him with a competitive market. If we all follow this course of action, none of us will shop carefully, the market will cease to be competitive, and all of us will be worse off than we would be had we all devoted extra time to careful shopping.

This quandary, known in the theoretical literature of economics as the "prisoners' dilemma," typifies many (though not all) of the cases we have considered here. Decisions on how much care to exercise, based on the rational weighing of the pros and cons of caring, are certain to inflict a loss on society and its members whenever caring yields benefits not fully taken into account by the individual either because they are too remote for him to perceive them or because they redound partly or wholly to other people's advantage. The shopping example illustrates a principle which governs many aspects of our lives. The remedy in all such cases is to rely not on individual rationality, but on enforced regulation or moral imperative as the motivating, or at least as a modifying, force governing behavior.

To establish, obey, and enforce general rules of behavior whose observance by all benefits all is a very rational thing to do. To distinguish it from the individual rationality discussed so far, one may call it social or higher rationality—higher, because we must have higher intelligence and more insight to recognize that we gain a greater advantage through an arrangement which subjects our behavior to rules than we do through an arrangement which gives us (but also others!) complete freedom of action.

Such higher rationality is sometimes codified into law. Consider the rules of the road. We are better off obeying them than we are if each of us drives according to his individual rationality. But the enactment of rules and their enforcement by authority are practicable only when the desired behavior can be assured by prohibition. Laws, bylaws, and regulations are of little or no use when socially optimal behavior calls for initiative and action.

Hence the need for moral imperatives and unwritten laws: guides to action contained in religious and ethical maxims, social conventions, the Boy Scout Code, rules of good citizenship and gentlemanly behavior, and the like. Such rules abound in every society and are closely interwoven with principles of individual and social rationality. The theoretical distinction we just made between individual and social rationality is simple and clear-cut, but most people's behavior, in practice, falls somewhere in between these logical extremes, and most of the time people are not aware themselves of the influences that motivate them and the relative importance of those influences.

Also, the comfort we derive from being useful to others is very much like a moral imperative, because it motivates behavior ideally suited to supplement our selfish individual rationality. Obviously, if a person gets satisfaction out of doing his fellow men a good turn, he will exercise more care than if he cared only for himself. In the economist's language, this form of status seeking *internalizes* the external benefits of caring and so causes individually rational behavior to come closer to bringing about a social optimum.

The argument that we carry the economy of care to excess amounts to this: our selfish, individual rationality is not modified, or not modified enough, either by ethical and religious maxims or by status seeking of the type just mentioned. Let me cite two examples where that seems to be the case and where the consequent social loss is apparent.

One of the many things on which we economize bother is dressing up when we go out to a public place. The gain in comfort from *not* dressing up is considerable, and the loss, in some people's eyes, merely one of bourgeois prejudice. Europeans are much more formal and tradition-bound in this respect than we are, which could, indeed, be due to their greater class consciousness. But is it? Evening dress rental to working-class men and women is big business in England, and the wearing of it, at least to opera and first nights in the theater, is no less common in socialist Stockholm or communist Budapest than in capitalist Munich or Paris. The custom lends a festive air to the occasion and makes the crowd much better looking. The result, almost certainly, is a better performance by players and actors and a greater enjoyment by the audience than would otherwise be the case.

That this is so is strongly suggested by all the evidence we have. An aesthetically pleasing environment *does* influence people's performance of whatever they are doing and judgment of whatever they are witnessing. Experiments have shown that people, without being aware of their different attitude or its cause, make significantly more favorable judgments of the same set of objects in a "beautiful" than in an "ugly" room, and that they also find the performance of tasks less monotonous, less fatiguing, and more enjoyable in a "beautiful" room than they do

in an "ugly" room.[33] These and similar findings have been applied many times in industry, yet we make no use of them in
consumption.

For the second illustration, let me return to our shopping example. Most of us believe that we act rationally when we save
ourselves the bother of careful shopping in our everyday purchases. The European attitude is very different. Europeans seem
never to give a thought to the time, attention, nervous energy,
and shoe leather spent in bargaining, arguing, comparing,
seeking the best brand, the lowest price, and selecting the best
specimen. It is as if they did it for sport, or for the principle of
asserting the consumer's expertise and ability to fend for himself by making sure that no shopkeeper cheats or exploits him.
Whatever the reason, such behavior does put pressure on producers to heed consumers' tastes, to offer variety and good
quality; it also increases the correlation of price with quality,
which in turn reduces the care and time needed for careful
shopping.

Let us turn to the question of evidence. If the careful behavior
of buyers causes market prices to reflect differences in quality,
then random differences in price, unexplained by differences in
quality, must be evidence of careless shopping. There is plenty
of such evidence in the American economy. The identical brand
and model of most appliances and other durable goods are
priced very differently in different stores, and the same is true
of most foodstuffs and articles of clothing. Most surprising to
foreigners visiting this country are the wide divergences in the
price of a product as standardized as gasoline. According to a
recent (August 1974) survey of San Francisco gas stations conducted by the San Francisco Consumer Action, the most expensive regular gasoline costs 30 per cent more than the least expensive, though their octane ratings are identical.

Even greater divergences exist in air fares. Quite apart from
the especially low excursion, night, youth, and family fares and
charters, the standard, one-way fare on regular airlines also
varies greatly between the different offices and agents even of

the same airline. The fare actually charged may exceed the fare prescribed by the Civil Aeronautics Board by as much as 31.5 per cent. A 1972 sample survey showed that of thirty-one purchases of one-way coach tickets for regular flights there was an overcharge on twenty, and the average overcharge was 20.7 per cent.[34]

All observers confirm that price differentials of that magnitude are unknown in Europe, but documentation is scanty. Only the French have official statistics, and they have no statistics on commodities for which comparable data would exist elsewhere. In this country, *Consumer Reports* alone publishes data on price dispersion; but of the similar European publications only the West German *DM* and *test* provide information in the same form, and washing machines and freezer refrigerators are the only two products for which I could find fully comparable data. The average percentage by which the highest price exceeds the lowest price of a given brand and model of washing machine was 32.8 per cent for fourteen U.S. models and 15.1 per cent for the same number of models marketed in Germany. The corresponding averages for freezer-refrigerator combinations were 33.9 per cent for thirteen U.S. models as against 12.5 per cent for the sixteen models available on the West German market. The difference between the two markets is very great, and it can only be explained by the much greater competitiveness of the German market, which is assured and enforced by the greater carefulness of the German shopper.[35]

Take another piece of evidence. Compare the nature and quality of American and European products, or, better still, look at their comparison by the buying public. All U.S. imports of manufactured consumers' goods from Europe are items we also manufacture. Indeed, we manufacture the great bulk of such items at home. Imports are seldom more and usually much less than 20 per cent of our total consumption of a particular item; the imported variety is typically a more expensive variant (at least by the time it reaches the American consumer), bought by the rich and the choosy, presumably because it is better made, better designed, better in quality, in styling, or in attention to detail than its domestic counterpart.

The days are long past when such differences would have been explained as the typical difference between our low-cost mass production and the Europeans' expensive, labor-intensive, handmade, customer-oriented craft manufacture. Nowadays, Swiss watches, Italian shoes, German beer, Swedish cutlery, and British cars are just as mass-produced as our own, and often on the same equipment. Why, then, are they better than American watches, shoes, beer, cutlery, and cars? Our own industries are as large or larger, as well established, with equally good access to raw materials; our quality control, engineers, designers, and stylists are second to none. Detroit surely has the technical knowhow and design capability to produce a car as good as a Mercedes Benz or as trouble-free as the Volkswagen; Wisconsin's breweries should be on a par with, say, those of Mexico or Canada; our food processors, shoe manufacturers, and so on should also be able to produce goods no worse than the imports. Yet the higher quality product always comes from abroad. Where is the explanation? We look in vain for it as long as we look only on the production side.

The explanation must be sought, instead, in the greater choosiness of the European buying public. European producers, catering primarily to their own, more demanding, more quality-conscious markets, are forced to provide more variety, greater subtlety in styling, better quality, and a greater range of qualities than American producers are. The American producers, who face a more easy-going and less discriminating consuming public, can best maximize profits by cutting corners and enlarging the market through lower prices, and, quite naturally, they do just that.

The American buyer of European imports benefits from the high standards which the careful European shoppers' finicky demand imposes on their producers; he does not have to be a careful shopper himself. In other words, he can be what is known as a free rider, enjoying the benefits of other people's careful shopping without paying his share of the cost, in terms of time and effort, that careful and aggressive shopping involves. That explains why American producers find it unprofitable to cater to his demand by trying to out-compete high-quality imports, despite the often exorbitant price they fetch. American consumers seem willing to pay a high price, in terms of money, for the *reputation* of European imports; that is, we pay cash to obtain high quality without having to pay for it in terms of careful shopping.[36]

Table 8 shows imports and domestic output in all the cat-

TABLE 8

U.S. Imports of Final Manufactures in Order of Importance, Expressed as Percentage of Total Domestic Supply

	1965–69	1982
Passenger Cars and Chassis	8	27
Radio and Television Receiving Sets	15	50
Distilled Liquors except Brandy	27	28
Wines and Brandy	19	
Shoes (except rubber)	7	38
Watches and Clocks	17	47
Cheese	3	4
Women's Handbags and Purses	14	46
Vitreous China, Table and Kitchen Articles	38	47
Musical Instruments and Parts	11	22
Silverware and Plated Ware	10	23
Raincoats and other Waterproof Garments	10	32
Cutlery	9	16
Pottery Products	22	43
Fine Earthenware Food Utensils	32	70
Leather Gloves and Mittens	29	28
Other Gloves	14	40
Carpets, Rugs, Mats (except woven)	20	53
Umbrellas, Parasols, and Canes	24	47
Perfumes, Toilet Water and Cologne	2	4

SOURCE: *U.S. Commodity Exports and Imports as Related to Output*, U.S. Dept. of Commerce, 1973 and 1986, issues for 1969, 1970, and for 1981 and 1982 respectively. Tables 1B and 2C.

egories of consumers' goods where imports are important. It is striking what a small part of total consumption imports were in the 1960s. Note that our 1960s export statistics confirm the argument. We exported mainly manufactures that were bought by professional buyers whose expertise and careful choosiness imposed high standards on the manufacturers. Aircraft, machinery, and medical furniture (as against other furniture) were some of the items. A list of our main manufactured exports is given in Table 9.

All of the above cases exemplify important aspects of the comfortable life, and they serve to establish my claim that we seek and secure them in excess—not in relation to a norm, but

TABLE 9

The Main U.S. Exports of Manufactures Four Digit SIC Commodity Groups in Order of Importance, 1965–69 Average
(in millions of dollars)

Motor Vehicle Parts and Accessories	$1427.4
Aircraft	1261.7
Construction Machinery and Equipment	1130.6
Electronic Computing Machines, Calculating and Accounting Equipment	608.7
Industrial Organic Chemicals	550.0
Aircraft Parts and Auxiliary Equipment	547.9
Plastics Materials and Resins	481.4
Farm Machinery	441.0
Industrial Inorganic Chemicals	407.6
Special Industry Machinery	364.6
Aircraft Engines and Engine Parts	318.9
Photographic Equipment and Supplies	318.9
Pumps and Compressors	312.1
Soybean Oil Mill Products	302.7
Milled Rice and By-products	296.4
Mechanical Measuring and Controlling Instruments	282.9
Pulpmill Products	249.1
Solid State Semiconductor Devices	234.0
Refined Copper	230.3
Chemical Preparations	227.9

SOURCE: *U.S. Commodity Exports and Imports as Related to Output, 1970 and 1969,* U.S. Department of Commerce, Bureau of the Census, 1973, Table 1A, pp. 10–13.

in the sense that we obtain them either in larger quantities than we can use, or to the point where they do more harm than good. For their sakes we pass up many other ingredients of the good life, to whose discussion we now turn.

CHAPTER NINE

Is It Too Dull?

The convention that Europeans are pleasure-loving, frivolous and sophisticated and that Americans are sober, hard-working, and frugal is well known and well established on the anecdotal level. Does that convention stand up today, in the light of hard facts and statistics? We have plenty of data to check on the consumption habits of the United States and Europe. Food is a natural starting point, because most of us spend a large part of our budgets on it.

FOOD

People get both comfort and pleasure from food, but societies differ greatly in the degree of pleasure they derive from it and in the amount of effort they put into getting that pleasure.

The French appear to enjoy their food much more than the British enjoy theirs, and the difference is well reflected in their expenditures. In the mid-1960's, the average standard of living and real income was just about the same in the two countries, but where the Frenchman spent 28 per cent of his income on food, the Englishman spent only 22 per cent.[1]

No such simple test can be used for comparing the pleasures we Americans take in food with those of people in other countries. Although we devote an even smaller part of our expenditure to food than do the British—or the people of any other nation—that means nothing, because we also have one of the highest standards of living. And one of the best established regularities in economic behavior is Engel's Law, which says that the higher a person's income, the smaller the proportion of it will he spend on food. We are compelled, therefore, to look elsewhere for evidence.

We are known for our interest in nutrition and our lack of interest in the pleasures of food. Our food is notoriously plain, designed to provide not pleasure, but health and sustenance. To quote the opening sentence of a scientific text on food selection and preparation, "In this country of lavish, almost shameful abundance, the great majority of Americans go through life without experiencing a single, technically evaluated, good, representative dinner." [2] That is a statement about supply, not demand, but when it comes to the stimulating, pleasurable qualities of food, supply is determined by demand.

The nutritive values of food are given by nature, but the pleasure and the interest are added by the cook, who provides variety, novelty, and subtlety by the way he selects and prepares the ingredients, blends the flavors, harmonizes the dishes, and controls their consistency, temperature, color schemes, and so on. Cooking, however, is a skill that requires no special talent beyond a genuine interest in the pleasures of food. In countries where almost everybody is a connoisseur of good food, almot everybody is also a good cook; and the enjoyment of cooking very often goes with the enjoyment of eating. According to the official French survey of leisure activities, 22.1 per cent of Frenchmen and 57.6 per cent of Frenchwomen enjoy cooking; 4.2 per cent of the men and 6.6 per cent of the women consider it one of their favorite activities. The making of pastry as an enjoyable activity seems more exclusively feminine: 8.5 per cent of the men and 67.0 per cent of the women enjoy it and 1.8 per cent of the men and 5.4 per cent of the women look upon it as a favorite pastime.[3] All this is well in keeping with the almost proverbial fact that food is a great and serious source of pleasure for the French.

We have no corresponding statistics in this country, so the reader must make his own guess of how very much lower our percentages would be if the data were collected. It is a pity they have not been, because they are probably the best evidence of people's enjoyment, not only of cooking, but also of eating. Few people will admit to themselves, or even be conscious of, their lack of skill in savoring food; we are more reliable and honest with ourselves when we judge our skill and pleasure in cooking.

Most people are also better at seeing the other person's shortcomings than their own; which explains one of the basic agreements between British and Americans, both of whom consider deplorable the other's food. To repeat, the primary skill which is wanting is that of exercising one's sense of taste; the skill of cooking is derivative and easily acquired by anyone who enjoys eating. Little is known about the distribution of the innate ability to exercise one's sense of taste, but it is very likely that, just as in the case of a musical ear, few people are born without the potential, though many fail ever to develop it.

American travelers to mainland China, Poland, and Hungary often express surprise at the excellence of the food, yet the ingredients are nothing extraordinary. The explanation can be found in the minimal adequacy of supplies combined with the population's great interest in the pleasures of eating. Conversely, if no foreign visitor to the United States ever comments on the excellence of our cooking, their lack of praise does not reflect on the quality of the foodstuffs we grow, but merely on our utter lack of interest in the pleasures of food.

All classes, rich and poor alike, can practice good cooking and enjoy good food. The tremendous range of materials used in European, Chinese, and Mexican cooking has much to do with poor people's having to eat everything edible; they use their ingenuity to make it enjoyable. Many of the best Italian and Hungarian dishes are based on pasta and are poor man's food. Some of the most exquisite achievements of French cuisine have brains, sweetbreads, or tripe as their main ingredient and were probably developed by the gourmet poor, who could not afford the better parts of the animal. The glory of bouillabaisse probably had its origin in the poverty of fishermen, which forced them to cook their entire catch indiscriminately; the rich had sense enough to benefit by the culinary skills born of poverty. Our American diet is the poorer for our turning up our noses at the innards considered delicacies elsewhere, for our passing up the delights of all but one of the many varieties of mushrooms, and for our many other dietary self-restraints. The resulting monotony of our diet constitutes the freely chosen poverty of the rich.

One could argue, of course, that a nation on a reducing diet can hardly be expected to have an interest in the pleasures of food, but that is not a sufficient explanation, because our dieting is of recent origin, while our lack of interest in food and the plainness of our cooking go back to the Puritan ethic of the founding fathers of the Republic.[4]

As a distinguished Mexican poet-diplomat put it recently,

> Pleasure is a concept (a sensation) absent from traditional Yankee cooking. . . . [It] is a cuisine with no mysteries: simple, spiceless, nutritious food. No tricks: the carrot is the honest carrot, the potato is not ashamed of being a potato, and the steak is a bloody giant. It amounts to a transubstantiation of the democratic virtues of the founding fathers: honest cooking, one dish after another, like the sensible and plain-spoken sentences of a virtuous speech. Like the manners of those at the dinner table, the relations among the different substances and flavors are direct . . . Interdiction of concealing sauces and garnishes that exalt the eye and confound the taste. The separation among the different ingredients is analogous to the reserve prescribed for sexual, age, and class behavior. In other countries a meal is a communion and not only among the people at the table but among the ingredients themselves; a Yankee meal is saturated with Puritanism, is made up of exclusions.[5]

It is hard to document such an eloquent statement statistically. Quality is notorious for defying quantitative measurement, and just as difficult is the separation of the stimulus or pleasure component from the nutritive value of food. Sauces are the one food aimed exclusively at adding interest, variety, and enjoyment to the nutritive value of whatever they are poured over. Their almost complete absence from American cooking is highly significant, the more so because sauces also hide the inferior quality or lack of freshness of what they are added to, and we do skimp on quality and freshness. Indeed, indices of the quality and freshness of the raw materials of cooking are our best available statistical index of the weight consumers attach to the pleasure component in food.

Vegetables, for example, taste much better fresh or frozen than canned or dried. The proportion, therefore, of fresh and frozen vegetables in the total of all vegetables consumed is a good indication of the cook's, and, ultimately, the consumer's, concern with their enjoyment and of his or her willingness to pay more money for it, or spend more time and effort on its preparation. The data show that the U.S. consumer buys only two-thirds of his vegetables, measured in terms of net weight, fresh or frozen, in contrast to the western European's three-fourths.

With fruit, which is best eaten raw, the dividing line is more appropriately drawn between fresh fruit on the one hand and all processed fruit (frozen, canned, dried, and juiced) on the other. Again, we buy 62 per cent of our fruit fresh, as against the western European's 87 per cent.

In the case of meat, the data do not separate the fresh from the frozen, and smoked sausage and meat are valued for their distinctive taste. Accordingly, the appropriate dividing line seems to be between fresh, frozen, and smoked meat on the one side and commercially ground meat, sausage meat, and sausage on the other. The U.S. proportion of fresh, frozen, and smoked meat in total meat consumption is two-thirds, compared to western Europe's nine-tenths. That tremendous difference is

Quality of Food (mid-1960's). Percentage of High-Quality Variants in Total Consumed

	Fresh fruit in all fruit consumed	Fresh and frozen vegetables in all vegetables consumed	Butter as a proportion of butter and margarine consumed	Fresh, frozen and smoked meat in all meat consumed [a]
Italy	97.9	76.7	99.9	93.9
France	93.3	79.4	84.7	94.7
Belgium	89.6	80.8	51.9	86.6
Sweden [b]	87.3	82.5	46.2	76.3
German Fed. Rep.	87.2	81.6	46.0	92.7
Netherlands	80.9	72.2	10.8	84.6
U.K.	72.8	72.5	67.8	(90.4) [c]
Weighted average for above countries	87.2	77.6	68.6	90.5
U.S.A.	62.0	67.4	34.0	66.0

[a] Excluded are ground meat, fresh sausage, and sausage meat.

[b] Swedish percentages are in value terms.

[c] Probably an overestimate: does not exclude ground meat, for which data are unavailable.

SOURCES:

Italy, France, Belgium, Germany, Netherlands: *Budgets Familiaux 1963/64*, Office Statistique des Communautés Européennes, Bruxelles, 1966, Série Spéciale 2, 3, 4, 5, 6.

U.K.: *Household Food Consumption and Expenditure: 1969*, Table 9, pp. 49–51, Ministry of Agriculture, Fisheries and Food, London: HMSO, 1971.

Sweden: *The Family Expenditure Survey 1969, Preliminary Results.* Meddelande No. P 1971:9, Stockholm: National Central Bureau of Statistics, 1971.

U.S.A.: *Food Consumption of Households in the United States, Spring 1965.* Household Food Consumption Survey 1965–66, Report No. 7, U.S.D.A. Research Service, 1968. Data on meat from private communication of Dr. T. Kreiling.

partly explained by our willingness to consume unimproved, in the shape of hamburgers, all the inferior cuts of meat, which others dress up with sauces and garnishes to offset or hide their inferiority.

A similar quality difference also exists between butter and margarine; here again, our butter consumption is 34 per cent of the consumption of all table spreads, as against western Europe's 68 per cent.[6] The full details of these data, together with their sources, are shown in Table 10.

For coffee, the corresponding data (sales of coffee beans as a proportion of total sales) are not available, but since pre-ground coffee loses so much of its aroma that no one can tell the quality of the bean that went into it, the processors of vacuum-packed ground coffee use inferior mixtures; and we seem to be rather special in drinking these. That shows up clearly in the statistics. Valued wholesale at world-market prices, the mixture we drink is 6 per cent cheaper than the average coffee of both eastern and western Europeans; it is 20 per cent cheaper than what the Swedes and the West Germans drink. Only Italian espresso is poor man's coffee, better roasted and freshly made, but from a mixture cheaper than ours.[7]

Surprising as they might seem at first, these data merely confirm the common knowledge and anecdotal evidence that we Americans are less interested in the pleasures of food than are western Europeans. We probably do not spend less on food (in absolute terms) than they do, nor need our diet be inferior to theirs in any sense other than that of taste. After all, we pay a lot of attention to nutritional values and to having a balanced diet; and our meat consumption is significantly higher than Europe's. At the same time, it would be false to attribute the lesser freshness of our food to urbanization and the greater difficulties of food distribution in urban centers. For one thing, the United States is no more highly urbanized than the more industrialized European countries are; for another, informal comparisons by housewives indicate that fresh vegetables and fruit are tastier and foodstuffs are of better quality in large European (and Canadian) cities than they are in American cities of comparable size. The tastiness of fruit depends largely on its ripeness when it is picked, and this is inversely related to in-transit spoilage rates and distribution costs. Our less tasty fruit, therefore, is often also cheaper, and if our producers and distributors sacrifice quality for cheapness, they are bound to do so in response to consumers' preferences and willingness to trade quality for a saving in price.

The consumer's lack of interest in the pleasures of food can undoubtedly save him money, and it very often can save him time and effort as well. His willingness to accept canned and juiced fruits and vegetables when fresh ones are available saves him all three; and his predilection for pre-sliced bread, pre-ground coffee and spices, vanilla extract, garlic salt, dehydrated onions and potatoes, pre-cooked rice, pre-mixed powders for gravies and dressings, and pre-cooked, packaged meals is presumably motivated by a desire to save time and effort.

Indeed, the food-processing industry lives by the consumer's desire to save labor, though usually it also profits by using artificial flavors, inferior raw materials, and cheap fillers. To avoid them is only a matter of cost; the fact that the cheaper and inferior variants survive best in this highly competitive market is again proof of the consumer's willingness to sacrifice flavor in order to save expense. For the better tasting, more expensive, processed foods (cheeses, jams, canned meats, beers) we rely largely on imports—presumably because our demand for these "fancy foods" is not large enough or not discriminating enough to warrant their domestic production. Given the excellence of our raw materials and the superior efficiency and knowhow of our food-processing industries, it is hard to imagine any other reason.

Most of our labor-saving preparations and processed foods contribute to taking the interest, variety, subtlety, and enjoyment out of our diet, and their effects, of course, are cumulative. One should expect them to have corresponding and similarly cumulative effects also in saving time, but the data, surprisingly enough, do not quite bear that out.

The internationally comparable time budgets of 1966 show that the average American spends 69.8 minutes a day at meals, almost a half-hour less than the 96.1 minute average of the western European. That difference is perhaps the most tangible and quantitative evidence of our lesser interest in food and lesser enjoyment of it. A historian of technology explained it by the preponderance in the American diet of foods processed to eliminate the effort of chewing, such as hamburgers (30 per cent of all meat consumed), juiced and diced fruit (31 per cent of all fruit), milkshakes, cole slaw, chopped sandwich spreads, and bread with "the resiliency of a rubber sponge, [which] is half masticated before reaching the mouth" (55 per cent of all bread),[8] but his theory does not contradict my interpretation.

Processed foods, however, are supposed to save not eating time, but preparation time, and such savings hardly show up at all in the time budgets. Americans spend 44.1 minutes a day on average in preparing meals; that is a mere 1.4 minutes less than is needed by the gourmet French, who would not touch a premixed, bottled salad dressing with a ten-foot pole, and only 5.8 minutes less than the western European average of 49.9 minutes daily. If one corrected for the greater frequency with which Americans eat out at restaurants, there would be no difference at all in time spent preparing meals.[9] In view of our great reliance on ready-to-eat and almost ready-to-eat foods, this is very puzzling. Could the explanation be that here again the consumer saves more time than he or she can put to good use, and that time saved in the kitchen is mostly also wasted there?

VACATIONS

After food, recreation is the main item of expenditure and area of human activity to look at in search of data which reflect consumers' preferences between stimulus and comfort. Much recreational expenditure buys comfort rather than stimulus; also, almost two-thirds of the expenditure so classified is spent not on recreation, but on durable goods used in recreation. For both these reasons, the statistics of total expenditure on recreation and entertainment, as defined and reported by the United Nations Statistical Office, are not very useful for our purposes, although they do show that we devote a smaller proportion of our total consumption expenditure to it than do western Europeans (see Table 11). For meaningful data, one must look at the detail.

Vacationing is probably the most clearly stimulating form of recreation. Whether used as an occasion for sightseeing, active sports, getting an extra dose of nature, catching up with our reading, exposing ourselves to some unusual entertainment, or simply getting out of our accustomed routines and doing some-

TABLE 11

Expenditure on Recreation and Entertainment, 1968

Country	Total consumers' expenditure [a]	Recreation and entertainment expenditure	
	(IN BILLIONS OF NATIONAL CURRENCY)		(AS % OF TOTAL EXPENDITURE)
Sweden	73.100	6.600	9.0
France	380.400	32.700	8.6
Belgium	657.700	54.700	8.3
Italy	29,740.000	2,404.000	8.1
Norway	34.727	2.758	8.0
W. Germany	297.300	23.400	7.9
Great Britain	27.020	2.088	7.7
Netherlands	51.240	3.110	6.1
United States	538.900	30.000	5.6
Canada	40.987	1.879	4.6
Luxembourg	23.446	.971	4.1

[a] Consumption of households and private non-profit institutions.

SOURCE: *Yearbook of National Accounts Statistics, 1969*, United Nations, pp. 220, 231.

thing different, vacations are clearly a source of stimulation in the truest and best sense of the term. Fortunately, there are many good and nearly comparable statistics on the subject.

Large-scale, official sample surveys of vacation travel are available in France for 1969, in the United States for 1972. They show that the number of "person trips" described as vacations was, expressed as a proportion of the population, 67.8 per cent in France and 54.0 per cent in the United States for vacations of at least three nights' or four days' duration. For vacations of at least six nights' or seven days' duration, the figures are 60.8 per cent for France, 30.25 per cent for the United States. The average duration of vacations was 20.24 days in France, 8.95 nights in the United States.[10]

The difference between the two countries is very great, and we find a similar difference when we extend the comparison to all of western Europe. Small, private sample surveys conducted in 1967 in all the western European countries show the proportion of the adult population taking vacations of six days or more away from home. Those figures differ from the United States data, available for the same year, in that they relate to adult instead of total population, count the number of persons taking trips instead of the number of person trips, and use six days instead of the longer six nights as the cut-off point, so they are not strictly comparable. However, by interpolating and using the very detailed 1969 French data for estimating correction factors, we can adjust the U.S. Census data for these definitional differences to obtain an estimate of the percentage of the U. S. adult population in America taking vacations of six days and longer, and that estimate is fully comparable with the western European data. All these are shown in Table 12.

It is evident from the United States National Travel Survey that vacation travel is a function of income: the higher the income group, the greater the proportion of people who go vacationing. The European data imply the same thing; they show a higher percentage of people vacationing in the rich than in the poor countries. It is the more striking, therefore, that the United

TABLE 12
Vacations, 1967

Country	Percentage of adult population taking vacations of six days or more
Sweden	66
Great Britain	64
Switzerland	62
Netherlands	59
Denmark	54
Norway	51
France	49
Luxembourg	47
Austria	41
West Germany	38
Belgium	37
Ireland (Rep.)	36
Finland	35
Spain	32
Italy	28
Portugal	27
Weighted average of above countries	44
United States	27.7 [a]

[a] My estimate, based on Census data.

SOURCES:
European data from *Survey of Europe Today*, Table 42, p. 139.
U.S. data from *1967 Census of Transportation*, Vol. 1, *National Travel Survey*, Table 8, p. 25.

States, perhaps the richest country of them all, should have a very much lower percentage of vacationers than western Europe as a whole does, and that it should rank with the poorest of the western European countries.

The explanation we first think of, the fact that we have much shorter paid vacations in America than people in Europe do, is no explanation at all. Paid vacations are one of many fringe benefits negotiated between employers and unions; if ours are less generous than those given in other countries, the reason is not the American employers' lesser generosity, but the American employees' lesser interest in this particular fringe benefit. Also, the median length of adult Americans' vacations away from home is less than four nights—far shorter than the shortest of paid vacations.

Indeed, it is often said that Americans, rather than wanting to take proper vacations, prefer to go away for several extended long weekends instead. But even if we assume that two extended weekends of three to five nights are the equivalent of one vacation of six nights or more, we can only add 11 percentage points to the U.S. figure, which is not enough to bring it up to par with the European average, and quite inadmissible, of course, because it leaves out of account the Europeans' extended weekends, of which we have no documentation. It seems, therefore, that we must accept the difference between our and other countries' vacation habits as the reflection of a true difference in preferences.

Vacations involve costs in the sense of discomforts, which may weigh more heavily with us than they do with other people. The austerity of summer housing, the noise of hotel rooms, the discomfort of unfamiliar beds and baths, the hazards of restaurant food, the crowding of resorts and beaches, the greater exposure to the vagaries of the weather, and the danger of mail going astray or a reservation not being honored are all discomforts which some people are less willing to undergo than others are. Our favorite form of vacation is camping, but our habit of roughing it in air-conditioned trailers, surrounded by all the gadgetry of modern comfort from electric toilets to portable refrigerators, shows our unwillingness to pay anything but money for the exhilaration of the great outdoors.

The evidence of the vacation statistics is confirmed and reinforced by data on other forms of recreation. The 7.9 minutes a day we spend on average in walking, hiking, playing outdoors, and engaging in active sports is less than a third of the 28.5 minutes a day western Europeans devote to those activities, and the disparity is even greater in the time we (3.3 minutes) and they (16.8 minutes) devote to gardening and pets. Visits to cafés and pubs take up 2.7 minutes of our day, 7 minutes of theirs; we spend 0.6 minutes a day in theaters and museums, less than a half of the 1.4 minutes they spend.[11] All these are instances of the individual's taking the initiative to expose himself to physical or mental stimulation, and in all these cases we take such initiative much less often or for much shorter periods than do western Europeans.

COMPANY

Much of man's mental stimulation comes from contact with others, and it is here that the time-budget data show the most striking differences. The average time Americans spend alone while awake (6.6 hours a day) exceeds by 2.5 hours, or more than 50 per cent, the western Europeans' time (4.1 hours a day) so spent,[12] and our tendency to keep to ourselves seems to cut across most of our activities. In the United States, employed married people with children are alone 44 per cent of the time they watch the mass media, compared to 21 per cent of the time in Western Europe,[13] and the ratio of their total free time spent alone to the time spent with their families is 34 per cent in the United States as against 18 per cent in Western Europe.[14]

Of the 2.5 extra hours a day we spend alone, fully half is due to the much longer *worktime* we spend alone (2.4 hours a day) than do western Europeans (1.1 hours a day).[15] This result seems to have upset the authors of the international time-budget comparisons, who went out of their way to make sure that every question they asked was understood and interpreted in the same way in the different countries and languages. For this very great disparity in the time spent alone while at work is virtually certain to reflect, at least in part, a difference between the Americans' and the Europeans' way of looking at essentially similar work situations. "The American office worker in an area with one or two other desks, for example, might describe himself as being "alone" during extended periods when the occupants of the room were all privately engrossed in their separate endeavors, . . . whereas workers [in other countries] tended more often to note the physical presence of co-workers." [16]

That is probably a correct explanation, but the difference between the American and European interpretations of the same objective situation is itself significant. Many office and factory workers who held, or were able to observe, similar jobs in Europe and America have commented on the Americans' greater concentration on their work and the Europeans' more easy-going, socializing attitude. Where French office workers go around to shake hands and exchange greetings with all their colleagues on arrival and departure every day, in addition to having many chats and friendly exchanges in between, their American counterparts do not even say good morning to a colleague already engaged in work for fear of disturbing him. The difference, probably, lies more in the workers' attitude than in the discipline imposed from above; it is proverbial, and great enough fully to exonerate the authors of the time-budget comparisons of negligence in the phrasing and translating of their questions.

A striking confirmation of our great tendency to keep to ourselves is the migration of the aged. Most people in most countries stay put on retirement because they want to be near their friends, relatives, acquaintances and former colleagues, whose company they want and cherish all the more when the routine of human contacts of their profession and workplace are disrupted. We do the very opposite. Many retired Americans move to a milder climate in California, Florida, or Mexico, others buy a camper or trailer and spend months, even years, moving from one trailer camp to another, and still others buy themselves into retirement homes, apparently willing to relinquish the company of all those they spent their active life with, whether as daily gossips or nodding acquaintances. The implication of that choice is that their human contacts were either not too numerous, or not very strong, or not very precious. We are much more mobile, of course, socially and geographically, than most societies (see p. 202, below); and our great mobility during our active life keeps us from forming the strong friendships which bind others to their home towns. Whatever the reason, the foot-looseness of the American aged confirms the statistics on our lack of company.

A very different source of stimulation is the physical environment of one's home and its furnishings. Its importance for man's well-being is well attested,[17] but its great dependence on durable goods makes any appraisal of the attention and expenditures we devote to it difficult. The only non-durable things we put into creating an attractive home environment are flowers, which are especially important because they are an unskilled input, require continuous attention, and provide continuous change and novelty. Data on consumers' expenditure on fresh flowers are available in many countries, but we cannot make them fully comparable. For one thing, we lack comparative price data; for another, one-quarter of all United States purchases at the florist's are destined for the garden, while in Europe the overlap between nursery and florist seems smaller and one-family gardens (like one-family houses) are rarer. Also, 10 per cent of the flowers we buy we give to someone in a hospital, and a correction should perhaps also be made for the higher incidence of our hospital stay occasioned by our much higher demand for surgery. None of these corrections is possible, but all of them seem to call for a downward revision of the United States figure. The reader should bear this in mind when he looks at the uncorrected figures of Table 13. They show that we spend on flowers a much smaller proportion of our income than all others do and a smaller sum of money than most others do. Correcting the data would, presumably, make the disparity greater.

A CONFLICT

The data just cited were small in number but fairly varied and representative; they clearly showed the average American's

TABLE 13

Consumption of Cut Flowers and Potted Plants, 1970
[in Fleurins [a] (Swiss Francs)]

	Denmark	Norway	West Germany	Belgium/ Luxembourg	Netherlands	Italy	U.K.	Weighted Average of European Countries Listed	U.S.
Total expenditure on flowers—retail (in millions)	318.9	193.4	3,139.1	393.6	491.3	1,205.5	597.0		6,922
Expenditure on flowers as per cent of national income	0.63%	0.54%	0.50%	0.44%	0.44%	0.37%	0.15%	0.39%	0.20%
Per capita expenditure on flowers	64.8	49.9	51.6	39.4	37.7	22.7	10.0	31.2	33.8

[a] The Swiss franc, under the name fleurin, is used as the unit of account when paying for flowers sent by wire from one European country to another. In 1970 it was worth 23 U.S. cents.

SOURCES:
European data from Verband des Deutschen Blumen Gross- und Importhandels, "Der Verbrauch an Schnittblumen und Topfpflanzen in einigen Westeuropäischen Ländern" [mimeographed]. These data were obtained by adjusting domestic production at wholesale value for exports and imports and adding an estimated retail margin to the figures so obtained.
U.S. data from U.S.D.A Marketing Economics Division, Economic Research Service, *Report No. 855* (1971) and *U.S.D.A. Agricultural Statistics,* 1971, p. 268.

lesser indulgence in stimulus enjoyment than the average western European's. What is the significance of that difference?

Individual differences in tastes exist and are often great; it is only natural to expect there to be national differences in tastes as well. Why should they not account for the differences just discussed? And why do I claim that America's life-style and consumption pattern are biased and in need of special explanation? In Chapter Two we came across differences in behavior that could be explained by differences in personality; and I noted that personalities can be, perhaps not yet measured, but certainly ordered according to average arousal levels. Every country has many different personalities among its inhabitants, but the frequencies with which different personalities occur differ from country to country and cause the average personality to differ also. Such national differences in average personality, and in the average personality's average arousal level, are the basis of an attempt, made by Professor R. Lynn, to explain national differences in behavior by national differences in personality.

From various indices of personality, Lynn pieced together a ranking of eighteen countries and correlated it with the same eighteen countries' ranking on a variety of measures of behavior and of outcomes of behavior. The most obvious measure is the per capita consumption of stimulants and depressants, since one would expect low-arousal people to be heavy consumers of stimulants and light consumers of depressants and high-arousal people to have the opposite consumption pattern. That expectation was fully borne out. The rank correlation coefficent, ρ, measures the similarity of two rankings and ranges from $+1$ for identical ranking to -1 for perfect inverse ranking. Its value for the correlation of national personality with the consumption of tobacco was -0.83, with the consumption of caffeine (coffee and tea) -0.81, and with alcoholism $+0.59$ –the last slightly lower but significant at the 5 per cent level.[18]

Lynn also correlated with the country rankings such other indices of behavior and outcomes of behavior as hospitalized mental illness ($\rho = -0.80$), motor vehicle accident deaths

(ρ = +0.62), deaths from coronary heart disease (ρ = −0.63), economic growth rates (ρ = +0.67), suicide rates (ρ = +0.41), calorie intake (ρ = −0.30), and so on, and he cited the other evidence that made him expect these correlations.[19] His results strengthen our belief that there are meaningful national differences in personality, differences great enough that we can predict behavior on their basis. His attempt to trace back the origin of such differences in personality to climate and racial composition has been less successful, but the concept is useful even if not fully explained. In view, then, of the existence and quantifiability of national differences in personality, why do we need to explain divergent tastes between Americans and western Europeans as far as diet, vacations, physical and mental stimulation are concerned? The answer is simple. Our national character may differ from those of other nations, and we may be expected, therefore, to behave differently from others in accordance with our different national character; but all our national peculiarities discussed in previous sections of this chapter happen, with one partial exception, to be out of character.

It is true that measurements of personality are far from accurate, and Lynn's ranking of countries by arousal or anxiety levels is not even unique. But the differences between his and other authors' measurements and rankings are slight. Great Britain, America, Norway, and New Zealand are always at the low arousal end of the scale, and Japan, West Germany, Austria, France, and Italy are always at the opposite end. We Americans, as a non-anxious, hard-to-arouse, extrovert people, live up fully to the psychologists' expectations with our high consumption of stimulants, low consumption of depressants, low incidence of suicides—which are mostly committed by the anxious—and equally low incidence of automobile accidents, which are also blamed on anxious people because of their greater aggressiveness and poorer muscular control. All the data referred to are, of course, relative to corresponding data in other countries.

Since both psychotic depression and chronic schizophrenia

are forms of pathologically low arousal, their incidence is likely to be high in populations whose average arousal is low, and the high United States rate of hospitalized mental illness bears out that expectation. Similarly, high arousal inhibits the appetite while low arousal enhances it, and we rank high among nations in our calorie intake.

Sexual activity is another form of behavior inhibited by high and enhanced by low arousal, but the only statistic available for all of Lynn's eighteen countries, the percentage of single men and women in the population, is a poor index of sexual activity—no wonder the correlation coefficient he obtained, though different from zero and of the correct sign, is statistically insignificant (+0.30 for men and +0.28 for women).[20]

Detailed sample surveys of sexual behavior seem to be available only for the United States and for unmarried university students in Great Britain and Western Germany. Data for the latter two countries include a rating of the subjects on an extroversion-introversion scale, and so provide a statistical verification of differences in behavior motivated by differences in personality. If one then compares the average behavior of all the German males with that of all the U.S. males in the corresponding educational, marital-status, and age group of the Kinsey Report, one finds that differences between Americans and Germans are very similar to those between extrovert Germans and introvert Germans. For example, our first coital experience is earlier, frequency of coitus higher, and frequency of masturbation lower than is the Germans'.[21]

It seems, therefore, that national differences in personality have good predictive power for behavior that is governed by strong physiological and psychological drives. But how about all the many other aspects of behavior which are less visceral? Personality probably has some influence on everything, and predictions based on it are not wanting. To quote a well-known writer on the subject, "Extraverts move their homes more frequently, they change their jobs more frequently, . . . We can now understand the very obvious pressure of extraverts for novelty, for change, for alternation; . . . the regular, the usual, the ordinary becomes anathema, and the search is on for new stimuli as well as for strong stimuli." [22] Here again, statistics clearly confirm that "labour turnover in North American manufacturing is significantly higher than in the European countries studied" (France, Germany, and the U.K.),[23] and a 1960 international comparison shows that in that year 20.5 per cent of the U.S. population moved to another community, as against 11.6 per cent in the U.K., 7.8 per cent in Japan, and 6.1 per cent in Western Germany.[24]

So far so good. But "the very obvious pressure of extraverts for novelty, for change, for alternation" is hardly manifest in our acceptance of dull food and drab surroundings, and our tendency to sit at home. Those aspects of behavior are subject, of course, to many influences, and, presumably, cultural, social, and economic influences go counter to the psychological ones and prevail over them. Therein lies the interest of my findings and the need and justification for discussing them further. For the conflict between our predisposition to do one thing and the outside pressures that make us do the opposite thing may well create a feeling of frustration and dissatisfaction with our own behavior.

Let me just add that I am not the first to discover and be puzzled by our incongruous behavior. When the multinational comparative time budget surveys became available, the door was thrown wide open for international comparisons, and the first ones made were published along with the surveys themselves. The authors of two of those comparisons were clearly disturbed by the way in which the U.S. data failed to fit into what seemed, to them, a normal pattern. The author of one comparison, which deals with loneliness, was so greatly puzzled by the evidence of our much greater loneliness that he questioned the reliability of the data (see pp. 195–96).

The other comparison is an econometric study of people's desire for variety in leisure pursuits and its dependence on their social and economic status. On the basis of a pilot study,

its author expected the higher strata among white-collar workers (professionals, for instance) to seek more variety than do
lower white-collar and manual workers, and Americans, because of their higher economic development, to seek more variety than do Europeans. Table 14 reproduces some of the results
and shows the average number of leisure pursuits of different
groups of men on weekdays. In Europe, social status seems to
have the influence it was supposed to have, and the better-off
western Europeans clearly make better use of their higher standard of living than the poorer eastern Europeans did, but the
U.S. data are "badly behaved" in every way. We seem to go in
for less variety than western Europeans, and our professionals
and other high ranking white-collar people are no more enterprising in their leisure hours than our unskilled workers are.
The author is baffled and does not hide her bafflement. I am
baffled too, by her data as well as by mine, which confirm hers.
The following chapters constitute my attempt to resolve the
puzzle.

TABLE 14

*The Average Number of Leisure Activities of Men on Workdays by
Country and Social Stratum*

Socio-economic groups	Belgium	France	German Fed. Rep.	Hungary	U.S.A.
high status white collar workers	5.25	4.07	3.61	3.12	3.04
low status white collar workers	4.42	3.17	3.04	2.57	2.98
skilled manual workers	4.09	2.58	2.97	2.27	2.80
unskilled manual workers	4.38 [a]	1.15 [a]	2.87	2.09	3.04 [a]

[a] The number of cases is less than 20.

SOURCE: Susan Ferge, "Social Differentiation in Leisure Activity Choices: An
Unfinished Experiment," in A. Szalai (ed.), *The Use of Time*, The Hague: Mouton,
1972, pp. 213–27.

CHAPTER TEN

Our Puritan Ghost

We have looked at a few of the more surprising features of our habits of living and patterns of expenditure, and found them the more surprising because not only do they go against what seemed rational or is appropriate to the rich, but they also go against what some psychologists consider, with some justification, to be our national temperament. If that is true, there must be strong influences at work to make us go against rationality and temperament all at the same time. I am thinking of cultural, educational, and economic forces whose cumulative effect might account for the conflict between what we want and what we get, and so explain some of our frustration. Before taking up those influences, however, I should like to dispose of one other influence which many of us might think of first: the influence of advertising.

Because advertising is so conspicuous and our expenditure on it so large, one naturally expects it to be highly effective in swaying consumer behavior. Testing its effectiveness, however, is difficult and seldom undertaken, and the most careful econometric study undertaken to date suggests that its impact on the public's expenditure pattern and consumption habits is not great.[1] Advertising seems to have much influence on brand preference but little on commodity preference, such as a preference for beer over wine or for tobacco over chewing gum. That does not exclude producers' having a strong influence on consumers' tastes; all it means is that advertising is not an important channel through which such influence is exerted.

Later I shall discuss the influence producers have on consumers' tastes, but in view of the negative evidence I will say no more on advertising. Instead, I shall turn at once to the first and most important influence to be explored: our well-known Puritan heritage and its effects on American consumers.

American puritanism goes back to the New England colonists who brought with them the philosophy of life we know as the puritan ethic. "Conscious that he is but a stranger and pilgrim, hurrying from this transitory life to a life to come, [the Puritan] turns with almost physical horror from the vanities. . . . Amusement, books, even intercourse with friends, must, if need be, be cast aside; for it is better to enter into eternal life halt and maimed than having two eyes to be cast into eternal fire." The Puritans were "an earnest, zealous, godly generation, scorning delights, punctual in labor, constant in prayer, thrifty and thriving, filled with a decent pride in themselves and their calling, assured that strenuous toil is acceptable to Heaven."[2]

The strength of these beliefs and precepts has greatly weakened over the centuries, of course, but some of that Puritan heritage remains and can be found to work its influence on our lives in two ways. First off, it tells us what to value and so affects our desires. In addition, it gives us great faith in the rightness of the values we hold, and that faith makes us impose those values on others by creating laws that curtail the production of some goods and render illegal the satisfaction of some wants. I shall deal with each of these influences in turn.

The Puritan ethic is ideally suited to sway people's preferences against stimulation and in favor of comfort. Puritans are against pleasure, but will allow, if somewhat grudgingly, the legitimacy of consumption necessary for a healthy and productive life. Pleasure, of course, accompanies the process of satisfying any need, however simple and biologically determined. Puritans are ready to accept, even to approve of, the "simple pleasures" that accompany the filling of simple needs, as long as they are not deliberately and artifically enhanced by the use of sophisticated techniques, in cooking, lovemaking, decorating, and so on. In other words, the Puritan disapproval and distrust of pleasure is not against all enjoyment, but only against activity and expenditure specifically and exclusively aimed at providing or enhancing enjoyment. The distinction is very similar to the one we made earlier between comfort and stimulation; it accounts for the early American disapproval of sports and theater, and it illuminates many features and aspects of our present-day behavior.

THE MORAL SUPERIORITY OF PRODUCTION AND MONEY-MAKING

When we divide man's activities and problems into those connected with production and those concerned with consumption, we find that in America the former are almost always considered more important and more serious than the latter. The high prestige we attach to all things having to do with production and the making of money is easy to explain in terms of the Puritan ethic, hard to explain in terms of anything else. The frugality and worldly asceticism of puritanism, its disapproval of spending on superfluities, cultural goods, and just about anything beyond the necessities of a plain and sober life, could not have been better calculated to deprive of prestige the task of housekeeping and the spending of money, along with cultural interests, aesthetic values, and all concern with the enjoyment of the good things of life. All these appear as unimportant, or at least as the less serious side of life. The more serious side of life is production, the creation of market value, one's contribution to production, and the earning of income in the process.

Originally, the Puritan ethic stressed the virtues of hard work and the diligent pursuit of one's calling, and it held out the rewards appropriate to these virtues—pride of craftsmanship and the recognition due to a man who does well in his calling. These values may have made sense in the craft society of the eighteenth century, because work was then an important source of satisfaction. The Puritan prescription—get satisfaction from work and rely on consumption merely to provide the necessaries and comforts of life—was probably attainable in the circumstances of the time.[3]

Since then, capitalist development has made most Puritan virtues meaningless. The very concept of a calling has lost its meaning today; only artists, writers, professional people, and members of a few remaining craft occupations still get satisfaction out of their work or feel responsible for and proud of what they produce. The majority of mankind has been alienated from its product. That must have been especially hard on the puritan countries, whose populations were indoctrinated to seek the main satisfactions of life in work at almost the same time that the Industrial Revolution took the satisfaction out of work. Practically every innovation that raised productivity and contributed to economic development did so by removing one more need to exercise human skill—and one more opportunity to derive satisfaction from its exercise.

We still retain some of the values of the craft society, but in a much attenuated and symbolic form. When profits or earnings are all a man has to show for his work, he transfers to them his pride of achievement and regards them as the symbol and measure of society's appreciation of what he does for society. Such was the interpretation the Puritan ethic put on money income, and it has been reinforced by the economist's theory of the competitive market, which holds that the market price of a man's services reflects the value of his marginal contribution to the national product. We use money not only as a medium of exchange, but also as the measuring rod of a man's worth, and we value income not only for the goods it will buy, but also as the proof of our usefulness to society. Being useful to society is

a source of satisfaction and comfort; money income is a token of
such usefulness and therefore becomes itself a source of satisfaction and comfort.

Here, then, is the moral basis of the higher place accorded to
money-making and production than to consumption. To produce goods or contribute to their production is to cater to market demand and so to perform services to others. Services to
others are services to society; it is natural to place a higher
ethical value on them than on selfish preoccupation with one's
family's welfare, which is what consumption activities are.
Hence people's concern with maximizing money income rather
than with getting satisfaction from the goods and services
bought with that income.

That system of priorities also has a counterpart on the collec-
tive level of public expenditure on public policies. We lag and
always have lagged far behind the European countries in welfare legislation that provides the disadvantaged with a minimum of consumption and brings the enjoyment of life within
their reach; but, until not long ago, we used to be far ahead of
them in providing free education which would enable everybody to learn to make a maximum contribution to production.[4]

Goods produced and services rendered to benefit others acquire monetary value as they pass through the market on their
way to the person they finally benefit, whereas services rendered to oneself or one's family are seldom valued in terms of
money. The distinction is similar to the one between production and consumption, and it accounts for the higher value customarily attributed to values expressed in money than to those
not so expressed. In short, the primacy of production over consumption, of monetary over non-monetary values, are both
manifestations of the moral judgment which sets service bene-
fiting others ahead of concern for oneself.

The lofty plane on which our money-mindedness originated
must not blind us to the wrongs and absurdities to which it
often leads. We welcome and consider progressive every technical innovation, every change in commodities and in ways of

doing things, which saves money, time, or effort, whatever the loss of quality or other non-monetary and non-measurable cost, manifest only to our eyes, ears, and senses of taste and smell. For generations we have ignored or belittled the nuisance value of the dirt, soot, fumes, and ugliness generated in the process of creating marketable products and monetary wealth—presumably on the ground that such non-monetary side effects of production are too frivolous and unimportant to be worth bothering about, let alone weighing against the cash value of its output. The poverty of such thinking has now become obvious, but it took the accumulation of many decades of filth around us to expose it, and even today, when government is actively trying to make us pollution-conscious, our Puritan money-mindedness still makes us close our eyes, ears, and noses to all forms of pollution which are merely unpleasant and reduce welfare without demonstrably causing illness, shortening lives, and reducing productivity.

We might justify such money-mindedness by arguing that whereas the benefits accrue to the person directly involved, the undesirable side effects are dispersed over so many people that they can safely be ignored. But that argument does not ring true. For one thing, we are far from being a selfish people; we have demonstrated our generosity and concern for other people's welfare in countless ways. For another, we show the same disregard for non-monetary costs and mere nuisance even when we ourselves bear the brunt.

An obvious example is noise pollution. The loudness, and so, presumably, the unpleasantness of noise declines by some factor between the square and the cube of the distance of its source. The person most exposed to the noise of power-driven saws, lawnmowers, and all the many other power tools is the user himself. Curiously, he seldom minds when the noise is of his own making. He seems to believe that the saving of time and effort outweighs the nuisance value of the noise—even when he has no better use for the time saved, when the many gadgets around him already save more effort than is good for him to save, or when the time saved benefits his employer, not him. Sometimes he seems even to enjoy the noise, perhaps as a symbol of progress and of the harnessing of mechanical power in the service of man, for whose sake a little discomfort, a mere assault on our senses should be well worth enduring. A recent survey showed that construction workers are notably unenthusiastic, even diffident, about attempts to make compressed-air construction tools quieter.

Noise abatement in cities, which has been standard policy for decades in many parts of Europe, has hardly begun in the United States—and, puritanically enough, it started only when it was discovered that noise is not merely unpleasant and grating on the nerves, but can actually impair hearing. Our general policy toward pollution is to leave it alone when it merely offends the senses and to do something only when it is proven to harm our health.

Our tendency to ignore the non-monetary costs of the production of monetary values is fully matched by our neglect of non-monetary benefits. That neglect inclines us to scoff at the value systems of other civilizations by belittling what they call "the higher things in life."

America's work ethic puts the earning of money ahead of the enjoyment of life. Every comparison of European and American work habits, among businessmen, professional people, administrative employees, and factory workers alike, shows that no matter whether we are driven by bosses or by internal compulsion, we always work harder, more persistently, more singlemindedly, and at a more relentless pace than the Europeans do. Our very much higher labor productivity, as shown by all the international comparisons, is one result of this difference;[5] another result may well be our greater need for rest after work, Everybody, when exhausted, puts comfort ahead of stimulation.

The way we seek status is also colored by puritanism. Some forms of status seeking benefit society, others do not; some appear noble, others seem objectionable. And paradoxically enough, our Puritan spirit often makes us choose the less beneficial and less noble forms. The reason is that the importance we attach to money income encourages us to identify status with conspicuous consumption rather than with ability to please. We want the kind of consumption that shows off high income, not the kind that exhibits high skill in obtaining or providing satisfaction from income.

Whereas the average European seeks status by showing off his expertise as consumer, displaying his knowledge of good but obscure and cheap restaurants, or demonstrating his ability to provide pleasant entertainment through unexpected and simple means, we Americans are more inclined to go in for austere ostentation, displaying our ability to spend a lot of money on goods distinguished from their cheaper counterparts mainly by their conspicuous expensiveness. In that way we maintain our puritanical disdain for the frivolous matter of consumption, as if it were not dignified to aim at getting the lowest price, let alone to display skill at doing it.

The same Puritan mentality is manifest in the way in which members of our counterculture seek status. They want to establish their rejection of the dominant culture and their membership in the counterculture at the same time, and they accomplish the feat by means of uniform grooming and dress which asserts their solidarity and appalls the Establishment. The western European young do very much the same thing, but with an important difference. They dress and do their hair in the same style and with the same calculated-to-outrage eccentricity as our young, yet they usually manage to add a dash of elegance and style in order to please their own·generation.

One more manifestation of a Puritan attitude is not bothering to dress up or take hair curlers out before going to a public place. I use this example to illustrate our excessive saving of the care others lavish on their appearance, perhaps as a means of seeking status in being easy on the eyes of their fellow men. But that is not our way of seeking status. Indeed, we have a puritanical distrust of all artifice aimed merely to enhance enjoyment.

Our dislike of dressing up in formal clothes for concert or theater is not unlike our dislike of dressing up food with sauces. Both seem impure and dishonest. We want the meat to be honest, not merely to taste good, the music to be enjoyed for itself, not for its trappings, and we want to be liked for ourselves, not for the good impression our clothes help us to make. Such preferences deny man's satisfaction as the primary aim—understandable enough in puritanism, an ethical system of religious origin. But if our main concern were to enjoy the taste of food, the sound of music, and our ability to please others, then anything we could do to increase that enjoyment would be desirable and legitimate, even including a mere change in appearances.

THE NEGLECT OF HOUSEKEEPING

It is strange that in our society, where people work so hard, and work for income, not for the fun of it, we should be so negligent in spending that hard-earned income. From the economist's point of view all economic activity aims at providing, assuring, or facilitating consumer satisfaction, now or later. Producing to earn income and spending that income are acts with the same aim: consumer satisfaction. And they stand in a peculiar relation to that aim in that neither can further it without cooperation from the other. Without production to generate earnings, there is nothing to spend on, and without consumer demand and spending, our profit motivated economy will not produce. That explains why a puritanical disdain for spending and consumption can impede production. No more output can be produced than consumers are willing to buy, and what is produced is neither better in quality nor more suited to consumers' wants than what they themselves are able and ready—if necessary, with expert help—to judge and to demand.

The Keynesian revolution was needed to make economists and the public recognize and accept the truth of the first part of the above statement. Thanks to Keynes we are now aware of the crucial importance of adequate effective demand to call forth the production of output, the utilization of capacity, and the employment of labor. The second part of the statement—that the nature and quality of output depend on the buyer's discernment and insistence on getting what he wants—is no less true, but its truth has yet to be established and generally recognized. It was glimpsed sixty years ago by Wesley Mitchell, the grand old man of American economics, when he complained about the backwardness of the art of spending money and deplored the "poor cooking and slipshod shopping" that went with it.[6] Noting the tradition that assigns the job to women, he asked if this might not explain the shoddy way in which it is performed. That was a preposterous question to ask, even in jest and even by the male chauvinist standards of his time; yet Mitchell was probably right in sensing a connection, except that he had causality run the wrong way around. A puritanical society, which looks up to the earning and down upon the spending of money, is apt to transfer the same hierarchy of values to the traditional practitioners of the two functions, looking up to men and down upon women. That would explain why the women's liberation movement started in the United States and has always been strongest here and in Protestant countries.[7] Since women, like men, have a Puritan hierarchy of values, their liberation movement is a fight not only for women's right to enter man's domain, but also for abandoning woman's. Both sexes want to concentrate on making money and are prepared to let housekeeping become no-person's-land and allow its skills and the skills of consumption fall by the wayside.

Mitchell did stress the much greater difficulty of the housewife's task of maximizing consumer satisfaction than her husband's task of maximizing income. That is important and will be discussed at length later, but it does not explain why we should be worse at it than are others, who, after all, face exactly the same difficulty. Yet, there is plenty of evidence to show that we are worse, some of which I cited when I discussed our happy-go-lucky attitude toward shopping and documented its effects.

The market is the place and shopping the occasion when producer and consumer, seller and buyer, can match wits on equal terms, aware that their interests conflict and that one party's gain is necessarily the other's loss. Although disparity in numbers and scales of operation give sellers the formal advantage of being able to set their prices and deal on a take-it-or-leave-it basis, competition among them enables buyers to regain much of the advantage so lost—if they bring discernment, intelligence, and determination to their shopping. In most societies, the majority of consumers never lose sight of this fact. They stand on their rights, are careful, choosy, critical, suspicious, aggressive, always on their guard when facing a seller, thus assuring that competitiveness which has such a beneficial effect on sellers' behavior.

I attributed such behavior on the part of Europeans to their acting on the supposedly "moral" principle of defending "consumers' rights," and our very different American attitude to our rationality, at least in the narrow sense of individual rationality. But is that a true and objective view? Might it not be colored by my bias, which would naturally make our own behavior appear to be more rational than other people's behavior?

American consumers are good-natured and easygoing. We find it embarrassing to bargain or even to engage openly in comparison shopping; we are ready to trust the seller's expert advice and to forget the natural conflict between his interests and our own; we are reluctant to make a fuss over minor blemishes and are willing politely to accept, sometimes even to praise, a badly cooked meal in a restaurant. Such behavior undoubtedly saves time and temper, both of which are valuable, and since they are worth more money to the rich than to the poor, it is, indeed, more rational for rich Americans to behave that way than for poor foreigners to do so.

At the same time, we do not behave at all that way in our capacity of producers and sellers. American sellers can be aggressive; automobile dealers and traveling salesmen are notoriously so. When on the selling side, we do not overlook the natural conflict between buyers' and sellers' interests, nor do we weigh the time and effort expended against the benefits gained nearly as heavily in the making of money as in the spending of it. If the passionate care Europeans bring to the art of spending seems exaggerated to us, our passionate pursuit of the dollar seems just as exaggerated to them, and, by their lights, it is in unreasonable contrast to our easygoing, happy-go-lucky attitude toward the spending of that dollar we so avidly pursue.

Who is right, or at least more nearly right? Since satisfaction cannot be measured, there is no simple way of deciding how best to allocate time, effort, and care between the making and the spending of money. But it appears that the Europeans do a better job. For whatever behavior is best from a narrow, individualistic point of view, it can be improved upon by devoting more care to shopping, given the external benefits this confers on others. In other words, the Europeans' undignified and unpuritanical obsession with getting their money's worth is very likely to bring them closer to what is best for society, even if our behavior looks better in the light of individual rationality.

PURITAN INTOLERANCE

So far I have been concerned with the subtle and intangible ways in which our Puritan attitude shines through our likes and dislikes, values and market behavior. I now come to the forcible ways of laws and regulations which curb our freedom of choice and impose the narrow path of approved behavior by turning deviant behavior into crimes, the so-called victimless or crimeless crimes.[8]

> With the possible exception of 16th century Geneva under John Calvin, America has the most moralistic criminal law that the world has yet witnessed. One area in which this moralism is most extensively reflected is that of sexual behavior. . . . As if the sex offense laws were designed to provide an enormous chastity belt encompassing the whole population and proscribing everything but solitary and joyless masturbation and "normal coitus" inside wedlock.[9]

But the bigotry and intolerance of our laws, while most glaring in the area of sex, also extend to drugs, drunkenness, loitering, gambling, and much else besides. The sheer number of victimless crimes on our law books is so great that much of such legislation remains dead letter, either unenforceable or capriciously enforced.

Even that part of our crimeless-crime legislation which is enforced diverts more than half of our law-enforcement resources from the task of exposing, punishing, and preventing crimes against persons and property. Almost half of all arrests in the United States are on charges of drunkenness, disorderly conduct, vagrancy, gambling, and minor sexual deviations (exhibitionism, voyeurism).[10] Drunkenness alone accounts for twice the combined total of all arrests for the seven most serious crimes (murder, manslaughter, forcible rape, robbery, aggravated assault, burglary, and theft) listed in the FBI's statistics of criminality.[11] One cannot even compare the data with those of other countries, because in most countries gambling, loitering, vagrancy, prostitution, and being drunk in a public place are not against the law, except when they endanger or annoy others.

The proportion of law-enforcement resources devoted to the pursuit of victimless crimes indicates a society's disregard for the principle of individual liberty. To quote John Stuart Mill's statement of it, "the only purpose for which power can be rightfully exercised over any member of a civilized community against his will is to prevent harm to others. His own good, either physical or moral, is not sufficient warrant." [12] Full observance of this principle is perhaps an unattainable ideal, but our observance, which falls short by more than 50 per cent, seems exceptionally low for a democratic country.

The illicit use of mind-altering drugs is the most important and most controversial example of victimless crimes. Prohibition of alcohol in the United States is now sufficiently remote for most people to have formed an objective judgment of its wisdom or unwisdom, and for most to have recognized the erosion of the respect for the law, the police corruption, and the encouragement of organized crime which were some of its costs and by-products. Prohibition was the assertion by rural, white, Anglo-Saxon, Protestant America of its preferences and the intolerant, if half-hearted, imposition of those preferences on the rest of the community. The attempt to impose them on our World War I allies failed fortunately.[13]

Prohibition was repealed long ago, but the moral taint on drinking and the criminal offense of drunkenness in a public place remain, as does our predilection for restricting consumers' choice through legislation in the name of morality or in that of protecting the individual from his own folly.

Very similar to Prohibition are our narcotics laws, except that in their case we did succeed in persuading other countries to help make the restriction world wide. Posterity may well judge our narcotics laws not too differently from the way in which we judge Prohibition today. For the known effects on physical and mental health and performance of the most common narcotics, opium, morphine, heroin and marijuana are very slight—such drugs are very much more benign than alcohol is. One of them, marijuana, is also much less addictive. The case, therefore, for outlawing marijuana is very much weaker than was the case for outlawing liquor. Yet our anti-marijuana legislation is extremely severe. In California, mere possession of marijuana brings a one- to ten-year prison sentence on the first offense, in Arizona, the sale of even a single cigarette is punishable by five years to life on the first offense, and in most states first-degree murder is the only crime more severely punished than the sale of marijuana. Yet the medical evidence stands unchanged. It is negative. As an index of the dangers of marijuana therefore, the severity of our laws itself constitutes a big lie—the more easily believed because of its bigness, though not less of a lie for that.[14]

More complex is the situation with opiates. Their effect on physical and mental health is also surprisingly slight—constipation and slightly reduced male potency and likelihood of pregnancy are the main effects.[15] In the nineteenth century, when their use was legal, they were widely and successfully used in medicine and as a cure for alcoholism. Since addiction is almost impossible to cure but fairly easy to transfer to another chemical substance, it was common medical practice in the United States to switch alcoholics to opium, which was cheaper, better for health, and enabled the addict to resume a normal and productive life.[16]

At the same time, the opiates are much more addictive than alcohol, and once a person becomes a narcotics addict he will stop at nothing to get his daily dose, just as a starving man will do anything for a bit of food. And since addicts seem to get no or almost no satisfaction—other than the relief of withdrawal symptoms—out of their addiction, to acquire an almost incurable life-long dependence on a narcotic for the sake of a short-lived initial period of positive satisfaction does seem a bit irrational.[17]

Yet wherever opiates are cheap and legal, and addicts are able to afford them, the personal and social harm seems negligible. This seems to have been the case in the nineteenth century, when social disapproval of addiction and the public's awareness of its incurability seem to have been sufficient to keep the number of addicts at a low level.[18] When these conditions are not fulfilled, or man's rationality cannot be trusted, the least objectionable restraint of freedom seems to be to restrict the sale of opiates and so prevent addiction, but to supply them freely to those already addicted. That is Britain's policy, and it seems to work well.[19] It is also India's policy with respect to alcohol. Our severe and uncompromising laws, combined with their poor enforcement, create the worst of all possible worlds. If addiction itself is the principal harm stemming from the use of opiates, then making that harm physically, morally, and socially painful is a very cruel way of dealing with the problem—not to mention the fact that doing so increases criminality.

The outlawing of gambling in most of the United States is another manifestation of our intolerance of life-styles unbecoming white, Anglo-Saxon Protestant Americans. The best defense of it would be exactly the same as for the opiates: the harm is the addiction. Here, however, our laws take full account of the fact that the addiction is harmless if the addict can afford it: the rich are free to gamble on the stock exchange, only the gambling of the poor is outlawed.

Interestingly enough, we do not seem to be gamblers. It is not known what percentage of people's total accumulated savings are held in the form of stock and other marketable securities in this and other countries, but data on the proportion of current savings people put into them are available. In the first half of the 1960's, when the stock exchange seemed to be a safe enough playground for rich grown-ups to play in, the proportion of our savings we put into securities was one-ninth to one-tenth of what Continental Europeans and the Japanese put into them, although we saved a smaller percentage of our incomes than they did. (Table 15 contains the detailed data.)

Many proscribed activities and satisfactions provide stimulation, and stimulation, let us remember, hinges on threat or potential threat to life. Safety and stimulus enjoyment, therefore, are often opposites and mutually incompatible. Their conflict, the need to find the best compromise between them, and differences of opinion on what is the best compromise are at the root of the problem of regulations protecting the individual from endangering his own safety.

There is an important exception to our tendency to restrict stimulation in the interests of safety. Hunting and shooting is the one sport for the sake of whose unrestricted pursuit America seems willing to endanger the lives not only of the shooters, but of everybody else. The unrestricted possession of firearms is an important cause of the danger to life and property in the jungle of American cities; and this danger, in turn, could be a contributing cause of our excessive fear of other dangers. For the effects of different stimuli on arousal are additive. If the tension of walking our unsafe streets in the everyday business of life is as much as we can bear, then we might well wish to

TABLE 15

Percentage Allocation of Household Financial Savings

		Deposits and Cash	Contractual Savings	Securities	Other	Total
Belgium	(1959–64)	46	20	34	0	100
France	(1960–65)	74	4	19	3	100
Germany	(1960–65)	54	26	20	0	100
Greece	(1959–64)	84	1	14	—	100
Italy	(1964–65)	62	11	14	13	100
Japan	(1958–64)	67	10	18	5	100
Netherlands	(1960–64)	—	42	—	58	100
Norway	(1960–65)	52	26	12	10	100
Sweden	(1960–65)	48	36	9	7	100
U.K.	(1963–65)	57	57	−21	7	100
U.S.A.	(1960–65)	70	38	2 [a]	−10	100

[a] The main reason, probably, for this very low percentage is our Anglo-Saxon habit of doing much of our saving in the form of buying a house and paying off its mortgage.

SOURCE: O.E.C.D., Committee for Invisible Transactions, *Capital Markets Study. General Report*, Paris: O.E.C.D., 1967, Table 18, p. 108.

legislate out of existence such further dangers and sources of tension as firecrackers, fast driving, swimming without a lifeguard in attendance, and so on. The idea that failure to outlaw firearms should lead to the outlawing of firecrackers in compensation may seem preposterous, but we are dealing here with the instinctive actions of a society which is impotent in the face of high crime rates, not with the statesman's rational choice between equally feasible alternatives. It is the same as loosening the clothing of a person in pain if we cannot eliminate his pain; we do the best we can under the circumstances.

If man's desire for stimulation and the excitement he can get from limited danger are blocked in too many directions by regulations and safeguards imposed by an excessively protective society, he will seek its satisfaction in areas where it is less blocked, or less effectively so, and that may well mean seeking an outlet in violence. Therefore, freedom of action, in the sense of letting everybody make his own choice between the excitement of danger and the comfort of safety, may turn out to be beneficial, not only to the individual, but to society as well.

Having dealt with the exception, the tolerance of firearms, let us return to the rule: legislation restricting sources of stimulation. Speed limits are an interesting case in point.

The number of automobile accidents and their severity increase with speed, and so does the exhilaration of speed and the enjoyment of driving. Each driver can balance safety against enjoyment as best suits his tastes; speed limits protect other people from his fast driving and him from theirs', but those limits also narrow the range within which he is free to seek his optimum satisfaction. Actual speed limits reflect our legislators' compromise between the driver's enjoyment and everybody's safety, and it is worth noting that our speed limits in the United States are quite a bit lower than those in most other countries, although our streets and highways are the widest and best designed for safe and fast driving.[20] Here is another bit of evidence of our bias in favor of safety and against stimulation.

There are many examples where harm to others is not quite so evident. Laws requiring seat belts for drivers, helmets for motorcyclists, life vests for sailors, laws and bylaws prohibiting firecrackers and swimming when no lifeguard is present, many of the "Don'ts" in National and State parks, are examples. Their sole aim is or seems to be to protect from harm the individual himself. One must bear it in mind, however, that even a person who harms only himself will often have to be rescued, patched up, nursed back to life, or buried with the aid of public services and partly or wholly at taxpayers' expense. It seems, therefore, that Mill's principle of liberty, which allows the curbing of personal freedom only in order to prevent harm to others, is not quite as unequivocal as it sounds, because the dividing line between crimes with victims and crimes without victims is not nearly as clear and simple as Mill would have us believe. Every dangerous activity is dangerous not only to the actor himself, but also to an invisible victim, the taxpayer. Should that empower the taxpayer, or the legislator on his behalf, to do what Mill cautions against—that is, protecting the individual against his own actions?

There seems to be no way out of the dilemma. We must weigh the benefits of greater individual freedom against the cost to taxpayers and judge each case on its merits. That is not easy, considering that the benefits can seldom be quantified.

But is the issue important? Two considerations make me doubt that it is. First, individual freedom versus cost to taxpayers is very much the scholar's pedantic debate; it is almost never mentioned in public discussion over such legislation, where the stress is always and only on safety. Second, virtually every case of this type I can think of takes place in the United States alone. In other countries, personal freedom is much more carefully cherished and guarded. They put out a good deal of publicity about hazards to life, limb, and health, trying to persuade and inform the individual, but they leave the final decision to him. Our intolerance makes us seek safety in coercion.

An innocuous example is the compulsory wearing of seat belts and motorcycle helmets, whose cost and inconvenience seem minor compared to the benefits. Helmets are mandatory in England, just as they are here, but in the recent general elections (1974) several candidates for Parliament ran on an Antihelmet platform, so strongly is the restraint on personal freedom resented.

More serious abridgements of personal freedom are the compulsory wearing of life vests for sailing, required in some states and supposed to take much of the fun out of sailing, and the frequent prohibition of swimming except where explicitly allowed and when lifeguards are on duty.

Two more restrictions on bathing are worth mentioning: one to protect the bathers, the other to protect the water; both are unjustified and both are further examples of our puritanical restraint on man's right to enjoy life.

To protect the bather, "it is agreed by most investigators that the bacterial quality of water for bathing need not be as high as that for drinking, but that natural bathing water should be maintained reasonably free of bacteria of known sewage origin." [21] Most advanced countries, therefore, find it necessary to test for bacterial quality and prohibit swimming where minimum standards are not met. Since bacterial quality cannot be judged by the naked eye, this makes sense—provided minimal standards are reasonable. The standard for water to be declared suitable for bathing and swimming is usually expressed as a monthly average of the maximum allowable number of coliform organisms per 100 milliliters, set at 50 in Utah and Washington, 100 in Maine, 240 in Montana and New Hampshire, and 1000 in the other states of the Union. The last figure is also the standard the U. S. Public Health Service sets for pasteurized milk. It follows that in the five States just named, the milk we (and they) drink would be considered too polluted to bathe in.

But if we may not swim in liquids not fit to drink, neither are we allowed to swim in water used for drinking. America is covered with beautiful lakes, but, since many of them are tapped for water supply, these are declared reservoirs, fenced in, and surrounded with No Swimming, No Boating, No Trespassing signs. Yet national conventions of water supply engineers discuss time and again the absurdity and lack of justification for this practice—which, incidentally, seems peculiar to the United States. They point out that all drinking water goes through filtering and purifying plants fully capable of eliminating at no extra cost all impurities recreational use would introduce into it; but such discussions usually end either with an appeal to the wisdom of leaving a venerable practice unchanged or with a reminder of an alleged old New England tradition: distaste even for the faintest suspicion of urine. [22]

CHAPTER ELEVEN

Our Disdain for Culture

Another important cultural force influencing our way of life is a bias in our education, which is likely to sway our consumption pattern in favor of comfort and against stimulus enjoyment. Measured by number of man-years of schooling per head of population, we are the world's most educated people. Are we also the best educated? The question I want to raise has to do not with the quality of our schools and colleges, but with what they prepare us *for*. Learning can have many aims; what do we try to achieve by staying in school so long? We are occasionally accused of lagging behind in culture; if we do, what does that mean in terms of our educational philosophy and the nature of our school curricula? To deal with those and related matters, we must first get a clear notion of what culture is. In Chapter Three I dealt at length with novelty as a source of stimulus and an intermediate degree of novelty as the condition that makes stimulus enjoyable. There we looked upon redundancy as something the stimulus source must provide in order to make the stimulus pleasant. But redundancy can just as well be looked upon as something the recipient's mind must contain if he is to enjoy the stimulus. We shall see that redundancy as a requirement in the recipient suggests a definition of culture.

For an art object or piece of music to be appreciated, it needs to be in or near a style or tradition we are familiar with; news and gossip to be interesting must be about people or places we know, or know about; a novel, to be enjoyable, has to deal with characters and situations that are credible and resemble those we have already encountered; a joke is funny to us only if the surprise and unexpected twist of its ending follows a familiar and unsurprising beginning. The supplier of the stimulus must see to it that he combines the new with the familiar in the right proportions, but the consumer of the stimulus cannot be completely passive either—after all, it is his education and previous knowledge that determine what is familiar to him.

Depending on their previous knowledge, different consumers are pleasantly stimulated by very different things; also, the difficulty of acquiring the skills of consumption varies greatly with the nature of the source of stimulation. The ability to enjoy a game of tennis, chess, or bridge is best acquired by training; the same is probably also true of the appreciation of literature and the arts. In addition, all these require a lot of practice and its careful sequencing from the easy toward the more difficult. At the other end of the range, enjoying a drive through the country requires familiarity only with other land-scapes—knowledge available to everybody who can see. Similarly, the pleasant stimulus of window shopping is also within the reach of everybody who has any familiarity with the uses of the merchandise displayed.

In short, all stimulus enjoyment is skilled consumption, but the time and effort required to learn its skills vary greatly from one stimulus to another and some of the consumption skills are so universal that they do not seem to be skills at all, because everybody acquires them as part of growing up and daily living. By "everybody," of course, we do not always mean literally everybody. The skill needed to enjoy music, for example, seems common to all or almost all in gypsy communities, among Welsh miners, and the people of Catholic central Europe; but it is very much the privilege of the elite in most other countries.

THE MEANING OF CULTURE

I shall define culture as knowledge; it is that part of knowledge which provides the redundancy needed to render stimulation enjoyable. Culture is the preliminary information we must have to enjoy the processing of further information. Consumption skills, therefore, are part of culture, while production skills are not. (Some production skills, however, are closely related to, and so impart, certain consumption skills.) Also, since only the enjoyment of stimulation is skilled consumption, while the enjoyment of comfort requires no skill, only stimulus enjoyment is a cultural activity.

All stimulus enjoyment other than simple physical exercise requires a certain degree of skill, but all of us acquire some of it so easily that we do not think of it as learning. It is useful, therefore, to define culture a little more narrowly, as the training and skill necessary to enjoy those stimulus satisfactions whose enjoyment requires skill and training. That excludes knowledge everybody picks up unwittingly in the course of everyday living.

Since the borderline between knowledge learned and knowledge casually picked up is often hard to draw, this is not a rigorous definition of culture; but its very vagueness makes it conform all the better to the common use of the term. To enjoy music, for example, one must know something about it, but what little it takes to enjoy a popular tune we learn automatically, just by being exposed to similar tunes and rhythms on TV, radio, and elsewhere. Accordingly, we do not consider a person musically cultured just because he enjoys popular music, although it clearly takes skill which someone from a totally different part of the globe would probably lack. Customarily, only the ability to enjoy serious music or true jazz is regarded as a sign of culture, presumably because to learn its skill requires effort. Indeed, the harder it is to learn a skill, the more it is respected, and that may be why some forms of culture are more highly regarded than others. The word "culture" usually makes people think of the ability to enjoy literature, music, painting, and other fine arts whose enjoyment takes effort and time to learn, although the appreciation and enjoyment of food, sports, games of skill and card games, political, economic and scientific news, and so on are also learned skills and must therefore be included in the definition of culture. The fact that a favorable family background enables some people to acquire certain consumption skills effortlessly does not make those people less cultured. The children of bookish parents often acquire a literary taste with no visible effort, just as the children of professional musicians and many American blacks pick up a musical culture at their parents' knee without even noticing. We should regard them as cultured because the majority considers their skill a cultural one.

Another basis for valuing some forms of culture more highly than others is the greater quantity of enjoyment they make possible. So far we have taken as given the objective information flow available and looked upon consumption skills as something that makes that flow accessible as a source of stimulus enjoyment, as if culture or consumption skills were windows through which to watch and enjoy a colorful procession that would pass whether or not it was viewed and enjoyed by anybody.

Luckily for mankind, much of the current flow of novelty can be preserved and stored up for the enjoyment of future generations and others who for some reason missed it when it was new, and canned novelty can be every bit as enjoyable as fresh novelty, though it usually requires more skill to enjoy. Literature, music, and the fine arts which create durable artifacts are the obvious examples. They represent vast storehouses of past novelty accumulated over the centuries, their contents' ability to give pleasure undiminished by the fact that they have already given pleasure to past generations. Since much canned novelty belongs to the distant past and has lost actuality, we need a little extra knowledge and skill to retrieve and enjoy it, but the return on that extra effort and extra culture can be very great.

In short, consumption skills differ not only in the difficulty of acquiring them, but also in the amount of enjoyment their acquisition makes available, and both render some forms of culture more valuable than others. In addition, a person can be more cultured than another in the sense of having acquired a larger number of consumption skills. And, finally, there is such a thing as being too cultured. After all, culture is the preliminary knowledge necessary to provide enough redundancy for the enjoyment of new knowledge, and there can be too much redundancy, leaving too little new knowledge. Not only can a picture or a piece of music become too familar for further enjoyment, a person may become too familiar with an entire field to derive much additional enjoyment from it. His tastes in that field have become jaded.

THE PURITAN ATTITUDE TOWARD CULTURE

My definition of culture helps to explain our ambivalent attitude toward it. To begin with, culture is the learning of the leisure class, which they developed, and needed, to enhance their efficiency in enjoying leisure. No wonder it is suspect in the eyes of productive, working members of society! Also, to our Puritan forefathers, skills and learning aimed solely at enhancing one's ability to obtain enjoyment looked like instruments of the devil. Fortunately, some consumption skills had other uses as well and so escaped censure, but most of them did not and were frowned upon. Today, puritanism is dead, but its ghost still haunts us. We have come to accept, even to admire Culture; but often only as something serious, noble, and elevating—like religion, good for the soul and perhaps also for prestige. The idea that culture should be there for pleasure, or even that its sole aim should be to give pleasure, seems frivolous or shocking to many people. *The Oxford Companion to Music,* in its good, if snobbish article on jazz, refers to that form of music as the music of pleasure. The implication that serious music is *not* for pleasure is unmistakable, yet what other purpose can it possibly serve? If it elevates the soul, by what means other than the feeling of pleasure is that achieved?

PRODUCTION SKILLS VERSUS CONSUMPTION SKILLS

Until the end of the eighteenth century, education was a privilege of the leisure class and consisted, appropriately enough, of training in consumption skills. Being educated and being cultured meant the same thing in those days. At the time, the skills of production seemed less important, less difficult, and more often acquired through apprenticeship than through formal training. Also, education was not very important as a source of income. Molière's *bourgeois gentilhomme* became rich first and only afterwards took lessons in music, dancing, deportment, and philosophy to learn the skills of enjoying his riches.

Since much stimulation is best enjoyed through mutual interaction, many members of the cultured leisure class became adept also as producers of stimulus enjoyment. One need only recall France's aristocratic men and women of letters, the gentlemen-architects of eighteenth-century England, and the many titled and wealthy composers and performers of music of all nationalities, from Henry VIII to Albinoni, from Frederick the Great to Mendelssohn.

In the nineteenth and early twentieth centuries, education in the United States became universal, but it also became more and more a training in production skills and less and less a preparation for the enjoyment of life. Our Puritan attitude and the requirements of our capitalist economy are equally to blame, or credit. After all, the worker's production skills increase productivity and profit, and there is plenty of evidence that the profound changes in the curriculum of our schools and colleges in the 1910's and 1920's were greatly influenced by the needs of industry and business.[1]

Even since then, economic forces have continued to press for the progressive crowding out of a liberal, humanistic education by the requirements of science and technology. Economic and technical progress are forever increasing the skill requirements of the productive system; moreover, the demand for production skills of the people wishing to acquire them is increasing even faster. Competition for leadership positions and for the more challenging and prestigious jobs is creating an excess supply of skilled personnel, which not only depresses the extra earnings to be had for extra skills, but also leads to unnecessary upgrading of skill requirements. As a result, many people find themselves overtrained for the job they get and the work they do.

There would be nothing wrong with salesgirls and gas-station attendants having, or even being required to have, B.A. degrees if those degrees enabled them the better to enjoy the books they read or music they listen to while they are waiting for their customers. Mostly, however, their diplomas give them production skills which lie fallow and whose acquisition crowded out the education that would have prepared them for the better enjoyment of their increased leisure.

THE RATIONAL BIAS AGAINST CULTURE

While professional and vocational training increasingly crowd consumption skills out of the curriculum, the need for such skills is growing with the rise in our standard of living. Greater affluence means more forms of consumption, and to enjoy them requires more consumption skills. We have access to more sports, more games, more pastimes than others, and to many more places to see and visit, but we lack the skills and knowledge needed fully to enjoy them and we even seem to lack the inclination to acquire such competence. It is as though we preferred unskilled consumption, trying everything once or twice, or in three easy lessons if necessary, but often remaining dilettantes and seldom aspiring to the more enjoyable higher reaches of consumption expertise. Unlike the English, French, and German *Who's Who,* all of which meticulously list people's favorite sports and hobbies, the American *Who's Who* does not list any consumption skills or preferences. Are we too puritanical to mention such mundane matters? Or is it that too few of us can boast of true expertise in enjoyment?

Why are we so uninterested in the skills of consumption? The majority of our population has ever-increasing access to leisure, and our schools and colleges increasingly offer adult education courses in which we can catch up on what we have missed in our youth, but almost three-quarters of the courses we sign up for are those which provide additional training in production skills.[2] One reason may be our puritanical hierarchy of values. If we are embarrassed to waste time on activities specifically aimed at providing enjoyment, how much more embarrassing must it be to devote time and effort to just learning how better to enjoy such activities?

But another, perhaps more potent reason is our rationality. Going to school to acquire a skill, whether the process itself is pleasant or unpleasant, is an investment which yields a return—additional income in the case of production skills, the better enjoyment of life in the case of consumption skills. Estimates of the rate of return on investment in professional and vocational training can be made and are available; nothing even remotely comparable is possible with respect to consumption skills. One cannot attach a dollar value to the skill of enjoying a concert or a ballet, even less can one estimate the time needed for or the chance of ever turning a neophyte into an enthusiastic melomane or balletomane through training and practice. With so many unknowns so utterly impossible to estimate, it seems rational, at least on a narrow interpretation of the term, to discount the benefits heavily and to opt instead for adding to our production skills and their easily quantifiable benefits. That seems especially true in our modern, calculating, quantifying society.

Here, then is another explanation of the oft-lamented American lack of interest in culture. Perhaps we have not quite shaken off the early Puritan prejudice against pleasure or recreation for its own sake; we also have a seemingly rational reason for not seeking more culture than we do and for not acquiring more of the training and skill needed to enjoy the skill-intensive satisfactions of life.

SKILLED VERSUS UNSKILLED STIMULUS ENJOYMENT

Whatever its reason or reasons, our lack of interest in culture does express our bias in favor of comfort and against stimulation. The way that bias works is, of course, neither direct nor simple. Man's desire for stimulation is far too deep-seated for him to abandon it just for a lack of skill at making the most of it. We saw that some forms of stimulation require less skill to enjoy than others, and some require virtually no skill at all. It is natural that lack of training in the skills of consumption should make us shift our interest in favor of those that require few or no skills. Insufficient novelty renders the stimulation so obtained unsatisfying or only moderately satisfying, which then biases us against all stimulation and in favor of comfort.

I have already mentioned a few forms of stimulation whose enjoyment requires virtually no skill and no effort on the recipient's part; there are many more. The entertainment industry provides much of it; for the rest, an open-eyed person can get a lot of stimulation out of just watching the world go by and following the change in political events and economic fashions. Time-budget surveys and various sociological studies tell us that the main sources of stimulation in the United States are watching television, driving for pleasure, and shopping—all of which are sources of stimulation requiring no skill.

Why do we find them less stimulating and satisfying than listening to music or reading literature? They are not less so, not as long as they provide a flow of information commensurate with our requirements for pleasant stimulation. Television, driving around, and shopping can all be very stimulating, up to a point. Many television programs are enjoyable and interesting; going to a colorful market or shopping center, browsing in a good bookshop, reading a Sears catalog, looking at the latest fashions in elegant department stores or inspecting next year's models of automobiles can all be fun. The same is true of driving. The constantly changing scene before our eyes provides pleasant stimulation; and when this is insufficient, the exhilaration of speed and the challenge of exercising our skill and trying our luck in weaving through traffic, gambling on what seems the fastest lane, beating the other guy to it and getting away with minor traffic violations in the process provide additional stimulation, adjustable almost at will to suit one's personal preference and the mood of the moment.

Yet the flow of novelty and stimulation available from those three sources is limited. What we get out of TV, shopping, and driving is fully adequate for pleasant, sometimes even maximally pleasant stimulation when the time devoted to their enjoyment is suitably limited, spaced, and selected, but it quickly becomes redundant, unsurprising, and monotonous as we devote more and more time to them in the vain hope that our intake of novelty will keep step with the increased time we spend on them.

Consider the survey of television which concluded that one-eighth of the viewers are almost always bored by what they watch. The flow of subjective novelty in the shows those viewers see must be way below their information-processing capacity. If the majority of them do not mind, and give evidence of not minding, the many commercial interruptions, the reason must be that the information content of the programs is no higher or not much higher than that of the interruptions. In general, all the evidence cited to show the very low value we attach to residual time was proof that our unskilled pastimes on which we spend our residual time are unable to provide enough novelty to keep our minds busy and unbored.

Technical progress, by freeing more and more time from work, increases man's demand for stimulation. The economy has responded by increasing our means of access to sources of stimulation, but it has failed to increase their stimulus content. Having a car makes it easier to enjoy the countryside; but the same neighborhood or countryside becomes less stimulating as one drives through it more often. Similarly, more retail outlets add but little to the variety and interest of the merchandise, whose attraction dulls on repeated viewing; and neither does the multiplication of TV channels, stations, and receivers increase, by itself, the flow of information transmitted. The novelty content in them depends mainly on the amount and quality of human imagination devoted to its production, and both are lagging far behind the great increase in our means of access. We will look into the reasons for that lag later. In the meantime, I ask the reader to accept, provisionally, as a fact of life our economy's inability to provide maximally pleasing stimulation to the unskilled consumer through TV, radio, window shopping, and similar pastimes for as many hours a day and as many days in a lifetime as he would wish to be stimulated.

The objection, therefore, to unskilled and effortless pastimes such as television, driving, and shopping is not that the stimulus they provide is inherently inferior, which it is not, but that it is limited in quantity and so provides only a limited quantity of enjoyment. That quantity can be adequate and satisfying when our demand for stimulus enjoyment is equally limited; but it ceases to be adequate when increased leisure increases our demand for stimulation and makes us spend more time watching TV, shopping, and so on in an unsuccessful effort to get out of them a larger quantity of stimulation than they can supply. For the source of stimulation and satisfaction is not the TV screen, the automobile, or the store, but the novelty to which they give access. It is helpful to think of television, driving, shopping, and other such pastimes as channels through which novelty is transmitted from the producers of novelty to its consumers. The channels are needed, and they must have adequate capacity for transmitting the novelty, but they cannot transmit more novelty than is there to be transmitted. Beyond a certain point, the amount of stimulus such pastimes provide increases not with the amount of time the consumer devotes to them, but only with the amount of novelty producers see fit to put into them. Without an increase in novelty content, more time spent watching television, driving around, or shopping merely spreads the novelty thinner, increases redundancy, and reduces the intensity of enjoyment. What would be pleasant stimulation on a moderate scale becomes, when pushed further, first, mere defense against boredom, and, ultimately, just boredom. That is how technical and economic progress and the ensuing increase in leisure often misfire.

Another important—and tragic—example of our economy's failure to provide adequate stimulation to the unskilled consumer is the problem of the aged. When people retire they are suddenly deprived of the stimulus satisfaction their work has given them, and, naturally, they try to fall back on the other sources of stimulation accessible to them. If they are unskilled consumers, they soon find their sources of stimulation inadequate; the result is the heartrending spectacle of elderly people trying desperately to keep themselves busy and amused but not knowing how to do so. Boredom seems inescapable, and boredom is a great killer. That may well be part of the explanation of the American male's relatively low life expectancy. American women are better off in this regard, for they have housework and cooking to keep them occupied and alive.

The remedy is culture. We must acquire the consumption skills that will give us access to society's accumulated stock of past novelty and so enable us to supplement at will and almost without limit the currently available flow of novelty as a source of stimulation. Different skills of consumption open up different stores of sources of stimulation, and each gives us greatly enhanced freedom to choose what we personally find the most enjoyable and stimulating, holding out the prospect of a large reservoir of novelty and years of enjoyment. Music, painting, literature, and history are the obvious examples.

Fifty or more years ago, those who correctly foresaw our phenomenal technical progress and increase in leisure also predicted a utopia of increased and increasingly universal culture.

Why did this part of their prediction fail to come true, and why does our greater need for culture fail to increase our demand for it?

The anti-cultural bias of our Puritan tradition, may well be the most important reason. The second reason, our narrowly rational bias against investing in consumption skills, looks less convincing now than when I first stated it. After all, our appetite for stimulation, the degree of stimulation and amount of novelty needed for maximum enjoyment, and the amount of leisure time our work leaves available for stimulus enjoyment over a lifetime are relatively easy to take into account. Moreover, weighing the costs of the time and effort we must invest in becoming cultured is of dubious rationality when having more time and energy than we know what to do with is the main reason for our becoming cultured.

And yet the desire to save time and effort seems so deeply ingrained in the American character that we just cannot help regarding their expenditure as a cost, to be weighed against the benefits of a cultural education. This may well be an example of the higher irrationality of behavior governed by narrowly rational calculation. That brings me to a third, if lesser, reason for our bias against culture, which also exemplifies the higher irrationality of narrowly rational calculation.

THE ART OF CONVERSATION

Conversation is an exchange of information and ideas; it is talk which is mutually stimulating. We enjoy pleasant conversation not only for the stimulus it provides, but also for the satisfaction we get out of knowing that our own contribution stimulates others. No wonder it is a major source of human satisfaction.

Since the pleasantness of conversation depends on the novelty and redundancy it contains, one may well ask how are they obtained. The novelty comes partly from the other person's information I do not share, partly from his different way of thinking, his different responses to shared information and shared experiences, which to be new to me must be not only different from mine but also unpredictable and surprising. For conversation to be mutually pleasant, it must provide the participants with novelty; this means that the thinking and responses of each must have an element of unpredictability for the other. In short, conversation is mutually pleasant when the partners are well matched and do not yet know each other so intimately as to rule out all surprises. The first part of this statement seems self-evident; the truth of the second part is easier to see by looking at its opposite. Many couples become bored with each other with the passing of years, because their long and close intimacy leads to a complete sharing of their memories and even enables each of them accurately to predict the other's response to every new situation and stimulus.

But if novelty is important for stimulation to be pleasant, familiarity or redundancy is no less so. The source of this is information shared by the participants. Shared knowledge of a common language is a necessary condition for a conversation even to take place; very much more knowledge must be shared for the conversation to be pleasant. The larger the common fund of information shared by a group of people, the more easily they can talk to each other, and the greater the scope for enjoyable conversation among them.

Contemporaries and people coming from the same country, the same town, the same school often find each other's company enjoyable. Having lived through similar experiences and witnessed the same events, their fund of memories has a large overlap; and it makes their conversation effortless. They do not have to search for suitable topics of conversation, because almost any random thought is suitable—that is, likely to conjure up similar enough memories in the other person to provide the necessary degree of redundancy. That explains why we feel so much at ease with people close to us, or with similar backgrounds. Needless to add, the optimum combination of novelty and redundancy, which provides the pleasantest conversation, is bound to be very different for different people. Presumably, extroverts want more novelty, introverts more redundancy, and advancing age probably shifts people's preference in favor of the latter. Thus extroverts seek many acquaintances, introverts close friends, and the old increasingly live on memories and enjoy exchanging reminiscences.

A major source of information, and so of the shared redundancy necessary for pleasant conversation, is education. Education, therefore, whatever its other benefits, increases our ability to engage in, and our chances of having, pleasant conversations; and for this purpose, education in the skills of consumption is especially effective. All of the knowledge we acquire by education we share with others, but because consumption skills are much less specialized than production skills, we share them with many more people. I can engage in shop talk only with those in my own field, and increasing specialization is forever diminishing their number. By contrast, a general liberal arts education, which is designed to provide the usual consumption skills necessary to enjoy society's accumulated stock of literature, arts, artifacts, ideas, and knowledge of man, society, and nature, makes me share a large fund of knowledge with all others who also learned the skills of consumption, and the broader this education, the larger the number of people with whom I will share it. In short, consumption skills open up much broader and greater possibilities of pleasant conversation than production skills do.

What is the significance of that rather obvious fact? Since conversation is a major source of human satisfaction, its facilitation is an important additional benefit of consumption skills. This is well known to people who appreciate the art of conversation and even to those whose desire for culture is snobbish, since such a desire usually stems from their wanting to impress others with their conversation. Why, then, are courses on literature, art, music, history, and other consumption skills not more popular than they are? The main reason, probably, is that conversation is very much a skilled consumption, and one must have acquired the skill before one learns to appreciate its benefits. Another reason, however, is that people who decide whether or not to invest in acquiring these consumption skills for themselves or their children on grounds of individual rationality are certain to demand less of them than would most benefit society.

The argument hinges on the fact that it takes at least two to share knowledge and make conversation, and that each person's conversation benefits at least two people: himself and his conversational partner or partners. When I acquire information and so improve my chance of having a pleasant chat, I also improve the similar chance of everybody else who shares the information I just learned. However, when I decide whether to learn or not to learn, I weigh only my own benefit and neglect other people's, with the inevitable result that I decide to learn less than would maximize the sum of society's total satisfaction derived from conversation.

We have here another example of an external economy whose neglect in the name of individual rationality leads to social loss. When each person makes an individually rational choice between consumption and production skills, the result of everybody's actions departs from the social optimum in the direction of too few consumption skills, and the magnitude of society's loss depends on the importance of conversation as a source of human satisfaction.

Here, then, is yet another reason, quite different from and additional to the others, why we are likely to opt for less culture than is good for us—good in the sense of providing the maximum enjoyment of life.

WHAT DO YOU KNOW?

The abstract theorizing of the last section was prompted by one of the most surprising facts we have considered (Chapter 9): the statistical evidence of our loneliness. According to psychologists, we are an extrovert, outgoing, enterprising people, hungry for stimulus, anxious to make friends, and uninhibited about talking to strangers; yet we spend 6.6 waking hours a day alone, 2.5 hours a day more than the average western European. About 10 to 12 per cent of this difference is probably explained by our commuting alone, in the isolation of our cars; Europeans, who commute just as much, do so in crowded trains and buses. But the remaining difference is still very great. Indeed, such a great difference would be statistically suspect if it were not confirmed by casual observation.

Talk is most certainly the Europeans' main source of stimulus, and conversational skill the accomplishment they most appreciate; it is what they mostly practice when they are together. One-half of the western Europeans' 2.5 extra hours of togetherness is at their workplace, and most immigrants from Europe who had similar jobs there and here will confirm that here workers are silent, while in Europe they talk.

More striking, or perhaps just more easily noticed, is the corresponding difference between the activities of Americans and Europeans during leisure hours. American tourists abroad are usually struck and often morally shocked by the much more leisurely and frivolous attitude toward life of just about all foreigners, manifested by the tremendous amount of idle talk they engage in, on promenades and park benches, in cafés, sandwich shops, lobbies, doorways, and wherever people congregate. On a small part of such socializing we even have statistical evidence.

The English, who resemble us the most in temperament, spend much of their free time talking with friends and strangers in the lively, social atmosphere of pubs. Visiting pubs is the second most popular non-home-based leisure activity in England, next and close to driving for pleasure, which holds the first place there, as it does here. The statistics are not very informative; they merely show that slightly more than half of the working male population visits a pub at least once a month, without specifying how often (see Table 16). You can get a good idea, however, of what this means even from a casual sampling of the innumerable pubs thickly strewn all over London and dotting the English countryside. Every noon and evening you will find all of them full of people and animated talk. Socializing rather than drinking is clearly most people's main occupation there, although a half-pint of beer is to talk as a bed is to making love—one can do without but does better with.

TABLE 16

Percentage of Employed Englishmen Engaging in Various Activities at Least Once a Month

	Professional and Managerial	Clerical	Skilled	Semi-skilled and Unskilled	All
Watching Television	95	99	98	95	97
Gardening	70	62	66	50	64
Listening to Music	65	70	52	44	57
Going for a Pleasure Drive	62	51	62	49	58
Going to a Pub	51	42	54	58	52
Going for a walk of a mile or more	56	63	41	36	47

SOURCE: M. Young and P. Willmott, *The Symmetrical Family*, New York: Pantheon, 1973, Tables 35 and 38, pp. 212 and 216.

Much the same thing happens also on the Continent, although France alone collects statistics. The French do much of their talking in cafés, and the proportion of Frenchmen who visit cafés at least once a month happens to be almost exactly the same as the proportion of Englishmen who visit pubs (see Table 17). That near identity of the British and French figures is the more remarkable because, as far as their alcohol consumption is concerned, the French and the English could hardly be more different. French per capita consumption is four and a half times that of the English.[3] If, despite this very great difference in their taste for drink, the frequency of their visits to café or

TABLE 17

Percentage of Frenchmen Visiting Cafés by Age, Income, Residence, Social Group, and Education

	More than once/day	AT LEAST				Rarely or Never	No Response	Total
		once/day	every other day	once/week	once/month			
All men, 14 yrs. and older	5.6	16.5	20.7	42.1	52.4	47.3	0.3	100.0
14 to 24 years	3.9	16.1	21.4	45.8	57.7	42.3	0.0	100.0
25 to 39 years	7.2	20.0	23.5	45.4	56.3	43.6	0.1	100.0
40 to 59 years	6.5	16.5	21.9	46.4	55.6	44.5	0.0	100.0
60 years and older	4.4	13.1	15.2	28.6	38.2	60.5	1.2	100.0
Incomes below Frs. 6000	5.5	11.6	16.7	31.5	42.7	57.2	0.0	100.0
Frs. 6,000 to Frs. 10,000	4.3	12.1	15.8	36.1	44.7	55.2	0.0	100.0
Frs. 10,000 to Frs. 15,000	5.7	18.3	22.6	45.1	56.4	43.3	0.4	100.0
Frs. 15,000 to Frs. 20,000	5.1	18.4	22.6	46.5	57.4	42.6	0.0	100.0
Incomes above Frs. 20,000	6.9	18.1	22.7	41.8	51.8	47.6	0.5	100.0
Income not declared	4.8	11.9	13.8	45.2	53.3	45.4	1.2	100.0
Rural communities	4.2	12.7	17.3	42.9	56.2	43.6	0.2	100.0
Cities with less than 20,000 inhabitants	5.7	15.3	19.8	46.6	55.5	44.1	0.4	100.0
Cities with 20,000 to 100,000 inhabitants	5.6	14.1	17.8	36.9	44.4	55.6	0.0	100.0
Cities with more than 100,000 inhabitants	5.2	15.2	19.6	38.6	48.1	51.7	0.1	100.0

Greater Paris region	9.0	28.8	32.3	45.2	53.8	45.4	0.8	100.0
Independent farmers	0.4	2.8	4.9	40.0	57.5	42.5	0.0	100.0
Farm Workers	0.9	14.8	18.0	32.3	40.2	59.7	0.0	100.0
Independent businessmen	9.6	25.2	34.6	54.5	64.8	33.6	1.4	100.0
Top management and free professions	2.0	11.1	14.5	39.0	51.4	48.5	0.0	100.0
Middle executives	7.1	15.5	20.0	36.6	46.2	53.8	0.0	100.0
Clerical Employees	7.3	21.4	23.4	37.0	42.4	57.4	0.0	100.0
Skilled and Semiskilled	6.0	19.8	23.8	49.1	57.8	42.0	0.2	100.0
Unskilled Workers	8.7	21.2	22.1	35.1	39.9	60.2	0.0	100.0
Other active men	7.1	18.3	22.4	31.5	43.2	56.8	0.0	100.0
Inactive men	5.7	13.9	18.4	33.7	44.8	54.9	0.3	100.0
College and preparatory school graduates [a]	4.0	14.1	19.2	37.0	47.5	52.3	0.0	100.0
High school graduates [a]	3.6	15.5	19.4	42.3	53.9	46.0	0.1	100.0
Junior high school graduates [a]	7.3	18.9	22.9	45.1	54.0	45.5	0.5	100.0
No diploma ("dropouts")	5.4	15.4	19.7	40.4	51.8	48.0	0.2	100.0

[a] These are the closest American equivalents of the very different French categories.

SOURCE: P. Debreu, "Les Comportements de Loisirs des Français (Enquête de 1967) Résultats détaillés," *Les Collections de l'INSEE*, Série M, No. 25, Paris: Institut National de la Statistique et des Etudes Economiques, Tables 241, 244, 247, 250, 253, on pp. 147–51.

pub is still so similar, that renders all the more plausible my contention that they go there mainly for the talk.

The very detailed French data also give much more insight into exactly who goes to a café, and how often. The habit seems not only universal but surprisingly uniform, cutting across all ages, income groups, and social classes of French society, with relatively small differences in frequency, and with skilled and semiskilled workers occupying a middle position between independent businessmen on the one hand and the free professions and top management on the other. One in six Frenchmen visits a café at least once a day—a high proportion, considering that this includes everybody, from fourteen-year-old youngsters to octogenarians. The corresponding English figures, when collected, may well turn out to be quite similar. Table 17 shows how deceptive and how empty a single figure that uses once a month as its cutoff point can be.

In other countries, such detailed statistics seem unavailable; but the 1966 time-budget studies show that the percentage of men and women who visit a pub or café at least once a day is almost as high in Western Germany (8.1) as it is in France (8.6) but not even half as high in the United States (4.0).[4] In our bars and cafés, we look in vain for visible or audible evidence of conversation as an important source of satisfaction. They are usually much less crowded, and most customers come to have a drink or quick snack, while few come to talk. The very arrangement of the typical American bar symbolizes its different purpose: the customers sit along a straight counter, facing the bartender, not each other, which is conducive to the ordering and silent consumption of one's drink, not to conversation. One of America's few sidewalk cafés, just off Waikiki Beach, displays the notice:

NO LOITERING
We certainly don't want to rush you but due to our lack of tables, please cooperate in making these tables available to the next customer.

The wording may be unusual, but the spirit is not. Much has been written also about subtler means of speeding the customer, making his seat uncomfortable so that he will yield it up soon to the next one. The practice reflects not so much on the café owner as on his customers, who good-naturedly accept it as a legitimate profit-maximizing weapon because they concur in the underlying assumption that people go to cafés to consume, not to loiter.

Yet, in most, perhaps all, other countries and civilizations, people go to cafés for the very purpose of loitering, and they consume merely in order to pay for the privilege and for the space the owner provides to facilitate meeting and talking to friends or just for the enjoyment of the sense of belonging to a group, whether for talking or merely listening.

Needless to say, foreign café owners are no less interested in maximizing profits than are Americans, but, being aware of the very different nature of what they sell, they act very differently. The last thing they want to do is speed the customer on his way. After all, those who come by themselves come for the crowd and the liveliness it imparts to the place, while those who come to talk need time to get into the swing of it and to find it worthwhile staying longer and consuming more. Instead of making the chairs uncomfortably small, the owner is more likely to reduce the size of glasses and coffee cups. That stratagem enables customers to stay indefinitely by consuming an unlimited number of portions, and probably comes closest to charging by time spent, short of metering the chairs. Nor can customers object if they come for the talk, not for the drink; it then seems perfectly proper to be charged by the quantity and liveliness of the talk.

If our visits to cafés and pubs are short and rare in America, do we make up for it by visiting more in each other's houses? Apparently not. One of our characteristics foreigners often comment on is the impossibility of dropping in unannounced on friends. Perhaps we want the advance notice merely to provide better hospitality or to make it into an event, but the number of visits is bound to be reduced as a result. Then too, our social events are not conducive to conversation, being too crowded and alcoholic as a rule. The common custom of providing background music also shows that the hosts do not expect conversation by itself to be stimulating enough to ward off boredom.

Largely missing in our country is the tradition of regular and frequent get-togethers of friends to argue, gossip, and exchange news. Most countries whose inhabitants have a strongly felt demand for such contact manage to develop facilities for practicing it. Our failure to develop them is a sign of not much demand. "What's new" is in many languages both a customary greeting and an invitation for a friendly chat; its American form, "What d'you know," is only a greeting and impossible to take literally for a question that calls for an answer. It is as though we lacked or begrudged the time for an idle chat, which may be idle but is also one of man's main sources of stimulation and satisfaction.

What I said earlier about education helps to explain why our gambit for a chat is so halfhearted and why we have failed to develop the locale and the facilities for idle talk. We lack the stuff conversations are made of. That could well explain the data here discussed. We engage in plenty of shop talk, as if to prove that we enjoy talking as much as anybody, but that is a narrow subject which allows few partners and keeps few people going for long. To go beyond it, we must also have—and share with others!—other interests in life: politics, sports, people, society, fashions, art, science, and so on, as well as the background knowledge and memory of similar and related things which enable us to discuss them. People must share a background to have a pleasant conversation, and since that background also constitutes the skills of consumption, those who lack these also lack conversation.

I cannot prove, of course, that we lack such a background; the reader must weigh the evidence presented here and elsewhere and judge for himself. That we are *presumed* to lack such background, however, is evident: witness the uniquely American journalistic tradition that requires every item to be written in a way that a newcomer from outer space could understand it. That is why the title or position of every public figure, however well known, the definition of every concept, however familiar, must be restated every day in every article. The practice is a cumbersome nuisance for the informed reader, but it is of real help to the uninformed. And the latter must be very numerous if for their sake it is worth inflicting all that boring repetition on the informed. The justification usually cited, that our news-paper-reading public embraces a broader segment of the popu-lation than it does in other countries, can hardly be valid: ac-cording to the *United States Statistical Abstract,* thirteen foreign countries have a larger per capita circulation of daily papers than we do, despite the fact that we receive more and longer schooling.

It is largely our narrow, individual rationality that makes us miss part of the fun others get out of life. My rationality is shortsighted if I choose not to acquire consumption skills that afterwards, with the benefit of hindsight, would have seemed worth having; it is selfish if I ignore the benefit from my be-coming more cultured to all those destined to share my com-pany. I have argued that the remedy is to move to a higher or social rationality, which takes a longer view and considers other people's welfare beside our own.

A higher social rationality and a willingness to act in society's interest are probably the best remedies, but in the case of cul-ture there are others, too. Since consumption skills are typically acquired by the young while they are in school, more manda-tory liberal arts courses in the school curriculum are one alterna-tive, and since much of the training in consumption skills is learning by doing, subsidies to the arts are another. All such measures, to be effective, must be based on a proper under-standing of the meaning and purpose of culture. It is hard to ram things down people's throats for the good of their souls.

CHAPTER TWELVE

What's Wrong with Mass Production?

Specialization, division of labor, mass production, economies of scale—all are names and aspects of the one principle, recognized and first stated by Adam Smith: that the division of labor increases its product. That principle is the foundation of our high standard of living, the guiding light of all economic progress, and it continues to shower benefits upon us. Yet it has drawbacks as well. Since the drawbacks affect us as universally as the blessings, it is essential that we have a balanced view of them together. The drawbacks, however, are as commonly ignored as the advantages are recognized; that is why I set out to redress the balance.

Mass production is a phase of the division of labor which originated in nineteenth-century America in response to a shortage of skilled labor. It consists in the partitioning of the skilled worker's complex sequence of operations into simple components, each to be performed by a separate unskilled worker. The resulting increase in speed and productivity is the basis of the modern economy's superior performance, but an inevitable accompaniment was the transformation of much interesting, demanding, challenging work into effortless but dull monotony for all but a small proportion of the labor force.

There is no way of telling at this late stage to what extent monotony was consciously accepted, the costs being judged worth paying for the sake of the benefits, and to what extent we merely drifted into it all. Let me, for argument's sake, assume that the transformation of the nature and conditions of work was fully conscious, freely accepted, and entered into with open eyes by all concerned. After all, the less interesting work, thanks to its much higher productivity, was also much better paid; it was rational for workers to accept its greater monotony for the sake of the higher pay in the belief that they could buy ample compensating stimulation out of their additional pay and enjoy it during their additional leisure time. What was wrong with this way of thinking was that it failed to take into account the concomitant change in the nature of products which has gradually changed our whole environment.

THE MONOTONY OF PRODUCTS

The monotony of mass-production work is fully matched by the monotony of its product. Stimulation depends on variety and novelty, some of which is provided by nature but most of which originates with man—after all, even the inanimate objects around us are mostly man-made. Man-made variety and novelty in turn depend partly on human imagination and partly on a human limitation: man is unable or unwilling to reproduce exactly anything that he or another has made before. Specialization inhibits imagination, while mass production eliminates the inability and unwillingness to replicate. The first I will deal with later; the second I can illustrate here with a simple example.

The dishes we eat from are among the many objects that surround us. When they are mass-produced, we look at them occasionally, observing their shape and design perhaps when we buy them and a few times afterward, but we soon take them for granted and use them forever after without seeing or caring what they look like.

Handmade or hand-painted dishes hold our attention much longer. Slight differences in shape or design and minor irregularities in execution give each piece an individual identity we cannot help noticing. Each piece has an interest that attracts and holds the attention, greatly postponing the day when complete familiarity makes us see it no more. Such characteristics do not necessarily have anything to do with artistic excellence. Many a mass-produced dinner service is better designed and more beautifully made than the average handmade set. An object does not become beautiful just because it is handmade. But it does become different from all others, and it is the novelty and variety due to this difference that makes it interesting and stimulating. A modicum of artistic quality will then render it more pleasantly stimulating.

This example of dishes also brings home the fact that any single item or set of items makes a small contribution to our total visual stimulation. But the arousing effects of stimuli are additive, and it is the cumulative effect of all objects being handmade and having individuality in the primitive economy, as against all being mass produced and lacking individuality in the advanced economy, that makes a great deal of difference to the total environment and its total stimulus impact.

Every primitive society develops a characteristic style in its clothing, pottery, furniture, architecture, and so on. The variety of primitive articles stems from people's inability and unwillingness to imitate exactly, and their attractive design is assured by a kind of natural selection: people have a natural tendency to select the best specimens as models to imitate and improve upon. The result is much redundancy, but also much variety, a combination which is usually pleasing. Man seems to have an innate aesthetic sense which is developed whenever and wherever a large part of the population is called upon to fashion objects.

That the ordinary objects made for everyday use in primitive societies provide plenty of visual stimulation is best shown by the fact that members of such societies are seldom aware of their need for stimulation. The need is discovered and the objects catering to it appreciated only when mass production puts an end to their manufacture or when foreigners, whose own economic development has deprived their own environment of visual stimulation, draw attention to the individuality of primitive manufacture. It is a well-known peculiarity of folk art that it is always unconscious and goes unrecognized as long as it flourishes.[1]

At the same time, one must guard against attributing more artistic sense to the appreciators of folk art than to its creators. We in this country are probably ahead of most others in appreciating and collecting contemporary primitive art, thanks partly to the magnificent pioneering collection of Mr. Nelson Rockefeller. But it would be wrong to conclude that we and Mr. Rockefeller have more understanding of this art than do the Melanesian, Polynesian, and African natives, who, after all, make the objects we collect and admire. We appreciate native handiwork more than they themselves do, because our environment lacks the stimulating objects they produce and have around in profusion. We attach a scarcity value to them, call them art, and pay high prices to possess them, just as we attach a high scarcity value to clean air and unpolluted bodies of water, which they likewise take for granted.

An example nearer to home is the patchwork quilt bedspread which the American housewife made even as late as the beginning of this century. Today such spreads are recognized as folk art. Their excellent design and color combinations are much appreciated, and they fetch prices ten to thirty times that of mass-produced equivalents. Yet the women who made them probably had no more artistic sense and skill than what normally comes from practice to everybody who can learn by doing (provided they do it not for quick sale, but in the expectation that they will live with what they make for the rest of their lives).

One may wonder why a handicraft, one seemingly so profitable, should have been allowed to die out. The answer is simple. Mass-produced objects are not inherently inferior to hand-made ones as sources of visual stimulation; they accumulate the inferiority of boring sameness only gradually, as more and more people acquire the same or similar items and so increase the frequency with which an individual possessor of an item encounters its identical twins. The final victory of boredom may take decades—as long as it takes for mass-produced goods completely to displace homemade or handcrafted objects. That is also the stage at which the mysterious transformation of old junk into valuable antiques takes place.

Indeed, when mass-produced furnishings and household objects first reached the market in the mid-nineteenth century, the age of Victorian gingerbread, the various national styles they imitated must have provided a welcome change from the lesser variety of locally handcrafted products, and it was probably a combination of such newness with cheapness that proved irresistible. Only very slowly did monotony get the upper hand, as thousands of homes filled up with identical products, their sameness unrelieved even by irregularities of manufacture.

The principal man-made source of visual stimulation is architecture. The architecture of pre-industrial societies provides plenty of interesting and enjoyable variety, whether it is the creation of professional architects or is, in the nature of folk art, an architecture without architects. For sheer volume of information designed to arouse and to provide interest and emotional impact, the Gothic cathedrals of France and England may well be unsurpassed, but many hill towns, fishing villages, and other agglomerations of buildings, through the clever choice of location and use of the natural features of the environment, have comparable visual interest and variety. *Architecture without Architects*,[2] the beautiful catalog published by the New York Museum of Modern Art, illustrates how simple means can achieve great impact; it also brings home the universality of this kind of stimulus, which seems to be produced by all ages, races, and civilizations, though rarely by the mass-production economy.[3]

An indication that we are relatively deprived of visual stimulation is the fact that we seek it abroad much more often than others seek it in this country. American tourists go abroad in much greater numbers than foreign tourists visit the United States. (Data on Canadian visitors to this country are lacking, so, to compensate, I am excluding U.S. tourists to Canada.) In one year, 3.3 million non-Canadian foreign tourists come here, while 7.6 million U.S. tourists go overseas and to Mexico.[4]

Our greater affluence will not explain the difference, because we take altogether much fewer and shorter vacations than many foreigners who are less affluent than we are. It used to be that vacations cost more in the United States than they did abroad, and, indeed, the disparity in numbers between American tourists abroad and foreign sightseers here was very much greater a few years ago than it is now. Today, however, cost can no longer be a factor, for repeated devaluations of the dollar and our slower rate of inflation have brought the cost of living and sightseeing in the United States down below that of many western European countries. That leaves as the remaining explanation the lesser interest and variety our cities offer the sightseer. We have our fair share of the beauties and wonders of nature, and the skylines and spectacular buildings of New York, Chicago, and San Francisco are pleasing and interesting to look at. But most of the man-made features of our environment were built in the age of mass production, and they look it, for little thought was given to and no money spent on making them beautiful as well as functional. They offer the tourist meager fare for his money compared to what he gets in poorer countries, with their picturesque towns and villages.

To go abroad for visual stimulation is not the only way, of course, to enliven an insufficiently stimulating environment. Another way is to import stimulation by embellishing our homes with decorative objects: curios, souvenirs, conversation pieces, antiques, works of art, reproductions of antiques and works of art, and flowers. Very often, the decorative centerpieces of coffee tables are the simple vessels and ordinary utensils of an earlier generation or a poorer society—a reminder that our decorative objects merely replace the sensual interest which mass production takes out of articles of use, in much the same way in which our vitamin pills replace the nutrients refined out of our processed foods. Grandmother's chamberpot used as a planter in modern living rooms symbolizes the poverty of the deprived, not the frivolity of the rich.

It is worth having an estimate of the money we spend on such decoration. From the Census of Business, our 1972 purchases of antiques can be estimated at $270 to $300 million. But since our imports of antiques and works of art by dealers *and* individuals amounted to $200 million, our total purchases of antiques and imported works of art may be put at $400 million. The sales of gift, novelty, and souvenir shops may be estimated at $900 million, but this comprises many non-decorative items and excludes the gift-shop sections of department stores and mail-order houses.[5] One gets closer to pure decoration with an estimate of the combined national sales of stores such as Akron, Pier I Imports, San Francisco's Cost-Plus Imports, Seattle's Pirate's Plunder, etc., which specialize on quaint, colorful, unusual, ostensibly handmade imports. A private estimate is that their total sales are $350 million, again excluding similar items sold by department stores.[6] Adding a rough estimate of the value of both department store and auction sales as well as sales of art, paintings, prints, reproductions, framing, and so on— items too small to merit separate Census listings—our total expenditure on antiques, works of art, and all other decorative objectives may be around $1.25 billion, certainly no higher than $1.5 billion.

Of our 1972 purchases of flowers and potted plants, estimated at $2.1 billion, 47 per cent is believed to have gone to hospital rooms, funeral parlors, and graves.[7] The remaining $1.1 billion worth of flowers, added to my above figure, yields $2.5 billion as a rough estimate of our total 1972 expenditure on adding interest, variety, and visual stimulation to our homes. That is one-third of 1 per cent of our total expenditure on consumption.

Objects designed or used purely for decoration, however, are not the only relief from the monotony of a mass-produced environment. Another and much more costly one is that quick succession of fashions which compensates for lack of contemporaneous variety. American women are supposed to be unique in refusing to wear the same outfit to the office on consecutive days; and fashions are said to be sooner accepted, more closely followed, and faster changing in the United States than anywhere else. Witness the ease with which we discard still usable clothing and furnishings just because we are tired of them. In New York City, many immigrants furnished their homes (as did a friend of mine who is a millionaire) with discarded furniture picked off the street on days the Sanitation Department designates for carting off bulky objects. I have already remarked on our habit of changing homes two to three times as often as the people of other nations do; we are also said to replace our cars sooner than others do. Fashion mongering may seem wasteful, but the human need for variety and novelty is as legitimate as the desire to survive. People can be accused of frivolity, and producers blamed for pushing them into frivolity, only if cheaper or better sources of stimulus satisfaction are available as alternatives.

Careful and reliable estimates of the cost of annual model changes in the American automobile industry show this to be a quarter of total costs.[8] In other words, we pay 25 per cent of the price of our new cars not for transportation, but for the novelty and variety which the annually changing appearance, features, and accessories of our cars provide. If we apply that percentage to our 1972 purchases of new cars, we find that our expenditure on novelty in automobile design can be estimated at $10 billion.

Since comparable estimates of the cost of novelty from changing fashions in clothes are not readily available, I propose to take automotive novelty as the symbol of frivolity-mixed-with-utility, and flowers, along with decorative objects, as the symbol of pure frivolity. Our four-times greater expenditure on the first than on the second is probably quite representative of the much greater importance of utilitarian frivolity in the consumer's budget.

Does the greater expenditure mean a correspondingly greater preference for that kind of frivolity? Not quite. For one thing, the novelty and the consumer's enjoyment of the novelty of his new car wears off, partly with his increasing familiarity with his new possession, partly with that gradual accumulation of sameness which results from his encountering increasing numbers of the identical model on the road. He is more likely to expect and discount the first process than the second, which latter is a kind of external diseconomy thrust upon him *after* he has made his purchase. To the extent that the consumer is robbed of his car's novelty after he has bought it, his expenditure on it overstates its worth.

For another thing, the consumer cannot usually choose between a new car with novel features and a new car without them. Apart from the few weeks at the end of the year when next year's models are already available but dealers also sell out their remaining stock of the old year's models, the consumer must buy his new car with its new design and new features whether he wants them or not. The cost of model changes therefore is partly borne by those who do not want them, which implies that society gets—and pays for—more model-changing than the totality of its members want. Such imposition on the whole society of the tastes, and the cost of the tastes, of part of its members is one of the drawbacks of the economies of scale— which are especially great in the automobile industry, where scale economies are important, but are present wherever the new fashions displace the old on the shopkeeper's shelves sooner than they do in the most conservative buyer's affection.

At the same time, the combination of novelty with utility also imposes an additional cost, one due to its being a package and not illustrated in the automobile example. All package deals are suspect, because if two separate things wanted by the buyer come in a fixed package, he is likely to get an excess supply of one of them, with society paying the extra cost. The automobile is an example of a package of practical use and frivolous novelty combined in fixed proportions, and so are virtually all consumers' durable and semi-durable goods. We get much of our stimulation in packages of that type from goods whose primary purpose is to provide some form of comfort, and the reason is simple: we have a strong preference for such combinations.

Our preference may have had its origin in our puritanical reluctance to take our pleasures straight, undiluted by practical utility, but in the course of time it became an aesthetic preference for simplicity and functionalism, for a simple environment uncluttered by useless objects, and for functional design in useful objects which declares their function rather than hiding it. We like our aesthetic stimulus to be built into useful objects by their good design and handsome appearance; most of us prefer the built-in elegance of sleek lines in a Cadillac to the added-on elegance of fringe curtains and flower vases in the Moskva. Our tastes as consumers are well reflected in our manufacturers' products: our industrial design is excellent and considered among the best in the world.

In the mass-production economy, such preference is satisfied at a cost. Stimulus satisfaction depends on novelty, which, in goods mass-produced in the thousands and millions, is used up much sooner than the comfort they yield. Clothing and furnishings become boring and unfashionable long before they are worn out; most of us get tired of our cars, appliances, gadgets while they still have plenty of life left in them; even toys often lose their attraction before they fall apart. In the modern economy, therefore, those of us who try to get our stimulation largely from such sources tend to replace durable goods sooner or accumulate a larger stock of them than purely utilitarian considerations would call for.

The faster-than-necessary replacement or accumulation of useful objects seems wasteful on the surface, because, with the additional stimulation one needs, one also gets additional use one does not need but has to pay for. Sometimes, however, the waste is more apparent than real. The automobile is a case in point, because cars are too expensive to be thrown away when replaced. Instead, people sell them to someone less affluent or less in need of automotive stimulation than they, and the effect on society's welfare is not bad. The total stock of cars we own is probably no greater than what we want for comfort. Annual model changes assure a reasonably stimulating variety of shapes and sizes on our highways, and if our cars are younger on average than other people's, the main reason, probably, is our large export of ageing vehicles.

Usually, our desire for change and novelty does lead to waste, but this must be looked upon as a cost, one to be weighed against the benefit like any other cost. Man needs stimulation and comfort, and most goods provide both, but, when they are mass-produced, they provide them in proportions very different from those in which people want them. Hence the dilemma. To get the right amount of stimulation, one must accept a little extra comfort into the bargain; to get the right amount of comfort, one must put up with insufficient stimulation. The first involves a cost, the second a loss of benefit; the individual ought to be left to make his choice by his own lights.

There is a way out of the dilemma, and I have discussed it already. Insufficient stimulation from an insufficiently stimulating environment can be supplemented by seeking extra stimulation from decorative and art objects and, more generally, from art, handicrafts, hobbies, and many other sources. If such resolutions of the dilemma are not more popular, it may be due to a distaste for pure decoration and stimulation, or to their requiring skills of consumption. The interest of our counterculture in handicrafts may look like a turning back of the clock, but it is a perfect resolution of the dilemma and the only one fully in the American tradition of simplicity and functionalism.

THE BANALIZATION OF ART

Having discussed modern industry and its mechanical perfection as a source of monotony, let me proceed to deal with its other source, scarcity of imagination. Technical progress and the rise in labor productivity are lopsided in our economy. They mainly add to the provision of comfort and increase the earnings of those who provide comfort. Thanks to competition in the labor market, such increases in the ordinary worker's wages enable also those who provide us with novelty and stimulus to demand higher earnings, which in turn raises the cost of stimulation in relation to that of comfort. For that reason, concerts, opera, ballet, and the legitimate theater, as well as most other artistic products and artistic aspects of products, are forever becoming more expensive. Hence the choking off of consumers' demand, though the process is slowed in the performing arts by their increasing subsidization by government and by philanthropic donations.[9]

The reason for such lopsided growth is simple enough. Thanks to our technical inventiveness, we have greatly increased the effectiveness of labor power in producing comfort; but novelty and its stimulus spring largely from imagination, and we have not managed to increase the effectiveness of human imagination in producing novelty. Thus the rising cost of imagination raises the price of novelty, while the rising cost of ordinary labor is offset by its increasing productivity and so does not raise the price of comfort. The rise in the relative price of novelty puts the squeeze on its supply and confronts its suppliers—artists, entertainers, and other such—with the uncomfortable choice between a reduction in their incomes and a decimation of their numbers. They can hardly be blamed for preferring the latter, but society suffers from the consequent reduction in the supply of novelty and stimulation. Matters are made worse by the rival claims of science and technology on the limited supply of imagination.

Such a bias in favor of comfort and against stimulation is not inherent in our technology and may merely result from the way in which we have chosen to use it. The new must be mixed with the familiar to be pleasantly stimulating; in some of the arts, such as music or abstract painting, a pleasing degree of redundancy is achieved by new variations, combinations, and permutations of familiar elements of a familiar style. Computer technology is well suited to producing limited novelty along these lines faster and in larger volume than can the human brain; it is possible that it could become an effective tool of the artist for increasing his productivity. The computer has already produced some tolerably good music, even if it has not produced great art, but such use of it is still in an experimental stage.

Although technology to produce enjoyable novelty still lies ahead, the technology to make existing novelty more accessible is already here. The communications industry is its main manifestation, but no less important are the mechanical reproduction of paintings, the recording and transmission of music, and the dissemination through film and TV of all the other performing arts. Even if the rising relative cost of originality has reduced the production of original sources of stimulation, what is produced is made available in so much greater volume and to so many more people that the total supply of stimulation available per head of population may well have risen. Democracy has been served, because many forms of stimulus enjoyment have been made available to a larger segment of the population. The question remains whether the individual has gained or lost as a result of his having less access to original and more to mechanically reproduced sources of stimulation.

The question is too large to be answered here, though I have already touched on one aspect of it. Another aspect can be dealt with by asking a related question: can mechanical reproduction in the arts ever be as good as the real thing? To take the example of music, musicians usually say no, audio engineers say yes or almost, and, apart from the purely technical side, whose further perfecting is just a matter of time, there seem to be two resolutions of their conflicting views. One has to do with the additional satisfaction most people get out of the human component, the physical presence of players and audience, and the tense, expectant, festive atmosphere their presence creates. I have discussed that element already. It is probably more important for many people than they care to admit.

The other resolution of the conflict of views on mechanical reproduction has to do with variety and uncertainty. Any given piece of live music can be listened to with pleasure much more often than any canned version of it. The reason is that successive live performances vary in tempo, interpretation, balance, perfection of execution, and they always involve some uncertainty as to how successful that particular performance will be. Live jazz is even more unpredictable, for improvisation is expected of the performers. The listener gains variety, novelty, suspense, even when the piece itself is already quite familiar to him. Indeed, some listeners brought up on canned music find the suspense so unsettling that they have to learn to accept it before they can fully enjoy live performances. None of that suspense and variety can be found, of course, in repeated hearings of the same record or tape.

Subjective novelty and stimulus enjoyment therefore diminish much faster with each playing of the same record than with each live performance of the same piece. People's tendency to listen to recorded music while reading or doing something else at the same time is perhaps also a sign that the record contains too much redundancy to provide a full measure of enjoyment or even to relieve boredom fully without additional stimulus from another source. The obvious remedy would be to own several recordings of each piece—which is not unfeasible economically, for recordings of a full-length concert cost no more than two good tickets to the concert. However, most people, once they own a good recording of a piece of music, will rather buy a recording of a new piece than a new recording of one they already own, thus to get more subjective information for their money. Similarly, many people will not go to a live performance of a program they own on records if they expect it to be less perfect than the recorded one they own. As a result, the modern music-lover goes through the repertory much faster than his predecessors did, because he gets less novelty and variety out of each composition and so needs more of them to obtain a given stimulus.

A closely related development with similar results is the increasing frequency with which, as a captive audience, we are made to listen to music in waiting rooms, offices, stores, public transport vehicles, and elsewhere. Such listening is usually a secondary activity, with our attention divided and the quality of reproduction inferior, but it does provide stimulation and also contributes to wearing out the novelty and increasing the redundancy of the piece, so affecting our ability to enjoy it during subsequent listenings.

Such banalization of art has occurred in other art forms. Seeing the same film repeatedly is much less interesting than seeing the same live play several times. Similarly, the wide currency of reproductions of some paintings greatly diminishes the interest and enjoyment they hold, especially when one encounters not only an occasional good reproduction on a friend's living-room wall, but many not-so-good reproductions in magazines, book covers, and posters. One more example, which I have already mentioned, is women's fashions. The quick and wide dissemination of fashions wears out the stimulus of their novelty very fast and explains the speed with which they change.

People's desire for the uniqueness of a painting, an art object, a dress, or any other possession therefore, however snobbish it may seem, is soundly based on a desire for maximum novelty and stimulus enjoyment. The owner himself, of course, quickly uses up the novelty content of his own possessions, but uniqueness enhances the enjoyment of others as well as the satisfaction the owner gets from other people's enjoyment.

Is the banalization of art good or bad from the individual's point of view? The great frequency with which we are exposed to poor reproductions of music or pictures clearly makes us use up their novelty faster than we otherwise would, though it does not yield correspondingly more enjoyment in the process. Professor Abraham Moles, who first raised this question, believed that the need for artistic imagination is likely to exceed the supply in the modern economy, and he called for computer technology with which to enhance the artist's productivity in creating novelty.[10]

The issue is unresolved, and it may look different to people who are willing and able to enjoy not only new but past novelty. To wring every ounce of novelty, variety, and stimulus out of an object, a play, or a piece of music before proceeding to enjoy the next one is desirable only if not enough of them of comparable quality are available to last for one's lifetime. When and where this is so depends on the art form and on one's breadth of interests, consumption skills, and appetite for stimulation. Music could well be, for some people, a source of stimulus whose stock, accumulated over centuries, is large enough to allow its wasteful use with impunity. Today's record buff probably knows and has enjoyed more pieces of music than many a nineteenth-century amateur musician ever did; who is to tell whether his superficial enjoyment of more music is worth more or less than the deeper enjoyment his predecessors got out of their more intimate and knowledgeable appreciation of a smaller repertory?

Here we must leave the question. The banalization of art is undoubtedly an important consequence of mass production; how it, in turn, affects the consumer's tastes, behavior, and enjoyment of art is hard to tell. This short discussion should introduce the reader to the nature of the problem, but it cannot resolve it.

CHAPTER THIRTEEN

What's Wrong with Specialization?

Having dealt with some of the implications of the economies of scale, let me now come to those of specialization more narrowly interpreted. Specialization is the key to the high and still rising efficiency of production in our economy, which perhaps explains the specialist's high prestige in our production-oriented society. But if narrow specialization is the necessary condition of efficiency in production, efficiency in consumption demands the very opposite. Humanity has many needs, and people's welfare depends on the balanced satisfaction of all or most of them. One of these, enjoyable stimulation, has a great variety of sources, and here again, a full and interesting life demands the ability to enjoy, if not all, at least a good selection also of them. To make good use of the available opportunities, therefore, and to make the best choices, the consumer must be a generalist: knowledgeable about the full range of satisfactions available, about all actual and potential sources of enjoyment, and about all the innumerable kinds of consumption it might be worth his or her while to make use of. The modern American consumer is a poor generalist. The purpose of this chapter is to explain why.

One form of specialization is the division of labor between

specialists and generalists. Consider the traditional division of tasks between husband and wife. Husbands must specialize on a particular occupation to earn the family's income; wives must be generalists to assure the family's welfare, and do it the better, the broader their knowledge of the world and of all the things that go into a good life. The specialist husband maximizes the output of, or the income from, whatever he is a specialist in producing; the generalist wife exercises judgment and makes choices when deciding how to allocate expenditure and what specialists to employ in order to achieve some broader aim—too broad an aim to entrust to narrow specialists.

The typical generalist's task, therefore, is different from and usually more difficult than that of most specialists. To quote Mitchell once again,

> In making money, nothing but the pecuniary values of things however dissimilar need be considered, and pecuniary values can always be balanced, compared, and adjusted in an orderly and systematic fashion. Not so with the housewife's values. . . . Her gains are not reducible to dollars, as are the profits of a business enterprise, but consist in the bodily and mental well-being of her family. For lack of a satisfactory common denominator, she cannot even make objectively valid comparisons between the various gratifications which she may secure for ten dollars—attention to a child's teeth, a birthday present for her husband, two days at a sanatorium for herself. . . . Spending money cannot conceivably be reduced to such a system as making money until someone invents a common denominator for money costs, and for all the different kinds and degrees of subjective gratifications that money can procure for people of unlike temperaments. Such household accounts as are kept doubtless have their value; but the most painstaking efforts to show the disposition of every cent spent still leave unanswered the vital question of what has been gained.[1]

Mitchell's appraisal of the housewife's difficult task applies *pari passu* to the task of every generalist. The housewife has to weigh many more factors than does the specialist, and she must exercise more judgment. She also needs to know about many more things, and not much less thoroughly than does the specialist. At the same time, the breadth of her goal usually defies its quantification and so deprives her of the powerful tool of quantitative measurement. Where judgment is important and measurement impossible, experience and wisdom must supplement formal training and knowledge by rote—yet another requirement of the generalist.

Most societies recognize the greater difficulty and more exacting nature of the generalist's task and the broader knowledge it requires; and such recognition is usually reflected in the high esteem in which he or she is held. An example is the high status enjoyed in most countries—though not in ours—by statesmen and politicians, who clearly are and have to be generalists to fulfill their proper function and fulfill it well. After all, they play very much the same role in the public household that the housewife plays in the private one.

The housewife also enjoys great respect in the Latin countries, especially in Italy, perhaps because it is there that the role of family generalist is the most clearly and exclusively vested in mother and wife. She combats the narrowness of her husband's preoccupation with money and work; she has decisive influence on the family's choice of satisfactions and sources of stimulation; she keeps the family budget, she determines the children's education and the family's social life and leisure activities.

At the other end of the spectrum from the Italians are Americans, who have a very low regard for the housewife and her functions. That downgrading is largely the result of the higher value we put on production than on consumption, on the earning of money rather than on the spending of it, which I attributed to our Puritan tradition and money-mindedness.

No single factor can fully explain, however, behavior so very different from other people's, and seemingly so irrational. Besides, even if our Puritan ethic could explain our uppity attitude toward the housewife and her tasks, it could hardly explain our similar attitude toward generalists other than the housewife. We have an equally low regard for politicians—a uniquely American attitude, which also goes far back in our history. Other generalists in our midst—handymen among workers, general practitioners among physicians, intellectuals (as against scientists) among academics—are also at the low end of the prestige and income scale within their groups, so much so that their professions are losing their attraction for the young and some of them seem doomed to gradual extinction.

Finally, the aged, who are respected members of society in most countries, are disenfranchised outcasts in America, which again shows our disdain and lack of use for the generalist. For the aged are also generalists—though by necessity, not by choice. They usually start out as specialists in their youth, but scientific and technical progress render most specialist knowledge and training obsolete over a lifetime. It is true that a life-long accumulation of professional and human experience enables the old to supplement their obsolescing specialist knowledge with judgment and wisdom, allowing them to shift roles and remain useful wherever these qualities are valued; however, it does them little good in American society, which sets little store by judgment and wisdom. Judgment and wisdom are the generalist's skills *par excellence;* to deprecate them is equivalent to looking down upon the generalist. The question is, why have we adopted that attitude?

The generalist's goals are broad and consequently difficult to quantify; it is hard even to identify success in achieving them. That difficulty usually leads to an underestimation of the monetary value to be placed on the services of generalists and accounts for the low earnings of those among them who sell their services in the marketplace. In our money-minded society, low earnings lead to low prestige. Also, in a society as mobile and impersonal as ours, we have to judge people's competence by their credentials, and many generalists have no credentials. The very breadth of the generalist's task usually makes it impossible to identify a training program, a diploma, or a particular type of expertise as the appropriate qualification; and broad knowledge, long experience, good judgment, and wisdom, however important, can almost never be documented. Many generalists, therefore, are professionals without credentials—one more reason, in addition to those already listed, for the generalist's low prestige.

Our deprecating and looking down upon the generalists' tasks is a bad and dangerous thing because it makes us neglect those tasks. Yet, performing our generalist's tasks well is much more important to our welfare than most of us realize—for three reasons. The first and most obvious one is that every family's well-being depends on how knowledgeably and intelligently its generalist apportions the family's income among the many alternatives available. The second, less obvious reason is that being a good generalist can be an important source of satisfaction to the generalist him- or herself, since to acquire the necessary general knowledge and make good use of it are themselves stimulating activities and sources of stimulus enjoyment; not to mention the pleasant feeling of belonging or superiority most people get from displaying their wide general knowledge.

The third and last reason is that the choices each of us makes in his or her capacity of generalist exerts an influence, however small, on the economy's total output. For there is truth to the saying that the consumer is king in our economy. To put that more generally, our society is steered by the aggregated outcome of ordinary people's decisions when they act as generalists in their various capacities as consumers, householders, parents, family members, friends, colleagues, jurors, voters, and so on. They use what knowledge, worldly wisdom, and intelligence they have to make the innumerable judgments, choices, and decisions that ordinary everyday life consists of; they also give advice to other people, influencing their decisions; and all of that contributes to determining how well society functions, what the economy produces, where it goes, what prices it puts on goods, what incomes it pays for different services.

In our democratic, private enterprise economy, therefore, all of us contribute by performing either the specialist's or the generalist's, or preferably both, functions: (1) the specialized professional work with which we earn our living adds to the economy's potentialities and gives us work satisfaction; (2) the way in which we organize and live our lives makes an impact on the composition of those potentialities, determines the satisfaction we get out of our share of them, and gives us a sense of achievement and pride when we have done it well. Since the two functions are equally important, we must bring just as much general knowledge, intelligence, and worldly wisdom to living our everyday lives as the amount of specialized skill, training, and knowledge we acquire the better to perform our work. That may have been natural in earlier, simpler ages when the generalist's task was correspondingly simpler, but it creates problems in today's complex world when the general knowledge needed for enjoyable living seems harder to come by than the specialized knowledge required for the average person's work. To make matters worse, that knowledge is getting ever harder to come by as the world becomes more complex.

The same scientific and technical progress that increases specialization by the division of labor and enhances the affected specialists' effectiveness by rendering their tasks narrower and easier, renders the generalist's task that much more difficult, since it requires one to know and make judgments about more and more specialties and issues. Greater specialization means more freedom of choice, which ought to be a good thing, but it is that only when people have the knowledge to make informed choices. When they don't, freedom of choice is a nuisance at best, a danger at worst. (Recall the time you first entered a Chinese restaurant with 246 dishes on its menu without a knowing companion at your side to advise you.) That is why generalists need to acquire ever more knowledge if technical and scientific progress and the greater scope for choice it creates is to improve our lives.

THE DECLINE OF THE GENERALIST

Given the ever-increasing complexity of the generalist's task and given our deprecating attitude to it, how do we go about it and prepare ourselves for the evermore difficult task of organizing our life, making it enjoyable, bringing up our children, fulfilling our citizens' duties, and so on? First, parallel with diminished faith in our own adequacy to the task, we tend to lose faith also in our parents', relatives', friends' advice and try to switch from lay to professional sources of information and advice. We glean whatever knowledge we find useful and can absorb from the wealth of information given to us by the mass media; and some of us subscribe to reviews, *Consumer Reports,* Medical School Health Letters, and other consumer and citizen aids to make us more knowledgable and worldly wise. Beyond that, we tend to abdicate our sovereignty, partly by shifting many of the judgments and choices we used to make ourselves onto professionals' shoulders, and partly by dropping some choices by default.

As to the latter, I laid much stress in earlier chapters on the fact that most stimulus satisfactions are the result of skilled consumption and require an initial investment of time and effort to expand our capacity to enjoy life. I also tried to explain our apparent reluctance to make such investments (see pp. 231 and 236). Here, we may have the most important explanation of all. When the increasing difficulty of our generalist's role makes us reluctant to make choices, we are likely to shirk and even to abandon the ones that are the most difficult to make, which typically are investment decisions; that is, commitments to accept present unpleasantness for the sake of future enjoyment, such as decisions concerning our children's education.

Our exceptionally flexible educational system gives pupils far too many optional courses from which to choose. Most youngsters, however, lack the foresight to prefer useful to easy courses, while school counsellors focus exclusively on work skills and vocational guidance, and few parents have the parental authority and strength of character both to overrule their children's preferences and to fly in the face of the ruling Protestant ethic. If training in the humanities and other consumption skills falls by the wayside, the more's the pity.

To come back now to the generalist's seeking of professional assistance, I have in mind his or her tendency to rely on the advice and services both of specialists and of such specialized generalists as politicians, general practitioners, psychiatrists, lawyers, brokers, realtors, travel agents, handymen, and so on. Most of that is undoubtedly useful and eases the generalist's task, but it also has its limitations, dangers, and costs, which I will discuss.

To begin with, note that some specialized generalists share the ordinary citizen's predicament and tend to abdicate their task or even to quit under the pressure of its ever-increasing difficulty. The best and most important example of that is perhaps the old-fashioned family doctor or general practitioner (GP), who, squeezed between low pay, low prestige, and the ever-increasing complexity of the task is slowly disappearing from the scene. The GP's job was both to relieve the specialists' burdens by performing their simpler tasks and to make diagnoses and judgments. The GP not only decided what specialist the patient needed, but also weighed the patient's age, general health, disposition, family situation, and economic position, and then made the judgment whether he or she would be better off with surgery, with medical management instead of surgery, or with the non-treatment of a benign ailment and acceptance of its minor inconvenience.

Such issues are vitally important, but our failure to recognize their importance and accordingly reward the physician most competent to resolve them has created the shortage of well-qualified GPs whose judgment we could trust. Instead, we tend to look to specialists of our own choosing to answer such questions, not realizing (or despite realizing) that even the most selfless and honest specialist has a bias in favor of exercising his or her speciality, if only because the specialist knows so much less about other specialties and the repercussions of other treatments. I already quoted evidence of our excessive use of surgery and its failure to lengthen our lives (see pp. 167–69); and lack of impartial professional advice is probably one of the reasons.

To some extent, the GP's task has been subdivided by the creation of such specialties as internal medicine and geriatrics, as well as the use of 24-hour clinics for emergencies and paramedics for home visits. The GP's disappearance, however, still leaves a gap, especially in rural areas. It has also rendered the relation between physician and patient much more impersonal.

The resulting replacement of personal trust in one's familiar GP by an often excessive faith in the medical specialist's powers and infallibility seems to explain why patients file so many malpractice suits and juries so readily vote for compensation. The consequent rise in insurance rates and excessive use of expensive diagnostic testing greatly contribute to the skyrocketing cost of medical care.

The example of the general practitioner has parallels. An obvious one is the disappearance of the handyman, who has been replaced by a number of specialized servicemen, mostly employed by manufacturers and representing the latter's interests more than those of the clients.

Politicians, unlike general practitioners and handymen, cannot disappear from the scene, but they can and occasionally do relinquish their main task. Traditionally, they have the double function of representing constituent's special interests and using their own privileged overview and access to expert opinion to form a more knowledgeable judgment of the public's general interest than most constituents are able to do and then to advocate that judgment and carry constituents along with it by convincing them of its rightness. This latter is their main and far more difficult task, of course, and one whose difficulty is increasing with the increasing complexity of our economy and society. That is why all-too-many politicians abdicate their responsibility for it and confine themselves to getting votes the easy way by uncritically accepting and adopting their constituents' less enlightened judgments even when they know those to be short-sighted and not in the public's best interests. Such behavior puts political decisions back into the voters' ballpark, which can greatly delay society's ability to forestall or deal with its problems.

PRODUCERS' CHOICE

Among those to whom the consumer relinquishes some sovereignty is the producer. Increasing specialization deepens the gulf between the producer's specialist expertise and the consumer's superficial knowledge of the nature and design of manufactured products; it is only natural that producer and consumer alike should have greater faith in the former's judgment of what it takes to give consumer satisfaction. The mistake is that, being on opposite sides of the market, producer and consumer may have conflicting interests; additionally, producers' notions of what satisfies the consumer may be influenced by what brings satisfaction to them.

The producer gains from reducing the time and effort needed to produce a given output because it adds to profit. What is more natural than trying to please the consumer the same way? Most of the consumer goods America has given the world save time and effort—no wonder we overdo saving both. We can only choose from what is available: dazzled by the colorful array of time- and labor-saving devices, we can hardly be blamed for choosing so many of them, especially when our faith in the producer's expertise makes us readily accept the saving of time and labor as the supreme good. Since what one wants depends very much on what one has or has access to, the producer's influence on our consumption pattern is difficult to demonstrate, except on those rare occasions when one gets a glimpse into "what might have been."

An example of such a glimpse is the very different development of the automobile in America and Europe. Increasingly, American cars have freed the driver from the need to know, to do, to think, to exert effort. Our cars are equipped with automatic choke, automatic transmission, power brakes, power steering, push-button windows, electric seat adjustment, idiot lights, and buzzers or lights to warn of open doors, unreleased brakes, unbuckled seatbelts, and so on. At the same time, European cars have moved in the opposite direction and acquired more gears, more gauges, more lights, light as well as horn signals, differential locks, and other such to give the driver more control, more to do. They cater to the driver's desire for challenge and the opportunity to display and exercise one's skill. Virtually all sports cars are produced in Europe; those we make provide the appearance more than the substance. The difference between our cars and theirs is great. It reflects our preference for comfort, theirs for excitement. But in view of the high proportion of European sports cars and the great number of other foreign cars sold in this country, it also reveals a significant difference between the American consumer's and the American producer's notions of what cars are for. It is noteworthy that our hot rods started life as ordinary sedans and were stripped down, souped up, and given extra controls and gadgets by the consumers themselves.

The automobile is a good illustration of the consumer's impotence once the producer has taken over decision making. During the postwar decades, Detroit made its cars longer, heavier, more impressive looking, allegedly in response to our well-researched wishes. The cheapest and shortest standard models grew almost a foot a decade, with their average length going from 185" in 1938 to 197" in 1948, 208" in 1960, and 217" in 1971; and the industry assured us that the public no longer wanted to buy yesterday's shorter and lighter cars. We would never have known better had not the existence of imported cars more than four feet shorter on average (160") enabled us to show our preferences not only within but also beyond the range of choices offered by domestic producers. Sales of imports rose from one-half of 1 per cent of new-car sales in 1948 to 10 per cent in 1958, 15.5 per cent in 1969, 22 per cent in 1974, and 35.9 per cent by 1987, which suggests quite a discrepancy between what market researchers surmised and what market behavior revealed about consumers' preferences. (Note also that more than 10 per cent of U.S.-produced passenger cars are locally produced Japanese cars.) That is why Detroit in 1960 launched its 181" long compacts, almost two and a half feet shorter than the cheapest standards though still quite a bit longer, wider, and heavier than the imports and growing more so. (They reached 186" by 1969 and 197" by 1974.) Only the launching of the subcompacts, another two feet shorter than the compacts, can be said to have fully restored consumers' sovereignty over domestic production. By 1970, 40 per cent of new-car sales were compacts and subcompacts, but that declined to 28.9 per cent by 1987.[2]

ARTISTS' CHOICE

Another one of the producers to whom consumers relinquish initiative is the artist. Artists produce stimulus, as distinguished from both comfort and stimulus blended with comfort. The use of works of art as stores of value is an important but unintended by-product. Artists may differ from other producers in abjuring mass-production methods, but, like them, they are specialists who have, and inspire, great faith in their superior knowledge of what they produce. They are also like them in often not producing what the consumer wants.

I have argued at length that for stimulus to be enjoyed, it must combine redundancy with novelty, and that the degree of enjoyable redundancy depends on a person's knowledge and previous experience. A given painting or piece of music therefore may provide too little redundancy for one person, too much for another, and perhaps just the right amount for the maximum enjoyment of a third. Professional artists naturally know more about their own and their fellow professionals' art than do other people, which is why almost any given work of art will contain more redundancy and less novelty for a professional artist than for an amateur. It follows that what is the most pleasing combination of redundancy and novelty for professional artists is likely to be too daringly new and unorthodox for their public; conversely, the art most enjoyed by the public will usually seem too routine and not innovative enough by the professionals' standards.

Those differences are inevitable and they explain why less innovative artists are usually more appreciated in their own time, while the greatness of the more imaginative ones is recognized only later, as the excessive novelty of their work—excessive by the public's standards—wears off. Great innovative artists, therefore, must live long to enjoy recognition in their lifetime. When the art public is knowledgeable, skilled in art appreciation, the difference in outlook between artists and their public is small, making it possible for many works of art to provide artists and the public alike with an enjoyable mixture of the new and the familiar. Only when the differences are large, because the public is unskilled in art appreciation, must the artist choose and either produce something that fellow artists appreciate but leaves an uncomprehending public cool and brings meagre or no earnings, or cater to the public's taste and produce work that sells well but other artists consider unimaginative or even downright banal.

Many people believe that the gulf between artist and public is greater today than it has been in the past. Much has been written on modern compositions' being understood and enjoyed by no one outside a small in-group of the composers and musicians themselves.

> The profession of composer discloses the singularity . . . of a person who troubles himself to produce something for which there are no consumers. . . . The contemporary composer is a gate-crasher trying to push his way into a company to which he has not been invited. The familiar spectacle of the contemporary work sandwiched between Beethoven and Brahms exposes the gate-crasher in full silhouette, sneaking into the concert hall under the coattails of the elect. . . . Few people like modern music much. Even fewer like much of it. Most people do not like it at all. But it continues to be written, played, talked about as if it mattered. Why?[3]

The music critic who wrote that blames the composer for paying no heed to consumers' tastes and foundations and universities for providing composers with the financial means to do so. Other writers, attacking him, have sided with the composer and blamed the public. But all seem to agree that there is a great gap between composers and the public.

I am not aware of similar complaints about a similar gulf between painters and their public, but the situation there is very different. Paintings, unlike pieces of music, are also investments[4]; and the more innovative, the better investments they are, since the less appreciated they are in the present, the more their value might grow with time. A patron of the arts, therefore, who seeks a good investment in addition to a source of stimulus enjoyment, has every inducement to acquire the professionals' taste, or at least to adopt their judgment in preference to his or her own. It is worth noting that in Soviet Russia, where the investment aspect of paintings played no role, there was a much-discussed gulf between what painters liked and what the public liked—or was supposed to like.

However similar the differences between producers' and consumers' tastes and between artists' and their public's tastes may be, our reaction to them is very different. We would much rather see consumers' tastes influence what producers sell them than the other way around; but many of us would hestitate to express a similar preference for the influence of the public's taste on artists' products. The reason is that when we weigh the artist's stimulus enjoyment against the public's, we tend to give the artist the greater weight. For works of art are durable sources of stimulus enjoyment that can last for years, or even centuries. Since the specialist's judgment is believed to be a better predictor than is that of the general public concerning what posterity's judgment is going to be, we attach the weight of future generations to the specialist's judgment. This, of course, outweighs that of the single present generation. Hence the feeling that artists should not prostitute their art to please the consumer's passing fancy and make more money. By sticking to what they themselves deem good, they may stay poor, but have a better chance of gaining recognition by posterity and of pleasing the more durable fancy of future generations of art connoisseurs.

DECORATING

So far, my concern was with the way in which generalists' abdicating or delegating some of their sovereignty affected the goodness of their choices. We now come to another possible cost of generalists' unwillingness or inability to cope with their tasks: the loss of that enjoyable stimulation and pride, which often comes from playing the generalist's role and playing it well. Accordingly, to relinquish one of the tasks one could easily perform oneself unaided may deprive one of a valuable source of stimulus.

A good example is interior decoration. In the last chapter, I discussed the monotony that mass-produced products create. But in an economy as large as ours, there is a great variety of mass-produced goods, a variety that provides ample room for consumers to exercise their individuality and ability to be different and to obtain stimulating variety in the way they select, use, arrange, and match mass-produced products and mix them with unusual ones. Doing that sort of thing happens to be one of the generalist's more manageable and rewarding tasks: it requires no formal training, and people who love to shop should enjoy and excel at it.

Take the furnishing of one's home. Throughout history, people have taken pleasure and pride in embellishing the outside and inside of their homes, with a view to creating a stimulating and pleasant environment for themselves and others. It was one of the housekeeping functions in which aristocrats were not too proud nor peasants too humble to take an active and creative part. Today, apartment houses and real-estate developers limit most of us to selecting colors, fabrics, wallpaper, and to choosing, matching, and arranging the furniture and decorative objects. It is a task well within the average householder's competence, requiring no special skill and minimal experience or training. Yet, most of us choose not to undertake it, which makes interior decoration a flourishing professional specialty in the United States. The American Society of Interior Designers today (1990) has 31,000 members, most of whose work is to plan, choose, buy, and arrange the furnishing of private homes; and they are serviced by many sellers of fabrics, furnishings, and antiques who sell exclusively to and through them. People who cannot afford to engage their own interior decorator often obtain the free advice of decorators employed by furniture stores. A telephone survey in the San Francisco Bay area has shown that all the large furniture dealers, whether good or bad, cheap or expensive, employ professional decorators who are involved in about half the value of the firms' furniture sales and who make home visits to between 30 and 40 per cent (by value) of the stores' customers. To assume that one-third or more of all

American householders seek some professional advice on decorating their homes does not seem unreasonable.

I lack comparable data for other countries, but in the judgment of American decorators knowledgeable about Europe, the situation there is very different. According to one who also works in Paris, the French counterpart to his American clients is too anxious to express his or her own personality and taste to hire a decorator. Only the super-rich do—more to have someone do the legwork than to provide the ideas. Independent interior decorators do not exist in France: they could not survive there for lack of that mainstay of their livelihood, sellers of furnishings and fabrics who sell exclusively through them. The few professional decorators in France are employed by decorating firms, which cater to institutional clients and the very rich. The same is true in Sweden, Europe's richest country, as well as in the other Scandinavian countries. Britain's few interior decorators cater only to owners of large country houses and the very rich. Germany seems to be somewhere halfway between France and the United States in this respect.[5]

There is a subtle but fundamental difference between relying on a fashion adviser's or decorator's advice and reading *Consumer Reports* before buying a dishwasher. *Consumer Reports* appraise what lies behind appearances, decorators appraise appearances and their ability to please. Does that mean that people who hire a decorator need an expert to decide what pleases *them?* Sometimes and to some extent it does. The enjoyment of visual stimulation is skilled consumption, and decorators and fashion advisers are competent to teach the skill. At the same time, for anyone genuinely interested, it is an easy skill quickly acquired. Most of those who employ decorators do so for lack of self-confidence, to impress others with a skill they lack, or to provide their guests with an enjoyment they themselves do not appreciate.

People who enjoy the stimulation of clothes and furnishings enjoy other people's as much as their own and get further satisfaction from sharing their enjoyment with others. Sharing enjoyment, of course, is a form of status satisfaction. Curiously enough, expensive clothes and furnishings yield status satisfaction even to those who lack the skill to enjoy their stimulation. The satisfaction comes from successfully standing out from among the mob or blending in with the nobs rather than from the knowledge of having given enjoyment to others by providing them with pleasant stimulation.

TOURISM

Another example of how a generalist may lose enjoyable stimulation by delegating one of his or her tasks to others is tourism. Alien places and peoples, natural wonders and the monuments and places of worship of ancient and alien civilizations are among our most easily accessible sources of stimulus satisfaction. All that has now been brought within many people's easy reach by the great advances in transportation and communication technology. The tremendous increase in air travel during the tourist season shows that many of us have seized the opportunity and are making plenty of use of it.

Note, however, that travel to the same foreign parts can yield widely divergent quantities of stimulus enjoyment, depending on how deeply one wants to immerse oneself in an alien civilization and how well prepared one is when setting out for its enjoyment. One can opt for any combination of stimulation and comfort within a wide range of possibilities according to one's age, temperament, mood, and the amount of time at one's disposal. It is not for me to interfere with other people's freedom of choice in this matter, but to make use of that freedom knowingly one must be aware of the alternatives, which people afraid of abandoning the security and comfort of packaged tours often are not. There are many kinds of pre-arranged package tours, some with excellent lectures on history, background, and art, and there are some without; most, however, involve the standardization of sights, meals, hotels, and the tourist's isolation from human contact with the people of the place, as well as one's loss of the sense of making one's own discoveries and of following one's own inclinations in one's own good time. Also, deciding where to go, what to see, where to stay and eat, how to cater to one's own and one's family's personal interests and special tastes used to be, and for many people still is, half the fun, with the necessary information and expertise quickly picked up from a good guidebook. But packaging saves a lot of bother and can make foreign travel almost as comfortable and effortless as sitting in an easy chair and watching a travelogue on television—and almost as unexciting. Another reason why most of us prefer joining tours is our ignorance of languages. Indeed, language skills are primarily consumption skills. Outside of tourist and transport industries, there is hardly a job that requires foreign languages. Those who admire the language skills of foreigners seldom realize that it is mainly leisure- and upper-class foreigners who learn languages; and that they learn them as a consumption skill, one which enables them to get around and see the world more enjoyably than they otherwise could.

CHAPTER FOURTEEN

The End of Sexism and Revival of the Generalist?

God has created man and woman and tied them together by mutual attraction; but man has tried to keep them asunder by dividing their labor into man's specialist and woman's generalist tasks. He may have aimed at securing the lion's share of leisure and comfort for himself, but that sexist division of labor had three other undesirable effects as well: it has tended to limit the sexes' mutual attraction and enjoyment of each other's company to the physical sphere, it has deprived women of economic independence, and it has deprived men of the stimulus satisfaction that accompanies the generalist's tasks.

By now, the great increase in the advanced countries' labor productivity has created a surfeit of comfort; and the parallel increase in specialization and the division of labor has rendered much work monotonous and unchallenging, leading to ever-increasing work dissatisfaction in the workplace. Both those changes affect mainly men, making their lives seem emptier, which may explain why the first noticeable manifestation of a revolt against our traditional division of labor between the sexes was the do-it-yourself movement.

DO IT YOURSELF

Do-it-yourself activity was the answer to the prayers of men bored by their jobs, surfeited by comfort, having more free time than they knew what to do with, sticking to the Puritan value system that sets work ahead of leisure, and believing that anything whose value can be expressed in money must be more precious than all else whose value cannot be so expressed.

Do-it-yourself is not the only, perhaps not even the most important, example of work partly undertaken for the fun of it, but it is the only one whose importance we can estimate. Originally, do it yourself referred mainly to gardening, ground and home improvement, home decoration (painting and papering), and home maintenance—the kind of thing our income tax renders worth doing on our own by making a dollar saved worth more than a dollar earned. At the same time that it saves money, however, do-it-yourself work is also enjoyable—all the more so because the fact that it saves money removes the Puritan objection to one's enjoyment of it.

A 1954 U.S. Government publication estimated the value of supplies and materials used in do-it-yourself activities at $6 billion, or 2.5 per cent of total consumers' expenditure.[1] The value that the work itself adds can range from double the value of the supplies used in the case of, say, papering and carpentering, to four times that amount in the case of house painting and to an even larger multiple in the case of gardening, which is probably the main form of creative and enjoyable do-it-yourself activity in America. I shall assume that, on average, the value of do-it-yourself work is three times the value of the supplies used, or $18 billion. That estimate can be related to our earlier estimate (Table 4, p. 102) of the value of non-market work, of which do-it-yourself is a part, and it turns out to be a mere 9 per cent of that total.[2] In other words, I am assuming that less than one tenth of non-market work is creative and enjoyable, while all the rest is household drudgery—surely a cautious and conservative assumption. That assumption implies, however, that the market value of what our more or less enjoyable do-it-yourself activities create was $24 billion in 1954, or close to 10 per cent of total consumers' expenditures.

That 10 per cent estimate holds for the early days of the do-it-yourself movement; comparable statistics for later years have not been published to date (1990). Do-it-yourself activity, however, is certain to have gained greatly in importance since then. For one thing, most tinkering around the house and garden is done by owners, and home ownership, as a proportion of all occupied housing, has risen from 55 per cent then to 65 per cent in the 1980s. For another, there are in print 14 U.S. Government publications, 126 "How to" manuals, and even encyclopedias on a wide variety of do-it-yourself activities, ranging from upholstery all the way to roofing and building solar-heating systems. For a third, there seems to have been a great expansion in the scope of activities engaged in for the satisfaction they yield. There is a great flowering of handicraft work in America, which apparently is unmatched elsewhere. It includes such things as leatherwork, jewelry-making, and pottery, undertaken by people willing to accept a lower money income for the sake of more creative work, and by those whose independent income enable them to do what they most enjoy. All that suggests that do-it-yourself is increasing in both scope and importance; and all of it is designed to provide challenge and stimulus for those doing it. At the same time, it makes or saves enough money to allay our Puritan consciences and arms us with enough competence to free us of the taint of dilletantism.

In short, even though our Puritan attitude, lack of consumption skills, and disdain for the generalist deprive us of much enjoyable stimulation as consumers, we can make up for the loss by seeking the creative satisfaction of productive work. The superior efficiency of American businessmen, managers, and scientists is often attributed to their single-minded devotion to their work, in the sense that work is their main source of satisfaction. It is very possible that those among us who find no fulfillment in their regular work should then seek fulfillment in some other work—the kind just discussed. We have an unfortunate tendency to underestimate the importance of goods, services, activities, and satisfactions that do not go through the market and therefore fail to acquire a monetary value. One purpose of the calculations just made was to guard against such myopia by providing at least a rough base on which to build a numerical value that can be attached to non-market work of the kind we are considering. Bearing in mind that the commercial value of what do-it-yourself activities produce was almost twice our total expenditure on recreation and entertainment already in 1954 ($13 billion), that its volume is bound to have increased substantially since then, to which the unknown and hard-to-estimate value of handicrafts must also be added, it seems clear that these newly discovered or rediscovered forms of productive work must be fairly important sources of stimulus satisfaction when compared with other sources of such satisfaction in our economy.

The great importance of such work is an outcome of the conflict between our tendency to seek rather *more* stimulation than people in other countries in sex, in stimulants, in frequent job and domicile changes, and so on, and our willingness to accept *less* stimulation than others enjoy in most areas of consumption. The first, according to psychologists, stems from our national character, our extrovert nature; the second I tried to explain in terms of the cultural and economic influences that make us choose or at least accept our impoverished consumption pattern—one that deprives us of so much of the stimulation that for other nations is an important ingredient of a satisfying life. If such deprivation really goes against our inborn temperament and needs, it is bound to be frustrating, unless it increases our hunger for stimulation in some productive activity where we can give it free rein. The evident importance of such activity is a sign that we do feel deprived of stimulation in other areas in our lives.

WOMEN'S LIBERATION

The student uprising of the 1960s, first for abolishing racial discrimination against blacks, then against the Vietnam War, was naturally followed by women fighting to abolish job and pay discrimination against themselves. That fight still has a long way to go, but it is already winning greater economic independence, more freedom of choice in marriage and sexual partners, and the prestige that money-makers enjoy in our society. It has also been largely responsible for the tremendous increase in women's participation in the labor force: from 37.7 per cent in 1960 to 46.3 per cent in 1975 and 57.4 per cent in 1989—which contrasts to men's labor-force participation rates at those same dates of 83.3, 77.9, and 76.4 per cent, respectively.

Women's entry into the labor force and into jobs and occupations previously closed to them is creating significant changes in several aspects of both women's and men's life-styles. To begin with, it is bringing men and women closer together by making them more similar in experience and interests, thereby turning them into comrades and friends, not only sexual partners. Second, it is drastically reducing the time women can and do spend on housekeeping chores and bringing up their children, although that still remains a multiple of what working men with wives working full time devote to them: the latter seem very reluctant to take over chores their wives no longer have the time to perform. As a result, working women leave themselves less leisure than do men. Other results have been the greatly increased demand for restaurant meals, cleaning services, and, above all, the services of day-care centers for babies and children.[3]

More interesting from our point of view is the question whether women also devote less effort to their generalist's tasks. Some undoubtedly do, either because they share their menfolk's scale of values, which puts work skills ahead of life skills, or because they find money making or their work so absorbing that it crowds out all other interests. Others, however, may not do so, despite having less time on their hands, because there are straws in the wind that suggest a newly emerging interest in life skills and life enjoyment on the American scene. That will be one of the topics of the Appendix, which reprints an address of mine, but its possible connection with women's liberation is worth mentioning here.

For an important consequence of women's, especially married

women's, entry into the labor force is its ending the traditional division of labor between male specialists and female generalists. That is likely to force women and men alike to rethink and reevaluate the relative importance of specialized work expertise and general life skills. The related great increase in the proportion of single-parent and non-family households is yet another change in our living habits that is also likely to force people into rethinking and revising their traditional scale of values.[4]

WHERE DO WE STAND?

In short, we seem to be in a period of transition as far as our work- and life-habits are concerned, although we don't know and lack the data to tell how far we have moved and how large or small a proportion of our population has been affected. That raises the question of what use, if any, this book can be to today's readers in this time of transition. Even at my most ambitious, I could only hope to open up a new field of enquiry, raise new questions, and provide a little reassurance that those questions are not as intractable as they first seem. But the book is open ended, because the subject is open ended. If it has provoked some readers into expanding, continuing, testing, contradicting, or at least thinking about my arguments, then I have done well. If it has helped them to shape their own behavior, so much the better.

The novelty of the book lies in introducing novelty as an object of desire and as a source of satisfaction. To write a whole book just to add one more source of satisfaction to the economist's already long list would be absurd, if it were not for the fact that the stimulus of novelty is among the most fundamental of human needs, and that novelty is a rather special commodity, as special as virginity or a delicate flower, and very unlike the economist's stock in trade. My fellow economists have been too earnest and puritanical to recognize the consumer's need for novelty, and many of us consumers have also been too earnest and puritanical to admit to ourselves our own desire for stimulation and novelty. We buy and enjoy novelty, but much less than we might; and even for that little we often need an excuse. Our consumption of stimulation, variety, and novelty is lower than average; and I have discussed some of the cultural, educational, and economic influences to account for such a consumption pattern. There would be nothing wrong, of course, with seeking comfort rather than stimulus if that would be one's ideal of the good life, except for the following reasons. First, we tend to overindulge in comfort. Second, economies of scale in the modern economy impose the majority's tastes on the whole society, and when the majority chooses to sacrifice the stimulus of novelty for the sake of comfort, the creation of novelty and the minority's seeking new ways of attaining the good life are both impeded.

Finally, we have seen indirect evidence of our undue avoidance of stimulus. Our extraordinary interest in do-it-yourself activities and in violence on movie and TV screens and paperback literature of the drugstore and airport variety suggests that our limited enjoyment of conventional stimulation leaves a void we are trying to fill. Yet another indication of our dearth of conventional forms of stimulation could be our remarkably great tolerance of crime, violence, and threats to life and property.[5]

There is no objective test for judging whether the stimulation we get from a concert or a game of bridge is as satisfying as the stimulus to be gotten out of reading a book by Stephen King or seeing a movie by Clint Eastwood; however, if more consumption of non-violent stimulation lowers people's desire and tolerance for violence, then a good case can be made for encouraging the enjoyment of such stimulation. That topic will also be taken up in the appendix that follows.

When I first posed the questions of the second part of the book—what is our life-style? how does it differ from other people's? what influences mold it?—they seemed interesting in their own right. To answer or try to answer them seemed an excellent illustration of the uses to which the first part's analytic framework could be put. Now, when environmental concerns become ever more threatening and we are in the midst of a third energy crisis, the subject seems to have gained in importance.

For whatever the merits and demerits of our way of life, it is the ideal that a large part of the world's population tries or hopes to emulate. We are leaders of fashion in life-styles; but the fashion we set is so expensive in terms of air, water, and soil pollution, ecological degradation, and energy consumption that it is very doubtful that our planet could maintain many more people for any length of time in the life-style to which we Americans are accustomed. If that is so—and most estimates and projections suggest that it is so—then it is high time for us to reexamine our life-style and find out how essential it is to happiness. I hope this book will give consumers and economists the tools for such reexamination.

We obtained and paid for more comfort than is necessary for the good life; and some of our comforts crowded out some of the enjoyments of life. Far from being bad news, that is really good news. It means that more people can attain the good life than would be possible if our way were the only one leading to it. Changes in life-style, however, are bound to be very slow and difficult. As long as we are leaders of fashion, we can hardly advocate for others a life-style different from our own, and to change our own and thus lead the world into a new fashion is almost as difficult. The irony is that what I have called our Puritan ghost is largely responsible for the high cost of our life-style, and we find it hard to accept the idea that one, perhaps the only way, of making it less costly is to make it less austere and more frivolous. Such a remarkable notion goes very much against our ingrained habits of thought, yet the findings of this book clearly point in that direction.

APPENDIX

Culture is a Good Thing

Culture comprises some of the best, most valuable things life has to offer. People involved in a cultural activity or interested in its products instinctively feel it to be so; but instinctive beliefs are not always easy to substantiate by logical reasoning. In the case of cultural activities, however, a very simple argument establishes them as superior sources of satisfaction, from the individual's as well as from society's point of view.

Alfred Marshall, the great economist of the turn of the century, fully recognized the great importance of what he called "activities pursued for their own sake." He thought them important not only for economics but also "for interpreting the history of man," as he put it. Recognizing that people's wants and desires for idleness are both satiable, he believed that economic progress and rising productivity are forever increasing the public's demand for activities pursued for their own sake. He cited evidence to bear that out and

[Address given at the Fifth International Conference of the Association for Cultural Economics in Ottawa on September 30, 1988. I am indebted to Professors Moses Abramovitz and Melvin Reder for their valuable criticism of an earlier draft.]

listed science, literature, the arts, athletic games, and travel as the main examples of such activities.

Marshall noted that the desire for excellence in the pursuit of those activities "exerts a great influence on the supply of the highest faculties," and he criticized his colleagues, especially Stanley Jevons, for regarding wants and consumers' desires to satisfy them as the sole mainspring of all economic activity, without even mentioning the important part played by activities that are their own reward.

Marshall's stress on the desire for activities as a motivation of human behavior and his criticism of his fellow economists for failing to take it into account in their theories are contained in the early part of his celebrated *Principles of Economics*[1]; yet his own theoretical work in the later part of the same book is subject to the same criticism. He, too, failed to incorporate the desire for activities into his own theory of economics.

My tentative explanation of his failure to practice what he preached is that he did not know how to do it. He seemed so struck by the difference between activities that are their own reward and productive work, which is onerous and only performed for money, that he failed to notice their rather obvious similarity: the products of both give satisfaction to passive consumers. Painting, sculpting, and music making are not only enjoyable activities, but their products, just like most other products, are consumers' goods or services, giving satisfaction to concert-goers, museum visitors, and the owners and viewers of paintings and sculptures. Had he paid attention to that similarity between productive work and enjoyable activities, he would also have realized that the difference between them, however important, is only a matter of degree, because many productive activities are often quite rewarding as well as onerous: while only undertaken for money, meeting the challenge and braving the dangers and obstacles that they offer also yield satisfaction.

Indeed, the close affinity between productive and cultural activities probably explains why the economist's neglect to introduce the latter explicitly into his model of human behavior has not detracted noticeably from its usefulness. Much greater and of far more significance are the differences between cultural activities and some of the other activities also pursued for their own sake.

Marshall showed great perception when he noted the ever-increasing importance of activities that are their own reward and attributed it to the progressive reduction of the time and energy required to secure our comfort and livelihood; however, he was overly optimistic in believing and implying that the impact of progress on human behavior was all to the good. His list of activities pursued for their own sake was not only incomplete, it was also lopsided and far too rosy, for it contained only benign activities, although malign activities pursued for their own sake are just as important and numerous, and always have been. Marshall, however, was a Victorian gentleman and a true child of the decorous, respectable, and hypocritical Victorian Age, which was much concerned with welfare but also managed to close its eyes to illfare. For violence and oppression, wife-, child-, and pupil-beating in the guise of discipline, as well as the conquest of other peoples and rule over them in the name of civilization, were also activities pursued for their own sake, whatever other motives and advantages they also had.

I am stressing the existence of those nefarious and questionable activities, and the fact that they, too, give satisfaction to those who pursue them, because in order to appreciate fully the value of culture, one must have a realistic view of the whole range of possible activities to which one's innate urge to be active and assert oneself can lead. For we all have the psychological need to engage in some physical or mental activity to vent our energies, provide stimulus and excitement, show off our strength, skill or daring, and give us a feeling of superiority. There are many very different ways in which to satisfy those needs, many influences to determine our choice among them, and that choice has a great impact on society's welfare, considering that one person's activity can give others pain as well as pleasure.

As a framework for discussing all that, it is convenient to classify human activities into three groups. The first, of course, is work, which is onerous, undertaken not for itself, but for the satisfaction its product yields, sometimes to the worker, but mostly to others who pay the worker for the disutility of performing the work. At the same time, depending on its nature and on the way it is organized, the work itself can also be stimulating, challenging, and even exciting, and provide the worker a chance to show off and excel over others. In short, work gives rise to both costs and benefits, but, when freely undertaken, the benefits can be assumed to outweigh the costs and the worker to be fully compensated for his or her time and effort. Only the distribution of the *Net* benefit from work can vary, depending on the bargaining strength of the various parties involved.

The second group of activities contains what may be called antisocial activities. They are the opposite of work in the sense that the roles of gainers and losers are reversed. These activities give satisfaction to the persons performing them, but they do so at the cost of inflicting pain, humiliation, bodily harm, or loss on others. I have in mind the many forms of violence, from sadism to vandalism, along with mental and physical domination of other people, torture, war, and rule over others. The costs of such activities usually outweigh the benefits, if only because a violent act yields only a passing, momentary satisfaction to its perpetrator, whereas the pain, harm, or loss it inflicts on others is often lasting or permanent. The distribution of the costs and benefits is extremely unequal, in the sense that all or most of the benefits accrue to the perpetrators and all the costs to others, with compensation in most cases neither paid nor even possible.

Somewhat similar to these activities is the taking of addictive drugs, which also gives rise to a passing, momentary pleasure but may, at a later stage, inflict a more lasting pain on the same person.

Finally, I come to the third group, which comprises all the activities that impose no burden, no harm on anyone, but give satisfaction and pleasure all around: both to those who actively engage in them and to others also affected. The very definition of these activities shows them to be the most benign and valuable of all. Note that this category includes both love, which our civilization regards as the greatest good, and learning for its own sake, for the wisdom and insight it leads to, which the Greek philosophers valued so highly.

Cultural activity also belongs in this exalted category. It is a labor of love, performed not for love of the person who benefits, but for love of the activity itself. That is one reason why I called culture a good thing. Another and no less important reason for calling it good, however, is that some cultural activities are potentially able to crowd out some of the antisocial activities listed in the second group. In other words, they not only create benefits all around, but are also capable of diminishing pain.

For one's need of stimulation and excitement is just as limited as are most of one's other needs and wants. Accordingly, if one activity (or set of activities) satisfies one's need for being active, then one's need for other activities is correspondingly diminished: they are, so to speak, crowded out. That is how the industrial revolution turned culture into a privilege of the leisure class when it forced working-class men, women, and children into factories for long, tiring hours of exhausting work, which absorbed all their energy and deprived them of leisure. The same relation of substitutability also exists, of course, among the various activities pursued for their own sake, which means that it should also be possible to substitute some benign activity or activities of the third group for some antisocial activities of the second.

To some extent that has always been known. We have long ago discovered that the best way of keeping children and idle youths out of mischief is to involve them in some organized game or competitive sport, provided that the sport is no less strenuous, absorbing, and exciting than the mischief would have been. Even the passive enjoyment of other people's activity can, if passionate enough, crowd out violence. In the early 1960s, when the Beatles' popularity among British teenagers reached hysterical proportions, many people credited that for causing the temporary decline of the street violence and rowdyism that occurred at the same time.

The big question is how to motivate people to prefer benign to malignant activities and make such choices on their own initiative—how to induce that ever-larger segment of the population, which has more time and energy on its hands than it knows how to use, to devote its excess time and energy to music, painting, acting, sports, or some other benign occupation rather than to drugs, rowdyism, cruelty, and violence.

Unfortunately, the obstacles in the way of achieving that are so formidable that their discussion will take up much of my time. Let me begin, however, with the one I can easily and almost completely dispose of, although it is the obstacle most often cited.

Many people expect cultural activities always to remain the privilege of a social and intellectual élite, believing that the enjoyment of such activities is restricted to people with book learning and a higher-than-average IQ. That is undoubtedly true of intellectual activities pursued for their own sake; and they are the first ones most people—certainly most intellectuals—tend to think of.

It is not true, however of the many other rewarding activities, which happen to comprise most artistic activities; although one is easily misled by the results of the many questionnaire surveys made of visitors to concert hall, opera, live theatre, and museum, all of which show that the great majority of those who visit them—about 80 per cent in the United States—are college educated, or at least have had some college courses.

Those surveys, however, merely show what kind of people enjoy exposing themselves *passively* to other people's cultural activities, which is a very different thing from the active pursuit of those same activities. Action can best satisfy the desire to be active and to provide the challenge, self-respect, and the feeling of accomplishment and satisfaction that I am concerned with here. Passive spectatorship is also enjoyable and stimulating, because it is not entirely passive, since it requires a mental effort to understand and appreciate what another person's cultural activity is driving at or what message it is trying to convey. That, however, is a much less strenuous and therefore much less satisfying effort, more of an agreeable pastime, which prevents boredom by adding to one's knowledge and keeping one's mind busy; but it seldom releases pent-up energies and satisfies people's amibition to assert themselves and prove their worth. Yet, paradoxically enough, it is usually only the latter, only one's passive response to and enjoyment of other people's artistic activity, that requires intellectual abilities and book learning.

It is art historians, art critics, and connoisseurs of art who have to have an élitist, intellectual education, not the artists. For artists' skills are very different; after all, most artists are manual workers, at least in the sense of needing the same skilled hands, eyes, and ears, and the same patient, perfectionist attention to detail that surgeons, craftsmen, mechanics, and most skilled factory workers need.

As an illustration of what I mean, note that many members of the sophisticated intellectual élite in today's United States embellish their homes with pieces of contemporary folk art imported from New Guinea, Mali, Ghana, Togoland, Dahomey, and other poor African and Oceanian countries. Most of these are ceremonial and ordinary household objects or articles of clothing, beautifully carved, painted, embroidered, or otherwise decorated, not by trained specialists, but by untrained simple people, who are certainly much simpler and less well educated than are those who buy and cherish their handiwork for its artistic qualities. Indeed, all folk art was and is created by ordinary people in primitive communities and agricultural economies as a means of occupying their free time and whiling away the enforced leisure of the winter months or the rainy season with some form of that slow, plodding, meticulous work, which we have come to call creative activity. In more leisurely times and civilizations, some such creative activity used to be engaged in by just about everybody who had less work to do than he or she had energy for because it was satisfying, could be shown off, and gave its creator a feeling of pride, accomplishment, and self-respect.

In short, the abject poverty of pre-industrial economies was made bearable by a more sedate and leisurely existence and the cultural activities that it made possible. The industrial revolution raised the standard of living and diminished poverty; however, in the process it eliminated the working classes' leisure, along with their ability and inducement to enjoy it in the form of cultural activities. That's what I was referring to earlier when I said that the industrial revolution turned culture into a privilege of the leisure class.

What I know of Europe's rich heritage of folk art and of the changing use of time seems to bear that out. European folk art was peasant art, which disappeared gradually when and where manufacturing industry displaced agriculture. In England, the first country to industrialize, folk art had already died out by the eighteenth century, whereas in economically backward Hungary, it reached its greatest flowering only in the middle of the nineteenth century and was still a living and lively art in my childhood. In between those extremes are countries like Germany, which started industrializing at the end of the eighteenth century and whose folk art reached its summit in mid-eighteenth century, declining thereafter. Germany is also a country with good data on historical changes in the use of time, which show that the length of an ordinary worker's working day increased from 8 to 9 hours in 1750 to about 12 hours by 1850, along with a simultanous increase in the speed and intensity of work.[2]

By now, the great strides technology has made since then would enable all of us to combine our much greater comfort and higher standard of living with even more excess energy and free time than the peasants of pre-industrial Europe used to have, which means that we ought to be able not only to match but to outdo them in the creation and enjoyment of some twentieth-century equivalent of folk art. What then prevents us from exploiting those new opportunities?

I will argue that the ultimate obstacle is the Puritan work ethic. The same Puritan ethic that made possible the industrial revolution by creating the belief that work and money making are the primary good, while culture and the beauty of nature and the environment are frivolous, secondary concerns, is still with us today and keeps us from recapturing those supposed frivolities. To show that to be so, however, I must first deal with an institutional and a psychological obstacle.

The institutional obstacle is simple enough. It consists of the fact that when technical progress reduces the labor effort needed to produce our accustomed standard of living, its impact effect is to create unemployment, not leisure. To convert unemployment of the relatively few into a little more leisure for the many by shortening the workweek or workyear requires deliberate action and consensus between employers and employees. As long as working hours were so long and exhausting that they encroached upon the time needed for rest and recuperation, workers wanted more rest and successfully fought for getting a part of their share of the benefit from rising productivity in the form of more leisure. But as the length of the workweek came down to 40 hours or less in the advanced countries and paid vacations became the rule, labor ceased pressing for more leisure.

Today's workers want unemployment to be cured by the creation of more work, not more leisure. Only as a last resort, when all else fails, as it did during the recent depression, have a few U.S. and European firms experimented with work-sharing and job-sharing.[3] These approaches proved quite successful and seemingly acceptable to employers and employees alike—but only as emergency measures to tide over periodic, severe depressions. The main obstacle today to shortening the workweek or workyear as a more permanent or standard cure for unemployment is that workers do not want more leisure, because they would not know what to do with it.

People's lack of preparation for making good and enjoyable use of their free time and energy is most apparent in old age and youth, when work is no longer or not yet available. When people unskilled for and unused to leisure activities reach retirement and suddenly find themselves with unlimited free time and no idea how to use it, they are at a loss; and evidence shows that they can face disorientation, depression, and premature death unless they find something constructive and satisfying to do, which at their age is not easy. Indeed, the main task of retirement homes is to ward off the inmates' boredom; and their atmosphere becomes depressing only when they fail in that difficult task, as they all too often do.

People's youth, when they finish or are about to finish secondary school, is another period in the lives of many when their need for stimulation and desire for excitement, challenge, and a chance to show their mettle is most pressing. At that stage, their youthful energy protects them from falling into torpor, as the aged are in danger of doing, but they face the difficult problem of choosing the right sources of stimulation and excitement. The risk they run of making the wrong choices is great because many of the most rewarding activities and virtually all the socially desirable ones require special skills, not only to perform and enjoy, but also just to find out whether one has any talent for learning those skills and whether their exercise is capable of providing the challenge, stimulus, and excitement one is seeking.

In other words, the problem of what to do with one's leisure and surplus energy stems from a lopsided education because informed choice from among rewarding activities requires not only knowledge of their existence, but at least a rudimentary skill in performing them as well. Without such skills one cannot even imagine that those activities could be rewarding to anyone, let alone to oneself. That is why people devoid of those skills tend to restrict their choice to sources of stimulation and excitement that require no special skills, such as sex, rape, drugs, violence, and crime.

Schools, along with homes, ought to teach all of us not only work skills with which to earn our living, but also the liberal arts, which impart the skills that render socially desirable leisure activities enjoyable, make life and people more interesting, and are necessary for making the informed choices essential for securing that balance between comfort and stimulation that best suits our temperament in different phases of our life and career. The two kinds of skills are equally important for both the individual's and society's welfare; unfortunately, however, our puritanical work ethic and money-mindedness have caused parents, teachers, and students alike to value income-generating skills much more highly than the skills that merely make life meaningful and worth living. That explains why work skills have been allowed to crowd life skills out of the curriculum. Without life skills to acquaint us with the many benign sources of pleasure in life, the excitement of violence and drugs tends to crowd out the excitement and enjoyment that art and culture have to offer.

Only kindergartens, elementary schools, and their teachers have remained relatively free from that bias and teach their pupils the skills of quite a variety of enjoyable activities. Thanks to them, we know that most children have good enough ears, eyes, dexterity, and artistic sense both to learn several artistic skills and to enjoy using them. Think of the surprisingly pleasing quality of many of the children's paintings displayed in our elementary schools and of the excellence of boys' choirs wherever they are formed and trained. Many of those skills could easily be developed further and retained to give meaning to later life; however, they are soon crowded out of the school curriculum, and then lost through disuse and forgotten.

Competitive sports are just about the only rewarding activities whose skills and practice are kept up throughout school and often remain a life-long interest. Unfortunately, the cheapest, most popular, and most exciting of those sports, football, seems too strenuous for most people to continue practicing beyond school or college, which soon reduces lovers of the game to mere spectators—an enjoyable pastime but much less satisfying and energy-releasing than being part of the action. That might explain the notorious rowdyism of football fans who, frustrated by missing the excitement they once enjoyed as active players, find an outlet in postgame violence for their pent-up energies and desire for active rather than passive excitement.

I brought up continuing sports education through all levels and grades of school because it is a fine example that cultural education easily could and ideally ought to follow. All it would take is to maintain and develop further the artistic skills and interests for which our elementary schools have so successfully already laid the foundations. If quite so simple and natural a thing still seems utopian and almost unattainable, the reason is that you cannot impose such a reform on the schools unless society is ready to accept the change in values that it implies.[4]

There are hopeful signs, however, that we are beginning very slowly to change our outlook on life and its priorities. For just as Marshall, a century ago, attacked his fellow economists for basing their theories on a narrow, consumption-oriented model of humanity, so the same critique of consumerism is leveled today in the United States, not against the economist's model of humanity— which, alas, proved only too realistic—but against an educational system that molds humanity after the economist's consumerist model and against the product of that education: people themselves.

The attack on U.S. education is in full swing and the narrowness and one-sidedness of the curriculum has become a much-discussed topic. Best known is Allan Bloom's critique of our failure to teach a common core of values, which he blames on excessive specialization in the universities.[5] If by values he means cultural and ethical values, I fully agree that they are badly neglected; however, they should be taught to everybody, not only to an élite of college graduates as Bloom suggests, because all of us need to learn how to lead a good life and lead it without encroaching upon other people's good lives. The high school is the proper place to do that because attendance is mandatory and reaches almost everybody, and also because the universities can ill afford to cut down on the amount of specialized training they offer, given the need to maintain and advance our extremely complex technical and scientific civilization.

As to the critique of humanity itself, that has taken the form of a revolt against our puritanical division of labor between the sexes. You may have noticed that the psychological problems I have been discussing were largely male problems. The disorientation of the aged afflicts mostly men; the violence of the young is the violence mainly of young men. The reason, obviously, is our sexist division of labor, at least among the middle classes, which assigned the prestigious task of money-making to men, and considered all other activities subordinate and relegated them to women. That has given men independence, but also an empty life whenever work was unavailable or unsatisfying. It also has made women dependent and burdened with the chores of householding and child care, but somewhat relieved by their enjoyment of two other subordinate tasks for which they were also made responsible: volunteer charity work and what there was of culture— gardening, home decorating, gourmet cooking, keeping up with literature, and dabbling in making music, painting, making quilts.

Both sides revolted against that sexist division of labor. The women's fight for greater equality and economic independence made great strides and was very successful, partly because it appealed to people's sense of fairness and did little violence to the work ethic.

The men's revolt in favor of a fuller life—soon joined by women and better known as the flower-children's revolt—was less successful and remained narrowly confined to a small élite, partly because it was the least important of several aims of the student uprising, and partly because it was a frontal attack on our Puritan ethic and its hierarchy of values.

Also, the revolt suffered an initial setback when the young enthusiasts for the arts and crafts expected more of them than they could deliver. They looked upon those activities as a full-time career to take up *in lieu of* other work, not as an addition to work for making life more interesting, oblivious to society's very limited demand for professional artists and craftsmen.

College statistics well illustrate what happened. At Stanford for example, which is my university, the number of students majoring in music and art tripled within the five years following the student uprising—an enormous increase. But as the graduating students entered and further depressed an already thin labor market for professional artists, they must have gotten very disenchanted, because in the next five years the number of students majoring in artistic fields declined just as precipitately and by almost as much as it had risen in the previous five years.

That does not mean, however, that the flower children's revolt has had no lasting effect. There are many signs to suggest a great increase both in the public's active participation in cultural activities and in its passive attendance at cultural events.

To begin with, even if Stanford trains hardly more professional musicians than it used to, it gives many more amateurs a chance to make music and improve their musical skills. Its instrumental and singing groups have proliferated and their membership has doubled over the past twenty-five years, although the university's total student enrollment rose by less than 30 per cent; and virtually all the additional members of choir and orchestra come from outside the music department. Today, the university's symphony, chamber, and baroque orchestras, its concert band, renaissance wind band, and two jazz bands have a total of 300 members, to which must be added the 200 members of the marching band, whereas the number of singers in the university choir, memorial-church choir, the Stanford Chorale, the Early Music Singers, and the Glee club add up to 350, although with some overlap between them. Only one fifth of all those instrumentalists and singers are music students, and four fifths of them are amateurs, yet the symphony orchestra is good enough to go on a world tour.[6]

The popularity of another cultural activity, acting, has increased even more in recent years. Today, the San Francisco Bay area has close to 130 professional and community theater groups, as against thirty or less in the 1950s. That is a more than fourfold increase over a period during which the area's population increased by 87 per cent. Nationwide figures are not available but the growth rate is said to have been very great. Today, professional, semi-professional, and amateur theaters and theater groups in the United States are believed to number in the thousands.

The 130 theater groups of the San Francisco Bay area employ, on and off, 700 professional actors and actresses and an estimated 1000 or more amateurs; and note that a professional among actors means one who is a member of Equity, the actors' union; not a person whose main occupation and source of income is acting. Considering that the unemployment rate of Equity members is 85 per cent and that most members earn between $115 and $175 per week when employed, it should be clear that not all the 700 professionals live on and for acting alone. About half of them are believed to have some other job or source of income and look upon acting more as a leisure activity. Only the other half are full-time actors, though half again of these live on a weekly $115 pay during the weeks they are acting and on unemployment compensation during the many other weeks when they are looking and auditioning for another acting job.[7]

Those are small but not unrepresentative samples of the American public's increased participation in artistic activities. According to a 1988 report of the National Endowment for the Humanities, they are paralleled by an even greater increase in passive audiences and the number of visitors to museums, art exhibits, Shakespeare Festivals, and so on, reported from all parts of the country.[8] The change is impressive when compared to what the situation was before, but our new interest in culture is still very much confined to a small educated élite.

Yet another benign leisure activity whose popularity has greatly increased in recent years is vacationing and tourist travel. According to a 1967 statistical survey, our interest in vacations was way below that of all but the poorest of the Western European countries (pp. 190–95). Although we ceased to collect statistics on the subject during the Reagan years, the more than threefold increase in the number of U.S. travelers overseas since then, with most of them crowded into the tourist season, suggests that we are catching up.

One final bit of evidence to suggest that America's Puritan ethic is beginning to erode is the increased interest of urban and suburban élites in the quality of life. That is manifest in the great proliferation of cookbooks, ethnic restaurants, kinds of bread and other bakery items, and the improved quality and ever-increasing variety of produce marketed. In the markets for clothing and durable goods, consumers are paying increased attention to design and workmanship, with unfortunate consequences for the

U.S. balance of trade because American producers have been very slow in responding to the American consumer's increased sophistication, while European manufacturers have long known how to cater to the luxury trade.[9]

Having focused so far on cultural activities people pursue for their own sake, let me close with a few words on the public's passive enjoyment of such activities and its reinforcing effect on their active pursuit.

The passive enjoyment of art and cultural events is satisfying and valuable in its own right, but no less important is the financial and psychological encouragement it provides for the more actively inclined to create art objects and artistic events. People enjoy engaging in artistic or any other activities only when they believe themselves to be good at that activity. The judgment of neophytes and non-professionals of their own performance, however, is often insecure and depends very much on how others judge it, which is one reason why they value all evidence of other people's enjoyment of what they are doing. Another reason is that passive observers' interest in and appreciation of one's performance gives one a feeling of superiority and accomplishment, which is an important additional source of satisfaction.

The general public expresses its art appreciation partly by applauding and partly by buying art objects and paying for admission to art events. Most people are lavish with applause, too often indiscriminately so, but stingy with money. Also, rich and poor alike applaud, but only the rich can afford to buy art. Those differences between the two ways of expressing art appreciation probably explain why acting and making music in community theaters, orchestras, and choirs seem to have become more popular as leisure activities than, say, painting, sculpting, or making pottery. For the performing arts are the only ones whose passive enjoyment can be expressed by applause, and it is common knowledge that actors, actresses, dancers, singers, and musicians enjoy what they are doing very much more when the audience's enthusiastic applause shows that it is with them and responds to what they are trying to convey.

Those who practice the other arts as a pastime must sell some of the objects they create, not only or not so much for the sake of the money, but just in order to find out whether and how others value their work. That symbol of the public's appreciation of one's artistic activity is much scarcer and harder to come by. One reason is that only the well-to-do buy original pieces of art. The other is that the demand for art objects is restricted by its very different nature, for plays and concerts give ephemeral pleasure, enjoyed only while they last, which renders the audience's demand for it a continuous, never-ending *flow*. By contrast, art objects are durable sources of enjoyment, of which most people want to own a limited *stock*. The demand for new art objects, therefore, stems mainly from the growth of the art-collecting public and from collectors' desires to replenish or add to their collection as part of it loses its attraction, goes out of fashion, or finds its way into museums and their vaults.

Those two limitations to the public's demand for art objects may well inhibit the creation of art objects as a pastime because the accumulation of unsold and unsaleable art in their creator's possession is likely sooner or later to deter amateur painters and sculptors from further artistic activity unless they—like Van Gogh and Henri Rousseau—are sure enough of their own artistic worth not to be discouraged by lack of public recognition.

Professional artists care about each other's, not the general public's, validation of their own judgment of the value of their work; but they need to sell their art to earn a livelihood and enable them to devote their full time and energy to art. Indeed, because market demand for art objects is mainly the demand of a rich élite, professional artists were probably better off in earlier times and civilizations when much greater inequalities of wealth and income created large aristocracies and so a bigger art market. If France has long remained the best home for artists, it must have been, at least partly, because her income distribution remained significantly more unequal than that of any other advanced country.

In more egalitarian countries, the State and/or the foundations have to take over or supplement the functions of the old-fashioned

Maecenas and rich art collector if artistic creation by professional artists is to flourish. It is a reassuring thought that in many countries they have already done so: in the West mainly by buying or commissioning art, in what used to be the people's democracies by paying artists salaries.

An increase in artistic activity as a pastime will probably help more than hinder the professional artist's career because a broader education and interest in art is likely to increase demand in the art market more than amateurs anxious to sell their art work add to the supply. In short, culture is likely to be a good thing not only for a sane society and people at large, but for artists as well.

NOTES

CHAPTER TWO

1 C. N. Cofer and M. H. Appley, *Motivation: Theory and Research* (New York: John Wiley & Sons, 1964), chap. 7.

2 Most of this section is based on D. O. Hebb, "Drives and the C.N.S.," *The Psychological Review*, 62 (1955), pp. 243–54, and D. W. Fiske and S. R. Maddi, "A Conceptual Framework," Fiske and Maddi (eds.) *Functions of Varied Experience* (Homewood, Ill.: Dorsey Press, 1961), pp. 11–56.

3 H. W. Nissen, "The Nature of the Drive as Innate Determinant of Behavioral Organization," *Nebraska Symposium on Motivation*, 1954 (Lincoln: Univ. of Nebraska Press, 1954), p. 314.

4 Fiske and Maddi, *Functions*, p. 39.

5 Hebb "Drives," p. 248.

6 D. E. Berlyne, *Conflict, Arousal, and Curiosity* (New York: McGraw-Hill, 1960), p. 209.

7 *Ibid.* p. 49.

8 *Ibid.* p. 193.

9 A. G. Bills, "The Influence of Muscular Tension on the Efficiency of Mental Work," *American Journal of Psychology*, 38 (1927), pp. 227–51.

10 Fiske and Maddi, *Functions*, pp. 30–36.

11 An alternative explanation which is sometimes advanced is that arousal is too high for efficient action.

12 S. L. A. Marshall, *Men Against Fire* (New York: Morrow, 1947), chap. 5.

13 W. H. Bexton, W. Heron, and T. H. Scott, "Effects of Decreased Variation in the Sensory Environment," *Canadian Journal of Psychology*, 8 (1954), pp. 70–76.

14 C. Burney, *Solitary Confinement* (London: Clerke and Cockeran), 1952.

15 A. Karsten, "Psychische Sättigung," *Psychologische Forschung*, 10 (1928), pp. 142–254.

16 Berlyne, *Conflict*, pp. 200–229; Fiske and Maddi, *Functions*, pp. 37–46.

17 J. McV. Hunt, "Intrinsic Motivation and Its Role in Psychological Development," *Nebraska Symposium on Motivation*, 1965 (Lincoln: Univ. of Nebraska Press, 1965), pp. 221–24.

18 The first person to introduce and analyze the concept of arousal and recognize its importance was Professor Elizabeth Duffy. See Duffy, "The Psychological Significance of the Concept of 'Arousal' or 'Activation,' " *Psychological Review*, 64 (1957), pp. 265–75.

19 This section is based on H. J. Eysenck, *The Biological Basis of Personality* (Springfield, Ill.: C. C. Thomas, 1967), and Eysenck, *Psychology Is About People* (London: Allen Lane, 1972), chap. 1.

20 An index of average arousal was obtained by measuring at frequent intervals and then averaging, in one test the amplitude, in another the frequency of the subjects' alpha waves. The mean values of the frequencies were 9.15 c./sec. for extroverts and 11.1 c./sec. for introverts; the mean and standard deviation of the amplitudes were 81 ± 14.9 for extroverts and 28.7 ± 8.55 for introverts. (The standard deviation is a measure of dispersion around the average. Usually, about two-thirds of the observations are within one standard deviation from their average.) Both differences are significant at the 1 per cent level. See Eysenck, *Biological Basis*, p. 178.

21 *Ibid.* p. 96; W. P. Colquhoun and D. W. J. Corcoran, "The Effects of Time of Day and Social Isolation on the Relationship between Temperament and Performance," *British Journal of Social and Clinical Psychology*, 3 (1964), pp. 226–31.

22 Eysenck, *Psychology*, p. 66.

23 *Ibid.* pp. 68 ff.

24 D. O. Hebb, *The Organization of Behavior* (New York: John Wiley & Sons, 1949), pp. 123–24; Hunt, "Intrinsic Motivation," p. 206.

CHAPTER THREE

1 The main sources for this chapter are D. E. Berlyne, *Conflict, Arousal, and Curiosity* (New York: McGraw-Hill, 1960), D. E. Berlyne, *Aes-*

thetics and Psychobiology (New York: Appleton-Century-Crofts, 1971), and J. McV. Hunt, "Intrinsic Motivation and Its Role in Psychological Development," *Nebraska Symposium on Motivation, 1965* (Lincoln: Univ. of Nebraska Press, 1965).

2 W. I. Welker, "An Analysis of Exploratory and Play Behavior in Animals," D. W. Fiske and S. R. Maddi (eds.), *Functions of Varied Experience* (Homewood, Ill.: Dorsey Press, 1961), pp. 175–226.

3 Berlyne, *Conflict,* pp. 4–6; *see also* Hunt, "Intrinsic Motivation," pp. 194–97.

4 According to *Duke University Longitudinal Study of Aging,* "the fact of having satisfying work to do in later life is very strongly related to subsequent longevity." I have lost the citation for this, but the conclusion seems to be well known and generally accepted by experts in the field.

5 Berlyne, *Conflict,* p. 174.

6 *Ibid.* p. 200.

7 S. Sharpless and H. Jasper, "Habituation of the Arousal Reaction," *Brain,* Vol. 79 (1956), pp. 655–80, quoted in Berlyne, *Conflict,* p. 174, and in Hunt, "Intrinsic Motivation," p. 210.

8 D. E. Berlyne, "Arousal and Reinforcement," *Nebraska Symposium on Motivation 1967* (Lincoln: Univ. of Nebraska Press, 1967), p. 59.

9 *Ibid.* pp. 58–59.

10 W. N. Dember, "Alternation Behavior," Fiske and Maddi, *Functions,* pp. 227–52.

11 Berlyne, *Conflict,* pp. 129–30.

12 W. N. Dember, "Response by the Rat to Environmental Change," *Journal of Comparative Physiological Psychology,* 49 (1956), pp. 93–95; quoted in Berlyne, *Conflict,* p. 131.

13 Quoted in Berlyne, *Conflict,* p. 98, from J. Piaget, *La Naissance de l'Intelligence chez l'Enfant* (Neuchâtel and Paris: Delachaux and Niestle, 1936).

14 Hunt, "Intrinsic Motivation," pp. 229–30.

15 Berlyne, "Arousal," pp. 71–72.

16 Hunt "Intrinsic Motivation," pp. 216–17; H. Helson, *Adaptation Level Theory* (New York: Harper & Row, 1964).

17 D. O. Hebb, *The Organization of Behavior* (New York: John Wiley & Sons, 1949), p. 233.

18 The binary logarithm of a number is the power to which 2 must be raised to give that number.

19 C. E. Shannon and W. Weaver, *The Mathematical Theory of Communication* (Urbana: Univ. of Illinois Press, paperback, 1949), p. 9. See p. 14 for a more rigorous definition.

20 That is the mean of a number of estimates. For a short account of these and other quantitative estimates, see H. Riedel, *Empirische Untersuchungen zur Kybernetischen Pädagogik* (Quickborn: Schnelle, 1965), pp. 26–29.

21 H. Riedel, "Einführung in die Informationspsychologie," H. Ronge (ed.), *Kunst und Kybernetik* (Köln: DuMont Schauberg, 1968), pp. 55–58.

22 R. Gunzenhäuser, "Zur Informationstheoretischen Betrachtung von Lernvorgängen: Konsequenzen für die Erzeugung und Betrachtung ästhetischer Objekte," Ronge (ed.), *Kunst*, pp. 88–96. For an information-theoretical discussion of mime, see H. Frank, *Informationsästhetik. Grundlagenprobleme und erste Anwendung auf die Mime Pure* (Quickborn: Schnelle, 1968).

23 Hunt, "Intrinsic Motivation," p. 199.

24 That seems at first to contradict an earlier statement (p. 40), that in view of the additiveness of different stimuli in raising arousal, an anxious person will seek lesser stimulation than will one who is relaxed, but there we were concerned with superimposing a sensory stimulus on another originating within the organism, whereas here we are dealing with the competition of mutually exclusive sensory stimuli for attention.

25 Only for some special purposes are the two combined in the concept of mathematical expectation, which is the numerical value of the consequences of an event discounted by the probability of its occurrence.

26 The difference between the two kinds of danger discussed in the last three paragraphs throws a much clearer light on the puzzle posed on p. 41, above: why should a violin concerto be more pleasantly stimulating to some people than is a mystery story?

27 Shannon and Weaver, *Mathematical Theory*, pp. 13–14. For a detailed estimate of the redundancy of French, see A. Moles, *Information Theory and Esthetic Perception* (Urbana: Univ. of Illinois Press, 1966), pp. 42–45.

28 That is equivalent to an information flow of between 3500 and 4000 bits per printed page. Recalling that the brain's information-processing capacity is approximately 16 bits/sec. or 1000 bits/min., we estimate an adult's reading speed to be 3½ to 4 minutes/page or 15 to 20 pages/hour. That is probably an underestimate, because the 50 per cent redundancy of English is an underestimate. We must also bear it in mind that that estimate refers to an unfamiliar text in an unfamiliar subject. Familiarity with the subject greatly increases redundancy and with it one's reading speed.

29 Riedel, *Empirische*, p. 45.

30 Moles, *Information Theory*, p. 23; *see also* K. Alsleben, *Ästhetische Redundanz* (Quickborn: Schnelle, 1962), pp. 22–23.

31 However, for an interesting attempt at measuring redundancy in musical programs offered at concerts, see Moles, *Information Theory*, pp. 27–32.

32 Berlyne, *Conflict*, pp. 283–88.

33 L. B. Meyer, *Emotion and Meaning in Music* (Chicago: University of Chicago Press, 1956), chap. 1.

34 P. A. Scholes, *The Oxford Companion to Music*, 9th Ed. (London: Oxford University Press, 1938), p. 370.

35 Frank, *Informationsästhetik*, pp. 21–23; Alsleben, *Ästhetische Redundanz*, p. 38. Frank gives estimates of the information-transmitting capacity of all the senses.

36 Berlyne, *Conflict*, p. 206.

37 *Ibid.* p. 207.

38 But see p. 68, below, for a possible explanation of the very different behavior of the gambler who, in the heat of the game, cannot stop and gambles away much more than he wanted to.

39 For a detailed discussion of the similarities and differences between food and novelty, see Berlyne, *Aesthetics*, chap. 16, section on "Intake of Food Versus Intake of Information," pp. 293–95.

CHAPTER FOUR

1 D. E. Berlyne, *Aesthetics and Psychobiology* (New York: Appleton-Century-Crofts, 1971), p. 84.

2 *Ibid.* pp. 84–85.

3 *Ibid.* pp. 81–94.

4 *Ibid.* p. 85.

5 D. W. Fiske and S. R. Maddi, "A Conceptual Framework," Fiske and Maddi (eds.), *Functions of Varied Experience* (Homewood, Ill.: Dorsey, 1961), pp. 46–49.

6 N. M. Bradburn and C. E. Toll, *The Structure of Psychological Well-being* (Chicago: Aldine Publishing, 1969).

7 D. O. Hebb, *The Organization of Behavior* (New York: John Wiley & Sons, paperback, 1949), pp. 199–200; *see also* J. C. Flugel, " 'L'Appétit Vient en Mangeant': Some Reflections on the Self-sustaining Tendencies," *British Journal of Psychology*, 38 (1948), pp. 171–90.

8 R. H. Bruce, "The Effect of Lessening Drive upon Performance by White Rats in a Maze," *Journal of Comparative Psychology*, 25 (1938), pp. 225–48.

9 That assumption is the starting point in the mathematical model of action presented in J. W. Atkinson and D. Birch, *The Dynamics of Action* (New York: John Wiley & Sons, 1970).

10 A. Marshall, *Principles of Economics*, 8th Ed. (London: Macmillan, 1920), Book III, chap. 5, sec. 2.

11 W. Nahrstedt, *Die Entstehung der Freizeit* (Göttingen: Vandenhoeck & Ruprecht, 1972), pp. 122–26; P. Pullar, *Consuming Passions—A History of English Food and Appetite* (London: Hamish Hamilton, 1970), pp. 87, 157, 196, 202, etc.

12 Hebb, *Organization*, p. 232–34; Berlyne, *Aesthetics*, pp. 91–92.

13 Flugel, " 'L'Appétit,' " p. 171.

14 F. D. Sheffields, J. J. Wulff, and R. Backer, "Reward Value of Copulation without Sex Drive Reduction," *Journal of Comparative and Physiological Psychology*, 44 (1951), pp. 3–8.

15 H. F. Harlow, "Learning and Satiation of Response in Intrinsically Motivated Complex Puzzle Performance by Monkeys," *Journal of Comparative and Physiological Psychology*, 43 (1950), pp. 289–94.

16 P. Le Roux, "Les Comportements de Loisirs des Français," *Les Collections de l'Insée*, Série M. No. 2 (1970), pp. 3–62. This impressive official survey of leisure behavior in France contains many statistical tables which give evidence of changing preferences with age, invariably in the direction of more comfort and less stimulation.

17 Habit-forming and the strength of habits will be further discussed in the last section of Chapter 6.

18 Berlyne, *Aesthetics*, p. 100.

19 *Ibid.* p. 218.

20 D. E. Berlyne, "Arousal and Reinforcement," *Nebraska Symposium on Motivation* 1967 (Lincoln: Univ. of Nebraska Press, 1967), pp. 44–45.

21 David Hume, "On Refinement in the Arts," *Writings on Economics*, E. Rotwein, ed. (Madison: Univ. of Wisconsin Press, 1955), p. 21.

CHAPTER FIVE

1 The subject will be taken up later in this chapter.

2 The fact that estimates of the national product always underestimate the value of its satisfactions is due to their valuing the total product at prices that reflect consumers' marginal, and *not* average, valuations. That shortcoming is well known to every economist, but it is often overlooked.

3 I. A-H. Sirageldin, *Non-market Components of National Income* (Ann Arbor: Institute for Social Research, Univ. of Michigan, 1969), pp. 56–76.

4 Quoted from Marx in E. Fromm, *Marx's Concept of Man* (New York: Ungar, 1961). The whole paragraph is based on Fromm's account of Marx's view of the subject, and all the quotations are Fromm's translations from the German original.

5 The experiment is described in D. O. Hebb, "Elementary School Methods," *Teachers' Magazine* (Montreal), 12 (1930), pp. 23–26; and it is referred to in D. O. Hebb, "Drives and the C.N.S.," *Psychological Review*, 62 (1955), p. 246.

6 Marx's discussion of alienation gives the somewhat misleading impression that specialization and the monotony and long hours of factory work made work that was previously enjoyable unpleasant. That may be true as a description of the change from handicrafts to factory work, but since the reserve army of labor was stationed on the farm, most factory workers started as farm hands, where their work must have been just as hard and tiring, if less monotonous.

7 H. L. Sheppard and N. Q. Herrick (eds.), *Where Have All The Robots Gone?* (New York: Free Press, 1972).

8 Sirageldin, *Non-market Components*, pp. 74–85.

9 In a 1955 questionnaire survey of 400 employed men, 80 per cent answered yes to the question: "If by some chance you inherited enough money to live comfortably without working, do you think that you would work anyway?" See N. C. Morse and R. S. Weiss, "The Function and Meaning of Work and the Job," *American Sociological Review*, 20 (1955), pp. 191–98.

10 U.S. Census of Population 1960, *Subject Reports, Occupational Characteristics. Final Report*, PC (2) – 7A Table 13, p. 184.

11 That is shown, for example, by the data compiled in January–February 1965 by the Survey Research Center, Univ. of Michigan, for their National Study of Working and Planning, Project 745, on which the Center's *Productive Americans* was based. I am indebted to Dr. Farley Bloch for calculating the correlation from the tape containing the full data.

12 M. E. Beesley, "The Value of Time Spent in Travelling: Some New Evidence," *Economica*, 32 (1965), pp. 174–85.

13 D. A. Quarmby, "Choice of Travel Mode for the Journey to Work: Some Findings," *Journal of Transport Economics and Policy*, 1 (1967), pp. 273–314.

14 Sirageldin, *Non-market Components*, pp. 77–78, esp. Fig. 4.6.

15 *Giving USA* (New York: American Association of Fund-raising Counsel, Inc.); also reproduced in *Statistical Abstract of the United States*.

16 H. L. Wilensky, "The Uneven Distribution of Leisure: The Impact

of Economic Growth on 'Free Time,' " *Social Problems,* 9 (1961), pp. 32–56.

17 For that approach, see S. B. Linder, *The Harried Leisure Class* (New York: Columbia Univ. Press, 1970), esp. chaps. 2, 3.

18 Wilensky, "Uneven Distribution," pp. 37–43.

19 U.K., *Final Report of the Civil Service Inquiry Commission,* Command Paper C-1113 (London: H.M.S.O., 1875), Appendices G, E.

20 From private correspondence with officials of the Department of Health and Social Security, London.

21 W. Nahrstedt, *Die Entstehung der Freizeit* (Göttingen: Vandenhoeck & Ruprecht, 1972), pp. 132, 137–38, 221–22, 228, 238.

22 P. Kevenhörster and W. Schönbohm, *Zeitökonomie im Management: Zur Zeiteinteilung von Führungskräften in Wirtschaft, Wissenschaft und Politik* (mimeograph, Bonn: Institut für Kommunikationsplanung, 1972), p. 30.

23 G. F. Break, "Income Taxes and Incentives To Work: An Empirical Study," *American Economic Review,* 37 (1957), pp. 529–49; M. Boskin, "The Effects of Taxes on the Supply of Labor: With Special Reference to Income Maintenance Programs," *Proceedings of the 64th Annual Conference on Taxation* (Columbus, Ohio: National Tax Association, 1971), pp. 687–89.

24 They were obtained by multiplying hours of leisure by the value of an hour's leisure, which was assumed to be equal to the hour's earnings given up for its sake. The flaw lies in neglecting the satisfaction (or burden) of that hour's work, although that is also part of the value of an hour's leisure.

CHAPTER SIX

1 R. G. Hawtrey, *The Economic Problem* (London: Longmans & Green, 1925), pp. 189, 192.

2 The main problem faced in making that simplification was faced also by Hawtrey, who drew a clear and careful distinction between creative consumption and "mere defense against boredom."

3 R. G. Hawtrey, "The Need for Faith" (presidential address to the Royal Economic Society), *Economic Journal,* 56 (1946), p. 361.

4 Hawtrey, *The Economic Problem,* p. 191.

5 There is a possible exception. I shall argue later that status consumption, in the sense of behavior aimed at establishing one's membership in a group, is a biological necessity, necessary for survival in both man and related non-human species. The demand for such consumption may be insatiable.

6 Hawtrey, *The Economic Problem*, p. 191.

7 The study of such behavior in animal societies is very recent, but it is highly relevant, *see* M. R. A. Chance and C. J. Jolly, *Social Groups of Monkeys, Apes and Men* (London: Jonathan Cape, 1970).

8 M. Moss, "Consumption: A Report on Contemporary Issues," W. B. Sheldon and W. E. Moore (eds.), *Indicators of Social Change. Concepts and Measurements* (New York: Russell Sage Foundation, 1968, pp. 456–62).

9 *Economic Report of the President, 1964*, Washington, D.C., G.P.O., 1964, Table 5, p. 64.

10 Estimate made by the author on the basis of personal income distribution and average secular growth rate data published by the U.S. Department of Commerce.

11 For an exhaustive and fascinating analysis of the subject in archaic societies, see M. Mauss, *The Gift* (Glencoe, Ill.: Free Press, 1954).

12 For a detailed discussion of such ineptness, see pp. 211, 214, below.

13 The scientific community has not yet resolved the 1969 controversy over whether regular physical checkups are beneficial or harmful, nor has anyone refuted the argument that high hygienic standards prevent the building up of immunities and so render people more vulnerable to some infectious diseases (e.g. mononucleosis). Equally doubtful is the wisdom of our high vitamin intake.

14 O. Paz, "Eroticism and Gastrosophy," *Daedalus*, 101 (1972), pp. 76–77.

15 For a survey of the entire subject, see E. R. Hilgard and G. H. Bower, *Theories of Learning*, 3rd Ed., (New York: Appleton-Century-Crofts, 1948).

16 O. H. Mowrer, "Two-Factor Learning Theory Reconsidered, with Special Reference to Secondary Reinforcement and the Concept of Habit," *Psychological Review*, 63 (1956), pp. 114–27.

17 J. S. Brown and I. E. Farber, "The Treatment of Emotions as Intervening Variables and a Tentative Theory of Frustration," *American Psychologist*, 4 (1949), pp. 211–12.

18 A. Amsel, "The Role of Frustrative Nonreward in Noncontinuous Reward Situations, *Psychological Bulletin*, 55 (1958), pp. 102–19; J. McV. Hunt, "Intrinsic Motivation and Its Role in Psychological Development," *Nebraska Symposium on Motivation, 1965* (Lincoln: Nebraska Univ. Press, 1965), pp. 208–9.

19 Hilgard and Bower, *Theories*, p. 112.

20 R. L. Solomon and J. D. Corbit, "An Opponent-Process Theory of Motivation: I. Temporal Dynamics of Affect," *Psychological Review*, 81 (1974), pp. 119–45.

21 *Ibid.* p. 131.

22 *Ibid.* p. 124.

23 The withdrawal symptom of caffeine, as that of such other stimulants as cocaine and the amphetamines, is depression, sometimes
severe depression. Stimulants differ in this respect from the depressants, like opium, heroin, morphine, alcohol, and the barbiturates,
whose withdrawal symptoms are heightened arousal and the discomforts (nausea, restlessness, etc.) that go with it. That is why addiction to depressants resembles more closely the homeostatic
drives, such as hunger and thirst, which also go with heightened
arousal.

CHAPTER SEVEN

1 Data similar to those shown in Table 6b are available for just about
all the survey dates. In addition, data on the dependence of self-
rated happiness on age, educational level, and skin color are available, and similar surveys have been conducted in many other countries. The interested reader should refer to the sources of Tables 6a
and 6b for further detail and information.

2 Some of the most interesting and important work of present-day
economists is their study of how individual members of markets receive and transmit market information. Thanks to that work we
now realize how far removed practical markets are from the economist's idealized, perfectly competitive market.

CHAPTER EIGHT

1 W. Beckerman, *International Comparisons of Real Incomes* (Paris: Development Centre of Organisation of Economic Co-operation and
Development, 1966), chaps. IV, V.

2 We hold twice the number of life insurance policies per head of
population than do the inhabitants of the more affluent countries of
western Europe. See *A Survey of Europe Today* (London: The Reader's Digest Assn. Ltd., 1970), Table 12, pp. 70–71, and *Life Insurance Fact Book 1970* (New York: Institute of Life Insurance, 1970), p.
26.

3 According to the 1967 Santa Clara County (Calif.) study in depth, we
generate 3.5 lbs./cap. domestic refuse a day, more than twice the
West German daily rate of 1.3 to 1.5 lbs./cap. See *Solid Waste Management in Germany—Report of the U.S. Solid Waste Study Team Visit
June 25–July 8, 1967*, U.S. Department of Health, Education and

Welfare, 1969, p. 1, and *Comprehensive Studies of Solid Waste Management*, First and Second Annual Reports, U.S. Department of Health, Education, and Welfare, Public Health Service, Environmental Health Service, Bureau of Solid Waste Management, 1970.

4 This section is largely based on J. Mayer, *Overweight: Causes, Cost, and Control* (Englewood Cliffs, N.J.: Prentice Hall, 1968), mainly chaps. 5 and 8, and S. M. Fox III and J. S. Skinner, "Physical Activity and Cardiovascular Health," *The American Journal of Cardiology*, 14 (1965), pp. 731–46.

5 A monotonic relation means that as one quantity changes one way, the other quantity will also change only one way.

6 Mayer, *Overweight*, pp. 71–73.

7 *Ibid.* pp. 102–4.

8 Fox and Skinner, *Physical Activity*.

9 C. W. Frank *et al.*, "Physical Inactivity as a Lethal Factor in Myocardial Infarction Among Men," *Circulation*, 34 (1966), pp. 1022–39.

10 J. N. Morris *et al.*, "Coronary Heart Disease and Physical Activity of Work," *Lancet*, 2 (1953), p. 1053; W. Zukel *et al.*, "A Short-term Community Study of the Epidemiology of Coronary Heart Disease," *American Journal of Public Health*, 49 (1959); D. Brunner and G. Manelis, "Myocardial Infarction Among Members of Communal Settlements in Israel," *Lancet*, 2 (1960).

11 Typically, the average blood triglyceride level in a random sample of a normal population is about 20–25 mg/100ml higher in men than in women. In a Northern California study, for example, plasma triglyceride concentrations were 146 ± 108 for men and 123 ± 92 for women; in an Albany, N.Y., study, serum triglyceride levels were 93 ± 38 for men, 73 ± 42 for women. See P. D. S. Wood *et al.*, "Prevalence of Plasma Lipoprotein Abnormalities in a Free-Living Population of the Central Valley, California," *Circulation*, 45 (1971), and D. F. Brown and K. Daudiss, "Prevalence [of Hyperlipoproteinemia] in a Free-living Population in Albany, N.Y.," *Circulation*, 47 (1973), p. 558.

12 J. Holloszy *et al.*, "Effects of a Six-Month Program of Endurance Exercise on the Serum-Lipids of Middle-Aged Men," *American Journal of Cardiology* 14 (1964), pp. 753–60; *see also* L. Oscal *et al.*, "Normalization of Serum Triglycerides and Lipoprotein Electrophoretic Patterns by Exercise," *American Journal of Cardiology*, 30 (1972), pp. 775–80.

13 A. Szalai (ed.), *The Use of Time* (The Hague: Mouton, 1972), Tables 2-2.2, 2-2.4, 2.2.6, pp. 583, 587, 591.

14 Very great disparities are shown by the most extensive comparative

surveys of household work by men and women, made by Professor Kathryn E. Walker of the New York State College of Human Ecology, Cornell University, Ithaca, N.Y.

15 Szalai, *Use of Time*, Table 2-1.1, pp. 576–77.

16 Many of us are so much below the lower limit of the viable range that dieting appears a lot easier than the substantial amounts of additional exercise that would be needed to reach or pass that limit.

17 At the moving walkways at some airports, a recorded voice does admonish one to let the hurriers pass by, but that is a minor exception.

18 Letter of Dr. Percy Stocks, *Lancet*, 1 (1951), p. 351. In 1952 the first large-scale statistical study was made; the subjects were London bus drivers, and bus conductors. See Morris *et al.*, "Coronary Heart Disease."

19 S. B. Linder, *The Harried Leisure Class* (New York: Columbia Univ. Press, 1970).

20 J. P. Robinson, "Social Change as Measured by Time Budgets," paper presented at American Sociological Association meeting, 1967 (mimeograph).

21 Those findings of the early Hartford experiment with pay TV are not contradicted by the popularity of today's (1990) cable TV explained by the much clearer pictures and the many more (including some specialized) channels it provides. For the former's wealth of documentation on the low value people attach to the time they devote to TV, see U.S. Congress, House of Representatives, Committee on Interstate & Foreign Comm., Subcommittee on Communication & Power, *Subscription Television*, Hearings. 90th Cong. 1st sess. (1967), esp. pp. 17–133 and 241–314.

22 Professor H. L. Wilensky, private communication.

23 V. R. Fuchs, "Some Economic Aspects of Mortality in Developed Countries," Mark Perlman (ed.), *The Economics of Health and Medical Care—Proceedings of a Conference held by the I.E.A. at Tokyo* (London: Macmillan, 1974), pp. 174–93.

24 R. P. Bolande, "Ritualistic Surgery—Circumcision and Tonsillectomy," *New England Journal of Medicine*, 280 (1969), pp. 591–96.

25 E. Vayda, "A Comparison of Surgical Rates in Canada and in England and Wales," *New England Journal of Medicine*, 289 (1973), pp. 1224–29; J. P. Bunker, "Surgical Manpower. A Comparison of Operations and Surgeons in the United States and in England and Wales," *New England Journal of Medicine*, 282 (1970), pp. 135–44; R. J. C. Pearson *et al.*, "Hospital Caseloads in Liverpool, New England, and Uppsala: An International Comparison," *Lancet*, 2 (1968), pp. 559–66.

26 C. E. Lewis, "Variations in the Incidence of Surgery," *New England Journal of Medicine*, 281 (1969), pp. 882–84.

27 J. P. Bunker, "Economic Incentives for Social Progress in Medicine," *Pharos of Alpha Omega Alpha*, 34 (1971), pp. 20–22.

28 U.S. Congress, Senate, Committee on Labor and Public Welfare, Subcommittee on Health, *Examination of the Pharmaceutical Industry, 1973–74*. Hearings, 93rd Cong., 1st and 2nd sess. (1974), Part 2, p. 568.

29 *Ibid.* p. 636.

30 *Ibid.* pp. 565, 642.

31 *Ibid.* p. 643.

32 For a detailed analysis of the last example, see B. Latane and J. M. Darley, *The Unresponsive Bystander: Why Doesn't He Help?"* (New York: Appleton-Century-Crofts, 1970).

33 N. L. Mintz, "Effects of Esthetic Surroundings: II. Prolonged and Repeated Experience in a 'Beautiful' and an 'Ugly' Room," *Journal of Psychology*, 41 (1956), pp. 459–66.

34 "How Airlines Overcharge on Connecting Flights," *Consumer Reports* (May 1972), pp. 321–24.

35 Unweighted averages, obtained for the U.S. from *Consumer Reports* (Oct. 1974), pp. 724–26; (Sept. 1973), p. 551, and for Germany from *DM*, April 1974, p. 87 and *test*, May 1974. Models sold through mail-order houses were omitted from both the American and German lists.

36 Indirect evidence that the American buyer of European imports is a less careful shopper than are other buyers of the same goods is the very much higher price he pays for them. Imported French cheeses, for example, cost twice or more than twice as much in San Francisco as they do in Vancouver—an enormous difference which cannot be explained by differences in duties and freight rates. In the case of many French perfumes, the producers charge higher prices to U.S. distributors than to their own, so to benefit by the lower price elasticity of our demand. All such cases constitute evidence of the less careful and less competitive buying practices of the U.S. consuming public.

CHAPTER NINE

1 Averages for 1965–67, based on U.K., *Annual Abstract of Statistics 1972*, p. 209, and J. Niaudet, "L'Evolution de la Consommation des Ménages de 1959 à 1968," *Consommation—Annales du CREDOC*, Nos. 2, 3 (1970), p. 79.

2 Carl A. Rietz, *A Guide to the Selection, Combination, and Cooking of Foods*, 2 vols. (Westport, Conn.: Avi, 1961–65), Vol. 1, p. v.

3 P. Le Roux, "Les Comportements de Loisirs des Français," *Les Collections de l'Inséé*, Série M., No. 2 (1970), Tableau 61, p. 48.

4 I am ignoring Southern and New Orleans cooking. It is a pity that the rest of the country has ignored them also.

5 O. Paz, "Eroticism and Gastrosophy," *Daedalus*, 101 (1972), p. 74.

6 One might be tempted to explain our lesser consumption of butter by our greater concern over high serum cholesterol levels and the consequent dangers of heart trouble, but these data, though the latest available, refer to 1963–65, a time when such concerns were not yet general in this country and margarine was not yet immune from these dangers.

7 *F.A.O. Trade Yearbook 1971*, Table 64, p. 245.

8 S. Giedion, *Mechanization Takes Command* (New York: Oxford Univ. Press, 1948), p. 204.

9 A. Szalai (ed.), *The Use of Time* (The Hague: Mouton, 1972), Table 2-1.1, pp. 576–77.

10 U.S. Census of Transportation, 1972, *National Travel Survey—Travel During 1972*, Table 12, p. 28; P. Le Roux, "Les Vacances des Français en 1969," *Les Collections de l'Inséé*, Série M., No. 6 (1970), Tableaux 11, 15, pp. 122, 128.

11 Szalai (ed.), *Use of Time*, Table 2-1.1, pp. 576–77.

12 L. Cseh-Szombathy, "International Differences in the Types and Frequencies of Social Contacts," Szalai (ed.) *Use of Time*, Table 1, p. 309. Eastern Europeans spend even less time alone, but that must be attributed to the severe and universal housing shortage in the communist countries.

13 *Ibid.* Table 8, p. 313.

14 *Ibid.* Table 6, p. 312.

15 *Ibid.* Table 2, p. 309.

16 J. P. Robinson, P. E. Converse, and A. Szalai, "Everyday Life in Twelve Countries," Szalai (ed.) *Use of Time*, p. 139.

17 A. H. Maslow and N. L. Mintz, "Effects of Esthetic Surroundings: I. Initial Effects of Three Esthetic Conditions upon Perceiving 'Energy' and 'Well-being' in Faces," *Journal of Psychology*, 41 (1956), pp. 247–54; N. L. Mintz, "Effects of Esthetic Surroundings: II. Prolonged and Repeated Experience in a 'Beautiful' and an 'Ugly' Room," *Journal of Psychology*, 41 (1956), pp. 459–66.

18 R. Lynn, *Personality and National Character* (Oxford: Pergamon, 1971), pp. 59, 84. The correlation between Lynn's country ranking and the average caffeine intake of different countries was computed

for the author by Mrs. Gita Sen. A statistical finding is said to be significant when the probability of its being due to chance is less than a specified fraction, usually less than one in a hundred or, sometimes, less than one in twenty. The first is called "significant at the 1 per cent level," the second, "significant at the 5 per cent level."

19 *Ibid.* pp. 59, 65, 74, 93.

20 *Ibid.* p. 89.

21 H. Giese and G. Schmidt, *Studenten-Sexualität. Verhalten und Einstellung* (Hamburg: Rowohlt, 1968); A. C. Kinsey, W. B. Pomeroy, and C. E. Martin, *Sexual Behavior in the Human Male* (Philadelphia: W. B. Saunders, 1948).

22 H. J. Eysenck, *Psychology Is About People* (London: Allen Lane, 1972), pp. 46–7.

23 *Wages and Labour Mobility*, Paris: Organisation for Economic Cooperation and Development, 1965, p. 50.

24 L. Long, "On Measuring Geographic Mobility," *Journal of the American Statistical Association*, 65 (1970), p. 1197; for Germany, *Statistisches Bundesamt*, Fachserie A (Bevölkerung und Kultur), Reihe 3 (Wanderungen), 1961, p. 9.

CHAPTER TEN

1 R. Schmalensee, *The Economics of Advertising* (Amsterdam: North-Holland, 1972).

2 R. H. Tawney, *Religion and the Rise of Capitalism* (New York: Harcourt, Brace, Mentor Books, 1926), pp. 166–67, 175.

3 For an excellent and well-documented discussion of the Founding Fathers' puritanism, see E. S. Morgan, "The Puritan Ethic and the American Revolution," *William and Mary Quarterly*, 3rd Series, 24 (1967), pp. 3–43.

4 I owe this bit of information to Professor Martin Lipset.

5 G. Hutton, *We Too Can Prosper* (London: Allen & Unwin, 1953), summarizes the findings of the many Anglo-American Productivity Teams of the postwar decade.

6 W. C. Mitchell, "The Backward Art of Spending Money," *American Economic Review*, 2 (1912), pp. 269–81.

7 K. E. Melder, "The Beginnings of the Women's Rights Movements in the U.S. 1800–1840," unpublished Ph.D. dissertation, Yale Univ., 1969.

8 "Victimless crimes" is the more customary term, but since they

include crimes against the State (e.g. spying), it is better to speak of crimeless crimes.

9 N. Morris and G. Hawkins, *The Honest Politician's Guide to Crime Control* (Chicago: Univ. of Chicago Press, 1970), p. 15.

10 *Statistical Abstract of the United States.*

11 *Ibid.*

12 J. S. Mill, *On Liberty* (London: Longmans, Green, people's ed., 1926), p. 6.

13 A. Sinclair, *Prohibition; The Era of Excess* (Boston: Little, Brown, 1962).

14 J. Kaplan, *Marijuana: The New Prohibition* (New York: World Publishing Co., 1970).

15 E. M. Brecher and Editors of *Consumer Reports, Licit and Illicit Drugs* (Mount Vernon, N.Y.: Consumers Union, 1972), chap. 3.

16 *Ibid.* pp. 9–10.

17 *Ibid.* chap. 10.

18 *Ibid.* p. 6.

19 E. May, "Narcotics Addiction and Control in Great Britain," *Dealing with Drug Abuse. A Report to the Ford Foundation* (New York: Praeger, 1972), pp. 345–93; *see also* H. F. Judson, "A Reporter at Large (Heroin in Great Britain)," *The New Yorker* (Sept. 24, Oct. 1, 1973), pp. 76–113 and 70–112.

20 If, as Lynn says, introverted, high-arousal people are the most prone to traffic accidents, then we should be among the nations least in need of low speed limits also on that account. *See* R. Lynn, *Personality and National Character* (Oxford: Pergamon, 1971), chap. 7.

21 J. E. McKee and H. W. Wolf (eds.), *Water Quality Criteria* (Sacramento: The Resources Agency of California, State Water Quality Control Board, 1963), p. 119. Most of the information and data of the paragraph come from this publication, which is considered the best in the field.

22 *Ibid.; see also* D. D. Baumann, "Perception and Public Policy in the Recreational Use of Domestic Water Supply Reservoirs," *Water Resources Research*, 5 (1969), pp. 543–54.

CHAPTER ELEVEN

1 W. N. Grubb and M. Lazerson, *American Education and Vocationalism: A Documentary History 1870–1970* (New York: New York Teachers' College Press, 1974), Introduction.

2 In the 1974–75 Metropolitan Adult Education Program of Santa

Clara County, Calif., less than 20 per cent of enrollments were in cultural, creative arts, and language courses, as against over 60 per cent in occupational, vocational, and diploma programs and another 20 per cent in home management, consumer education, etc. These proportions, obtained from statistical information published by MAEP, seem quite similar to corresponding data in other parts of the country.

3 R. Lynn, *Personality and National Character* (Oxford: Pergamon Press, 1971), Table 7, p. 56.

4 A. Szalai (ed.), *The Use of Time* (The Hague: Mouton, 1972), Table 2-1.2, p. 579. These data refer to both men and women and therefore are not comparable to those shown for men only in Tables 16 and 17. It is reassuring to find, however, that the French figure (8.6 per cent) quoted in the text from Szalai is almost identical with the corresponding figure for men and women in medium-sized cities given by Debreu, who is my source for Table 17, and whose survey was quite separate and independent from Szalai's.

CHAPTER TWELVE

1 See the article on Folk Art in *Encyclopaedia of World Art* (New York: McGraw-Hill, 1959).

2 B. Rudovsky, *Architecture without Architects* (New York: Museum of Modern Art, 1965).

3 For an exception, see B. Lassus, "Vers un Paysage Global de l'Habitant au Professionnel," *Society and Leisure,* 1972, No. 4, pp. 139–42, 1–26.

4 The figures pertain to 1972 and come from U.S. Immigration and Naturalization Service, *1972 Annual Report,* and U.S. Census of Transportation, *National Travel Survey, Travel During 1972.*

5 The 1972 Census of Business had not yet been published at the time of this writing. All the figures in the text are my estimates, derived by extrapolating from earlier censuses.

6 I am indebted to Mr. L. A. Henderson, president of Pier I Imports, Inc., Fort Worth, Tex., for this estimate.

7 The 1972 estimate is extrapolated from the data contained in Table 13; the percentage of flowers going to hospitals, etc., is from U.S.D.A. Marketing Economics Division, Economics Research Service, *Report #855,* p. 3, Table 2.

8 F. M. Fisher, Zvi Griliches, and Carl Kaysen, "The Costs of Automobile Changes Since 1949," *Journal of Political Economy,* 70 (1962), pp. 433–51.

9 T. Scitovsky, "What's Wrong with the Arts is What's Wrong with Society," *American Economic Review* (Proceedings), 62 (1972), pp. 62–69.

10 Abraham A. Moles, "Information und Redundanz," H. Ronge (ed.), *Kunst und Kybernetik* (Köln: DuMont Schauberg, 1968), p. 27.

CHAPTER THIRTEEN

1 W. C. Mitchell, "The Backward Art of Spending Money," *American Economic Review*, 2 (1912), pp. 277–79.

2 The sales figures come from various issues of *Automobile Facts and Figures;* the data on length are unweighted averages calculated by the author from information contained in *Consumer Reports*, Feb. 1938, May 1948, Sept. 1958, Apr. 1960, Jan., Apr., Jul. 1969, Apr. 1974.

3 H. Pleasants, *The Agony of Modern Music* (New York: Simon and Schuster, paperback, 1955), p. 7.

4 B. S. Frey & W. W. Pommerehne, *Muses & Markets, Explorations in the Economics of the Arts* (Oxford: Basil Blackwell, 1989), especially chap. 3.

5 For all this information I am indebted to Shirley VanCampen, executive secretary, California Northern District Chapter, American Society of Interior Designers, and to Michael Vincent, ASID, and Emerson Whipple, ASID of San Francisco, and to Lilian Grassman of Stockholm.

CHAPTER FOURTEEN

1 U.S. Department of Commerce, Small Business Administration, "Summary of Information on the Do-It-Yourself Market," *Business Service Bulletin*, No. 84 (Nov. 1954).

2 The 1954 figure in Table 4 is expressed in 1958 prices and had to be scaled down to make it comparable to estimates given in the text.

3 See "The Economy's Impact on Family and Social Relations in America" in my *Human Desire and Economic Satisfaction* (Brighton: Wheatsheaf Books Ltd., 1986), esp. pp. 164–67.

4 A simple index of the increase in single-parent and nonfamily households is the ratio of all households to the total population, which rose between 1960 and the mid-1980s from 29 to over 36 per cent.

5 On our increased tolerance for and vicarious enjoyment of violence, see my "The Desire for Excitement in Modern Society" in *op. cit.*, pp. 128–35.

APPENDIX

1 Alfred Marshall, *Principles of Economics*, 8th Edition (London: Macmillan, 1930), pp. 88–91.

2 Cf. The article on "Folk Art" in *Encyclopedia of World Art* (New York: McGraw Hill, 1961); Tamás Hofer & Edit Fél, *Hungarian Folk Art*, (Oxford: Oxford University Press, 1979), Introduction; and Wolfgang Nahrstedt, *Die Entstehung der Freizeit* (Göttingen: Vandenhoek & Ruprecht, 1972), pp. 138, 222, and *passim*.

3 Cf. Stanley D. Nollen, *New Work Schedules in Practice: Managing Time in a Changing Society* (New York: Van Nostrand, 1982).

4 Cf. R. F. Harrod, "The possibility of economic satiety" in Committee for Economic Development, *Problems of Economic Development* (New York: C.E.D., 1958), pp. 73–74 for a short account of the problem and the difficulties of resolving it.

5 Allan Bloom, *The Closing of the American Mind: How Higher Education Has Failed Democracy and Impoverished the Souls of Today's Students* (New York: Simon and Schuster, 1987).

6 I wish to thank Mr. John A. Planting of Stanford's Music Department and Mr. D. N. Namboothiri of the Registrar's Office for making available the data here used.

7 I wish to thank Misha Berson and Dean Goodman, theatre historians, Jean Schiffman of the Bay Area Theatre Association, Jay Moran of Actors' Equity, and Mr. David Motroni and Professor Wendell Cole for information on the live theatre.

8 Cf. *Humanities in America: A Report to the President, the Congress, and the American People*, Sept. 1988, National Endowment for the Humanities, Washington.

9 A large part of the great increase in our reliance on imports shown by the comparison of the two columns of Table 8 on p. 179 must have been due to the American public's increased sophistication.

INDEX

Acting and actors, 304, 306. *See also* Theatre

Activities: antisocial, 294; artistic, 296; cultural, 294, 296; enjoyable, 31–32; passive 295, 296, 306; rewarding, 291–92, 294

Activation, 17, 19, 20, 23. *See also* Arousal

Adaptation level, 40

Addiction, 63, 74, 127–32, 137, 138–39, 217–18, 219

Advertising, 5, 9, 204–5

Affect, positive and negative, 61, 128

Aged, 267; preferences of, 48–49, 73, 196–97, 238; problems of, 116–18, 225, 299

Alcoholism, 199

Alienation, 90, 143, 207

Alpha waves, 18

Alsleben, Kurt, 313

Alternation experiments, 37–38

Altruism, 121

Amsel, A., 317

Anxiety, 19, 21, 24, 25, 40, 113, 132, 200

Appetite, 63, 71, 154–55, 201

Appley, M. H., 309

Architecture, 229, 252

Arousal, 16–25, 62; additiveness of, 19, 21, 22, 39, 219, 250; appropriate level for efficient action, 20–21, 26, 29, 33; average level of, 25–27, 41, 122, 199–200, 201; changes in, 61, 62, 71; optimum level of, 23–28, 61, 62, 68, 71, 75, 76, 93; raising of, 31, 36, 59–61, 68–70; reduction of, 28–30, 59–61, 68, 125; system, 19

Art, 41, 68–69, 76, 91, 225, 227, 238, 246, 292, 303–4; abstract, non-representational, 56; banalization of, 258–63; computer technology in production of, 260, 263; distortion in, 56; investment in, 276–77; mechanical reproduction of, 260–62 (*see also* Folk art)

Art historians, 297

Artists, 275–77, 297; skills of, 297

Aspiration, 106

Atkinson, J. W., 314

Automobile: accidents, 199–200; model changes, 273–74. *See also* Driving for pleasure

Aversion system. *See* Pain center

Backer, R., 314

Baumann, D. D., 324

Bathing, 220–23

Beating, 293

Beatles, 295

Beckerman, Wilfrid, 318

Beesley, M. E., 315

Bentham, Jeremy, 15

Berlyne, Daniel E., 24, 309, 310, 311, 313, 314

Beta waves, 18, 43

Bexton, W. H., 310

Bills, A. G., 309

Birch, D., 314

Bloch, Farley, 315

Bloom, Allan, 302, 327

Bodily exercize. *See* Exercise, physical

Body weight, 154–58

Bolande, R. P., 320

Boredom, ix–x, 24, 31–33, 41, 59, 75, 77, 162, 233, 235, 237, 246

Boring, Edwin G., 55

Boskin, Michael, 316

Bower, G. H., 317

Bradburn, N. M., 313

Break, George F., 316

Brecher, E. M., 324

Brown, D. F., 319

Brown, J. S., 317

Bruce, R. H., 313

Brunner, D., 319

Bunker, J. P., 320, 321

Burney, C., 310

Butterfly diagram, 40

Cafés and pubs, 194–95, 240–45